SENTENCE

SENTENCE

TEN YEARS AND A THOUSAND
BOOKS IN PRISON

Daniel Genis

VIKING

VIKING
An imprint of Penguin Random House LLC
penguinrandomhouse.com

Library of Congress Cataloging-in-Publication Data

Names: Genis, Daniel, 1978– author.
Title: Sentence : ten years and a thousand books in prison / Daniel Genis.
Description: [New York, New York] : Viking, [2022]
Identifiers: LCCN 2021017315 (print) | LCCN 2021017316 (ebook) |
    ISBN 9780525429555 (hardcover) | ISBN 9780698405769 (ebook)
Subjects: LCSH: Genis, Daniel, 1978—Imprisonment. | Genis, Daniel,
    1978—Books and reading. | Prisoners—New York (State)—Biography. |
    Drug addicts—New York (State)—Biography. | Drug abuse and crime—
    New York (State)
Classification: LCC HV9468.G46 A3 2022 (print) | LCC HV9468.G46 (ebook) |
    DDC 365/.6092 [B]—dc23
LC record available at https://lccn.loc.gov/2021017315
LC ebook record available at https://lccn.loc.gov/2021017316

Printed in the United States of America
10 9 8 7 6 5 4 3 2 1

Set in Sabon LT Std
Designed by Cassandra Garruzzo

Dedicated to Petra Szabo,
for waiting for me
&
dedicated to the prisoners of New York State,
for teaching me

CONTENTS

SENTENCE

1.

GUILTY: AN
INTRODUCTION

In the beginning was the word. That word was "guilty." Upon my pleading so in open court, my existence for the next ten years was locked onto a narrow path winding through a part of America unknown to most . . . except for those who know it most intimately. When I became a convict, I joined the latter. However, the Incarcerated Nation is taken for granted by the select few who typically and sadly make a lifetime out of walking back and forth on that path. I've written this account of my journey behind the wall, a trip on which I saw many arcane and unusual things. Some were frankly atrocious, while others were strangely noble and life-affirming.

My own arrival there was fairly humdrum, as far as violent felonies go. All the armed robberies to which I pled guilty were committed during one bad week in August 2003. The heroin habit that drove me to crime was about nine months old by then and my second rodeo. I had managed to stay clean a year after the first, having become addicted at the age of twenty-two, sober a year later, and then back again. The scale of my relapse was increased by a credit card; some idiot issued me five grand of credit even though I was an unemployed drug addict. I spent all of it in the form of cash advances that went right to my dealer. The crime spree began when the credit limit was reached. Visa said I was done, but the opiate receptors in my brain still expected the bundle of heroin they had grown used to getting intravenously.

I had no way of coming up with a hundred dollars a day, and the withdrawal got very bad very quickly. Sick as a dog and desperately wandering downtown, I worked up the courage to show someone the same pocketknife I had once camped with and announced that this was a robbery. When my victim turned over the money, I apologized profusely. I repeated this pattern with varying degrees of success. When told no, I fled. Once, I had a pizza thrown at me. It was stressful and humiliating, no different from the awful things I had read about junkies doing in the many memoirs of addiction I swallowed up at the time. After a week of this and less than a thousand dollars stolen, I had an epiphany: the risks I took for small rewards, and the large compromises made with my own morality, were ludicrous. I threw my folding knife away and never held anyone up again.

The detectives who eventually caught me originally thought the sudden end of this pattern crime spree had been the result either of my arrest for some other misdeeds or of my death. They had apparently combed through the admissions to Rikers Island and the morgue dating from the afternoon when I realized I shouldn't be doing this. My crimes had been reported in the slow summer press as the work of the "Apologetic Bandit," due to the contrition I mewled at my victims at the crime scenes, but without an arrest the story did not make much of a splash. On the November day I was finally arrested, so was Michael Jackson, which left no room in the papers to report on my capture. Catching me was no great feat of detection. I had stopped my need to commit crimes by going to detox for heroin addiction and then stabilized myself with methadone, until I relapsed and returned to the very block I had mildly terrorized, because that's where the dope was sold. The day I returned to the scene of my crimes I was recognized by one of my victims. The woman I had robbed in August followed me and called the cops. She waited outside Barnes & Noble while the police were on their way, to make sure I did not slip away. I had been reading Luc Sante's *Low Life* in the store after taking a fix in the bathroom and then stole it to finish at home. This was the first of many resonances between my fiction and my facts, as the book was devoted to the very Bowery I was now apprehended on to the tune of "On the ground, motherfucker!" When I was searched, empty heroin bags were discovered in my briefcase; *Low Life* was abandoned as unworthy of evidence. Books and drugs, the two entities that determined so much of my existence, were both present when and where I had my last breath of free air for over a decade.

Low Life was exactly the type of book that had led me to this juncture. My love of obscure tales, printed artifacts from a city devoted to words, and the seamier side of the past primed me to become a bookish New York junkie with my head in the opium clouds of the nineteenth century. Sometimes my interests resounded. Years later I found a bilingual edition of Dadaist poetry with Luc Sante's handwritten name in it; he had donated the volume to the prison I was in, and no one else had yet picked up the French text. Herbert Asbury's *Gangs of New York* had influenced Sante to write about hop joints and blind tigers but had also inspired me to emulate the archaic antisocial characters it described. Villainy in sepia attracted me. I relished the idea that I was copping dope on the same blocks that William Burroughs had when he lived in his Bowery bunker; I had read *Junkie* several times by then, more as a users' manual than a work of art. Delving deeper, I read the only published collection of Herbert Huncke's mediocre work when the ancient dope fiend was still alive, and I lived for the streetscapes described in biographies of

Beat Generation figures because they were my streets, too. Of course, when things got a little too real and I found myself on Rikers Island, I lost my taste for the gritty and retreated into science fiction. On the day of my sentencing, I read William Gibson's *Neuromancer* twice in a row to avoid contemplating what awaited me.

Being the Apologetic Bandit did nothing to mitigate my sentence in court, despite the smoke blown up my rear by the $25,000 attorney my parents hired or the opinions of the numerous jailhouse lawyers who promised me that they could get me off . . . for a small fee. Although I was obviously disinclined to commit crimes I would have never thought of without a heroin addiction riding me, I was sentenced quite harshly as a person who "should have known better," as the judge put it. Of course I did know better; it may have felt unfair because a different standard was being deployed to deal with me, but its rationale was accurate. For each of the five counts of armed robbery to which I pled guilty, I would serve the mandatory minimum sentence: two years—a decade in total, twelve if I lost my good time.

The consequences of my crime and ultimate cost of my brief addiction were hard on my family as well as the woman I had recently married, who will get her own chapter. My family was once a loving clan of Jewish intellectuals. My father is a successful writer in the Russian language world, and my mother was a corporate computer programmer. They had emigrated from Russia in 1977, and I was born a year later, an only child. My addiction came as a big surprise after my accomplishments at Stuyvesant High School and NYU. I graduated from the latter in 2000, moving on to a job at a literary agency, a shared apartment on the Lower East Side, and the dalliance with heroin that soon took over everything else. When my parents came to visit on Rikers, the cops inevitably tried to shuffle them into the separate room where attorneys see their clients. For the ten years that they continued to visit, they kindly brought food and books, sent a hundred bucks a month, and never let me forget how much of a disappointment this all was.

Being from the 97 percent of Americans for whom the walled lanes of prison were either a mystery or a mistaken impression committed by Hollywood, I had much to learn about the ways and means of this world. My education came from my fellow prisoners, that 3 percent of countrymen who are either current convicts or have been behind the wall at some point, whether consciously instructing me or demonstrating the hidden truths and unwritten laws stringing the world inside together. To supplement this intense schooling, as well as to stay sane and give purpose to the years to which I was sentenced, I also read 1,046 books behind the wall. The list I kept of my reading proved to be the ultimate aide-mémoire for these years, and I will refer to it frequently in these pages. It proved easy for me to remember what was going on in the yard or in my breast when I look back through the batch of mismatched handwritten pages of my booklist and see that I was reading, say, *Ulysses*, in January 2012. Prison is a transformative experience, very much like war. You can't help changing. In my case, reading's evolution into writing made the difference between merely surviving ten years of incarceration and finding meaning in it. Even though my life was a daily shit sandwich, metaphorically speaking, my future was also in doubt. My location was an unspeakable secret to the social world of my parents, and they introduced my wife to others as "our relative," even though everyone knew the truth and were just being polite. Denying my very existence made things easier for them then but harder for me later, and few friends had my address to write to.

I was all of twenty-five years old when I was sent to a maximum-security prison called Green Haven Correctional Facility to start serving my ten-year sentence. I was still called "kid" by the older cons with whom I shared the big house. I was less than a year in when I saw an old man called Pop fed an actual shit sandwich. The impression left by the sight of Pop grinding a human turd between two slices of prison-issue Wonder Bread was indelible. It was an assault on most of my senses, including my understanding of right and wrong, and not something I will ever forget. The world of my coddled upbringing and life lived in between the covers of leather-bound books was suddenly so far away that it might as well have been make-believe, while ten years of a life in which men amuse themselves with raw cruelty and debasement was the only thing real now.

I FIRST MET POP early on in my bid, in 2004. He was a black man with sharp features, gray hair, and mental impairment. The cops had to bribe him with cigarettes to shower, and he learned to let himself grow foul in order to get free smokes. The one time Pop was forced to bathe rather than being cajoled, he marched from his cell in the nude to protest.

Pop was to be a ward of the state for the rest of his life, even though he had initially come upstate with only a skid bid. He had been given a one-to-three-year-long sentence for knocking a lady over in midtown Manhattan while riding (and then fleeing on) a bicycle. The man was clearly a low-functioning addict and alcoholic, but he had blatantly hurt somebody. The felony conviction of someone mentally handicapped is no less of a notch in the DA's belt than sending me up the river was. Upstate, Pop was immediately transferred to a "satellite unit" for psychiatric cases. Because of his short sentence he was presumed to be not very dangerous and housed in a dormitory of medicated men. There Pop noticed an old white convict sleeping off his meds. He didn't like the looks of the man. Pop proceeded to beat him to death with a fire extinguisher. The next sentence he received was twenty-five to life. Murder convictions are particularly valuable for DAs, while the line between mental illness and crime is drawn by the kinds of lawyers one pays by the hour rather than the court-appointed clock-watchers defending Pop.

Accustomed to begging from a lifetime of homelessness, Pop would ask for anything in his line of sight. "Can Pop have a cookie?" he'd ask. "Can Pop have a cigarette?" With resources severely limited in prison, charity is usually left up to the generosity of the donor. Constantly asking, claiming hunger and other evocations to pity, is considered in bad taste in a world where no one ever has enough of anything. For that reason, admittedly not a good one, an inmate with a cruel streak decided to teach him a lesson. He defecated on a slice of bread and capped it with another. Pop was used to handouts and received the sandwich with delight. He trustingly bit into it, mashing it with his tongue and gums in the absence of teeth.

"Oh no, they done fed Pop shit!" he exclaimed morosely. Nevertheless he took another little nibble to make sure it was all shit, and didn't contain anything edible like a slice of cheese. That extra bite was heartbreaking. Years later, when I read Marquis de Sade's *120 Days of Sodom*, I did not encounter this particular act in the chapters on coprophagic deviance but did see echoes of it in all the discussions of sadism, which I often felt exposed to in its purest form.

That was the world in which I landed. Where were my books now? My family, my friends, my entire previous life felt impossibly far away. After observing such a thing, or rather a decade of such things, was I even fit to return to the world that had so woefully underprepared me for this? In my disgust and pity, I also wondered whether I was really any better than the sandwich's chef. After all, I was the only one responsible for finding my way there, so it would seem I was in the right place. But having witnessed a deed beyond the realm of what I had once thought possible, I realized I would have to expand that category. And I would do so again and again; there was always a deeper circle of hell, however much I saw that was noble and good inside.

I had experienced a little of the brutality possible in life during my time as a drug addict, but it had lasted only a short time and had occurred so early in my life that I was cushioned from its sharpest edges by my family. Immediately after my arrest I could no longer count on any kind of protection, nor could I hide in books. I could only use them as I went on my journey. It was along a narrow path, but I had my eyes wide-open.

In the following pages, I will share what it was I learned over ten years behind the wall, where I aged from twenty-five to thirty-five, read more than a thousand books, and met a sizable percentage of my fifty-five thousand fellow New York State (NYS) prisoners. Because I quelled my hopelessness and terror by imagining myself to be an anthropologist sent to learn as much as I could about prison culture, *Sentence* is not arranged as a chronological account of my incarceration. Instead, I have organized it by subject, with each chapter devoted to either a specific demographic slice of the incarcerated population or a facet of prison life whose details are utterly unknown to the outside world. Some names and identifying details of certain people mentioned in this book have been changed. My reading often informed me in these studies in unexpected ways; I learned as much about modern prison from Solzhenitsyn and Dostoyevsky as I did when trying to make sense of what I experienced directly. Those many books enabled me to understand my fellow man and my own corrupted self quite handily at times, as I also read to comprehend my own fate; Proust saved me by showing me where the lost time went. Reading might have been the very thing that made it possible for me to return from inside whole. I hope the authors who inspired me will also help me as I try to make sense for my readers what I saw, whom I met, what I did, and why and how.

2

TEN YEARS, THREE MONTHS, AND SIX DAYS

Three years after graduating from New York University, cum laude and a semester early, I passed through a pair of steel gates leading through the four-story bastion walls of Green Haven. About a decade later I was released into the parking lot of Fishkill Correctional Facility, where my parents waited for me along with five years of parole. In the time between becoming a state prisoner and returning to civilian status, I was housed in a dozen compounds and traveled the state to its northern border with Canada and its western edge at Buffalo. My grandparents died, and George W. Bush was replaced by Barack Obama. When I look back, my extensive reading of the travelogues of nineteenth-century explorers was how I sought succor on my own trip through the Incarcerated Nation. I read James Boswell's *Journey to the Hebrides with Samuel Johnson* and Evelyn Waugh's collected travel writing, as well as Paul Theroux, Ryszard Kapuściński, and other genteel travelers, but it was Richard Burton's *Pilgrimage to Mecca* and Henry Stanley's *Through the Dark Continent* with which I most identified. I had no Livingstone to presume, and the Royal Geographical Society did not sponsor my travels, but as I moved through the treacherous terrain of the state's penal system, I took my own versions of notes on the varieties of human experience little known in the outside world.

I made sure not to forget who I was before I became prisoner

04A3328. This was a common theme in the literature of prison. Henri Charrière relied on his butterfly tattoo to survive the challenge in *Papillon*. Jean Valjean's torment over becoming #24601 in Victor Hugo's *Les Misérables* was clarified for me by my struggle to remain Daniel Genis and not the 3,328th prisoner to be processed into New York State prison in the year 2004. I had read *Les Mis* years before but returned to it for the description of its hero's decades of confinement and escape. My first name was never uttered by the guards, not once during my entire bid. They called me Genis if they were being nice and Inmate 04A3328 if I was in trouble. For our part, we were strictly forbidden from knowing anything beyond the first letter of their Christian names. This made for great fun when I accidentally learned that an irritating little bully's name was David, as well as "CO Creep." My friends and I would walk by him and say things like "The pictures of David online are going to get him fired," or "She said David has a genital deformity," leaving him visibly unsettled. In another case, a sexy and flirtatious young female correctional officer was only known to us as "E," so we all proposed names suiting her. I thought I did well with my classical "Electra," but it was my friend Billy Barovick who took the cake with "Erotica." The rules regarding names seemed random, but the intention behind them was clear: replacing our names with numbers was deliberately dehumanizing, while secreting the correctional officers' first names was an attempt to discourage fraternizing.

In any case I certainly tried to remain a free citizen of the world while the system put me through a conversion process I recognized from Primo Levi's account of being processed into a death camp for Jews by the Nazis. The fact that much worse than I experienced was suffered by innocent people in *The Drowned and the Saved* made my flicker of self-pity laughable, but much of what I read in the books of the German and Russian camp life was familiar. Downstate Correctional Facility was an hour north of New York. It was like the Sorting Hat in the Harry Potter books, though I guess we all went to Slytherin. Being the first prison that a convict sees, it had a processing procedure that was conducted with barked orders, insults, and even occasional violence; Elie Wiesel described something like it in *Night*, so I knew that such abuse was deliberate. Treating us badly right at the beginning of our confinement tested our attitudes toward this new and lower status in life. We were being checked for defiance.

The clothing I had arrived in from Rikers was thrown out with fury and mocked as "gay-wear." My orifices were rudely peered into, a part of the process supervised by a man wielding a club because so many failed to keep their cool when ordered to bend and spread. My legal papers, the only possession allowed to pass into the Incarcerated Nation from the various county jails from where we were each coming, were examined by a cop who made it clear it was disgusting for him to handle my effects. The hair on my head and face was shaved off by inmate barbers, and I was ordered to put lice-killing suds into my armpits and pubic hair, and then wash it off in freezing water. Refusing to apply the burning chemicals was another step that led to occasional outbreaks of violence, useful to the cops who needed examples to demonstrate their monopoly on it.

I attended to it all very carefully because I didn't understand everything that was being said. Every first-time prisoner has to quickly pick up the jargon in order to function in the Incarcerated Nation. Coded into the specialized vocabulary of doing time are entire penological philosophies, as well as the countercultural venom of a population held against its will. There's also racial and otherwise tribalistic tension, moral codes, and surprisingly much that is humorous. But the general gist is an attempt at professionalese in a world very far from professional.

Acronyms and abbreviations were common. CF means "correc-

tional facility" and shows great optimism on Albany's part. It's a
fairly new term and one that appeared as part of a cohort of fresh
institutional language. The retirement of traditional terms like "war-
den," "guard," and even "prison" came as part of a wave of penal
reform in reaction to the Attica prison riot of 1971, which some histories identify as marking the end of the 1960s. That event had prisoners of various minority groups joining together to demand an end
to their disenfranchisement. Inmates protested, much as black people, women, and gays had earlier done to demand an enhancement of
their civil rights. Albany was charged to respond.

The symbolism was as far as most of the good intentions got; in
essence, the changes were superficial. Doing away with the term
"prison" did nothing for the recidivism rate. I always preferred the
archaic, tough monikers like "clink," "big house," and "hoosegow"
(from the Spanish *juzgado* [court], also the source of "jug"). Nevertheless, there was a specific vocabulary to learn, and no dictionary to
brush up with in advance. You'd hear the guards say that someone
got dragged to the "shoe," and it turned out to mean SHU, or "special housing unit." These are entire jails built for solitary confinement, though only in theory, because New York typically locked you
in a room with another prisoner, often a maniac—a shoe à deux. If
you had a lexicon, it would tell you that prisoners never used that
term; it was always the "box" or the "bing" in common parlance.
CO, short for "correctional officer," is neither a proper description of
the men in blue nor what they are ordinarily called, unless it was to
their faces, in which case they are always addressed with the title.
Cops are also "hacks," "turnkeys," "guards," or "pigs," if one wishes
to sound hard on the cheap. We prisoners were officially "inmates,"
a term with pejorative connotations, while the out-of-fashion "convict" has today acquired a positive one.

Being a tribal society, we had flags. Our color was green; the coppers' was blue, because of their uniforms. Things resonate; in my quest to read the longest of books, I turned to Edward Gibbon's *Decline and Fall of the Roman Empire*, and then a few more works on things Byzantine. I was not completely surprised to learn that the factions tearing Constantinople apart during the long Byzantine twilight were aligned according to the blue and green chariot racing teams. Constantinople's violent urban class war had blues versus greens, like us!

What one cannot help but learn about prison, should one find himself there, is that violence hovered over every transaction and interaction in an environment starved of resources. Everyone stole whenever they could, and there was sabotage, too. I knew a man who would throw unopened cases of copy paper into the trash as his contribution to bringing down "the Man." The prison yard was also Adam Smith's dream; while transactions between prisoners were technically forbidden, capitalism arose out of the bare earth as the men bought and sold from one another in a hive no less active than the trading floor of Manhattan's Stock Exchange. The nature of our gray-market economy was made clear to me almost immediately, for while Newports and stamps may have been the official currency, addictions to gambling and drugs set the prices, and violence was the ultimate stock-in-trade.

Inside, the invisible hand of the market was naked and visible. In the Malthusian competition of all against everyone, the allegorical hand often functioned as a clenched fist. Dostoyevsky's *House of the Dead* describes nineteenth-century czarist prisons in a similar way. One can purchase so much in a prison yard. Packs of Newports will buy something to eat, various drugs, weapons, porn, and art, with carved bars of soap and photorealistic portraits being the most common. One can also acquire services like barbering, chiropractics, blow jobs, having someone stabbed, or having a love letter written. The latter was the only hustle I ever did much of, but every experienced prisoner had some way of making enough money for a joint or a meal.

The explorers whose works I studied also navigated a world defined by violence, even if tempered by wonder. Captain Sir Richard Francis Burton took a spear through both cheeks while penetrating the forbidden city of Harar in Somaliland, as I read in *First Footsteps in East Africa: Or, an Exploration of Harar* in the cheap Dover reprint, leaving him with devilish scars for the rest of his life. One of the first observations I made about my fellow prisoners was that scars were common. Many bore thick keloid cicatrices from ear to mouth, known as "telephone" scars because of how and why and where they were usually acquired. Others had split lips or cuts extending down from the eyebrows to the cheeks, making "window curtains." Also popular were "buck-80s," denoting the 180 stitches required to close a full facial cut. One man even had a ragged tic-tac-toe game on his forehead. I managed to avoid facial scarring, but that's not to say everyone I knew did.

Every prison also has a gambling operation or three, weekly sport tickets that cost a pack of Newports to play. Picking the right teams could pay off with fifty to one hundred packs, and sometimes there were multiple winners. These were professional operations, run by men who had been bookies in the real world. Every ticket had a secret bank, where a stash of cigarettes was kept to pay winners and ensure that the rest of the populace kept playing. But because transactions between prisoners were technically illegal, there was room for the law to fatten itself.

A few weeks before my arrival at Green Haven there had been an atrocious incident. The victim was a crooked cop who had boiling oil splashed in his face. Like much violence in prison, this did not happen because of raging tempers, an inability to control vicious tendencies, sadism, or general antisocial sentiment. The attack occurred because someone acted outside protocol and caused financial repercussions.

Identifying where the bank for a sports gambling operation was kept was a coup for a crooked cop, who could legally confiscate anything over two cartons. He used paid snitches to find out which cell had the hundreds of packs of cigarettes and confiscated them, right into the trunk of his car. Such a big loss shut down the ticket operation, but even worse was that a precedent could be set. It was one thing for the convicts to have been caught misbehaving and made to pay the price; being intentionally targeted and robbed was another. Such a breach in the accepted code could not be allowed to pass, and as a result the officer was disfigured. Violence emerged for the final settlement of accounts.

The man who did it was serving life anyway. He got years in solitary for the attack, and the box time would hurt, but he would be taken care of by his fellow convicts during and after, and he expected to die inside. I suppose on the day it happened, part of the crooked cop did, too. I actually managed to read about the incident in a local newspaper. It reveled in describing the horrible damage done to human tissue by boiling oil but did not even try to determine why this had happened. The only reason offered was that the assailant was a prisoner and his victim was the law.

Years later, in a federally funded class meant to teach us how to solve problems without violence, I encountered the same pigheaded belief that violence was always the wrong solution. Prison taught me that the opposite was true; there were times when violence was the only one. Being rather meek-mannered in my life up to this point, I wished this wasn't the case. But I was clever enough to know better. And I knew to be sure to pay my debts, lest I had to pay in blood. The violent life of prisons and their crushing limitations was mine for a decade. The tests and challenges and pain were a crucible for forging a better, harder man out of the boy who came in.

From that first incident on, violence often proved the theorems and derivations prison taught me. Mostly I learned about people, and if I include myself in that category, it's all I learned. One can't ask for a better subject, or for a better institution of learning. No wonder the Mob calls the joint "school." But it is a place to learn about the naked self. With all the fripperies we buy and drape over ourselves to occlude or manipulate the expression of our true natures removed by the brutal limitations of prison, one is left bare to see and be seen. And the consequences of being a slow learner can include a ruptured colon, so there is every incentive to get things right. I had my books to learn from, and my human subjects. The books could cause anomie, solipsism, and paper cuts if used unwisely. The men cut deeper and aimed for the face.

BECAUSE I WAS A QUICK learner I did not experience much personal violence over my decade in. This is not to say everyone had as placid a bid as mine. My first bunky, Mario, was stabbed in the face within a few weeks of our arrival in the summer of 2004, in my first month in my first max. His was the first attempted murder I witnessed. If the attack on the crooked cop demonstrated the role of violence in our economy and the importance of finance in the Incarcerated Nation, then the assault on Mario was a lesson in the specialized culture that prisoners have developed and the role violence plays in it. When I arrived I was alone in a double-bunked cell for a few days; they were waiting for another white prisoner to bunk me with. I was kind of shocked by the policy, but that kind of de facto segregation is what the cops learned is the safest practice after years of experience with bunkies fighting in the shockingly small confines of a max cell. The mandatory initial six months of double-bunking was inescapable. Perhaps living in such confinement was enforced to make the eventual move to single quarters so welcome as to appear spacious.

After my first few days with an empty cot below me, Mario showed up, with such an air of proprietorship that I thought he was there to fix the plumbing. He was a mountain of a man, soon proven to be the strongest white guy in the prison. Mario could lift a concrete table—considered a safe hiding spot because it took two regular men to budge—under which was a stash for razors and shanks. He would have made a great sumo wrestler or linebacker; at five feet ten he was my height but weighed more than three hundred pounds. Some of it was accumulated fat from his 100 percent diet of pasta and greasy red sauce, but most of it was dense muscle. Mario was pop-eyed and had a massive head. He had recently concluded an eight-year term, which he spent as a powerlifter and Italian yardfather. His existence crossed into celluloid stereotype, as Mafia movies operate in a feedback loop with these kinds of guys. It was hard to tell what they picked up from seeing on a screen and what the movies had learned from studying authentic Italian Americans of the organized crime subspecies. Mario used a contraband razor to slice his garlic, like they did in *Goodfellas*; he couldn't believe it could be done in any other way.

Mario himself wasn't a made man, though his father was. That, as well as his superhuman strength, gave him some expectations that weren't shared by everyone. While I was just feeling my way out with the other Caucasian mutts on the Irish court, Mario immediately sauntered over to the Italian court and chomped cigars with the older guys. There he felt himself at home, and then some. The old men didn't appear to have much use for all the weight-lifting equipment over which they ruled, so they weren't that impressed with Mario's flamboyant exercising and didn't agree with Mario's belief in the preordained rank he imagined for himself. Somehow Mario had a blind spot for how the Mafia actually runs, despite having seen all the movies and his own father soldiering for the Bonannos. He was not immediately promoted to captain of the Italian court, and he took it personally. He also underestimated the guys who had held down that court for decades.

Meanwhile, things in our cramped cell got scary. The bluster he displayed outside was a whole different world from the psychological torment he shared with me, and not in a healthy way. If he was to be miserable, then I had to join him, and he would take care of the reasons. Mario put it best in words I can recall him uttering sotto voce: "If I can't get along with a nice guy like you, what the fuck is wrong with me?"

He would make confessions I didn't want to hear, knowing I'd have to pay for the dubious privilege somehow. Mario told me that the truth about the three-decades-long sentence he got was nothing he could brag about to his *paisans*. He was serving the rest of his life for committing thirty daytime burglaries, kicking in suburban doors to steal enough to feed his carefully concealed drug addiction. He was in prison for being a crackhead, not a mobster. Sometimes he would weep. After those episodes, Mario would grow paranoid about my revealing his vulnerabilities in the yard. I never did, but the regret he felt over letting me see him cry drove him mad. I'd wake up to his walrus face too close to mine, swearing me to silence, threatening my life before the gates even opened for breakfast.

Life wasn't easy in that cell for me; after Mario bragged about ejaculating on some old bunky's toothbrush, I started to hide mine. He noticed and started to hide his. I began to dread nightfall. Perhaps the experienced elders of the Italian court took notice of some of this through the Cohiba smoke, or maybe they began to wonder why the son of a wiseguy never got his own "button." At his age, he should have been made. When Mario reacted, poorly, to their rejection of his offer to helm the Italian court, things got worse. The old men told him he should wait awhile, see how things go before jumping into the shoes of Teddy Persico, the last skipper of the court. Mario cursed them, hocking a big loogie on their court and moving over to the Irishmen to silently lift weights in a rage that didn't pass.

THE HIT WASN'T TOO long coming. I was doing bicep curls on a warm summer night; it was already dark. Mario was lured away from our court by two Irishmen who must have owed the Italians a favor. He was facing Paddy Irish, the one with the fearsome reputation, when the other moved out of his sight. The first stab went through his cheek and into his tongue. The man who'd been in conversation with him until that point suddenly became another assailant. Mario was stuck by two knives and was bleeding in spurts. The mountain went down on one knee and let out a groan deep enough that I felt it in my sore elbows. I had recently quit smoking; I immediately took it up again.

Despite the blood, despite the moan, Mario straightened up from his crouch. Realizing that the two Irishmen had scattered, he picked up a rock heavy enough to cave in a skull and set out for revenge. He knew he did not have much time and wanted to catch at least one of them. But too much blood had flowed for the cops to miss. Because of his size and the possibility he had a weapon, they came out in a phalanx, quickly surrounding him. They took Mario in without any resistance. Snitches later fingered the two fellows, but when Mario appeared as a witness at their disciplinary hearing, he said, "Never saw this piece of shit in my life," making himself the legendary stand-up guy he had wanted to be recognized as in the first place.

The man hated rats, but he also thought if his two assailants weren't found guilty, he wouldn't have a separation order against them and would one day be able to take revenge personally. They put him in involuntary protective custody for a while, since his attackers were technically unknown, and then they moved him out of the jail. He ended up in a different joint with a different jawline.

I learned so much from this nightmare. Not to underestimate old men in prison. Not to blow your own horn. Not to put yourself in another's control—Mario had not been able to get along with me because he worried about my betraying him. Not to take confessions. I also learned not to tell and how to do so with class. Mario was a much finer teacher than he gave himself credit for. But I think I'd rather share a cell with the devil.

PRISON WAS EXACTLY LIKE my short life with Mario: dull, menacing, and full of frustration for long periods, punctuated by the lightning-fast, staccato atrocity of violence at unexpected intervals. And strength hardly mattered; the mightiest man in the yard was brought to his bloody knees by two quick micks with ice picks. Witnessing such a thing at the very outset of my bid was healthy. I have to admit going through a phase of being glad it was Mario rather than me, though violence in prison was never random or senseless, so there was no reason for it to have been me. Nevertheless, I tried not to earn myself such a fate as his. For the next decade I factored in the potential for violence and Irishmen in all my decisions.

I READ AS MANY books as I could on the condition of incarceration in general to understand my new life better; Solzhenitsyn became an old friend, and I wonder if I'm not the last person to read all three volumes of *Gulag Archipelago* in the twenty-first century. However, it was Jack Henry Abbott's *In the Belly of the Beast*, written just a generation and a half earlier, that was the most relevant description of the exact system I was living under. The man himself had been freed thanks to his pen, or rather the impression it made on Norman Mailer, whom I met once. Despite honestly depicting Abbott as a determined lifelong criminal, Mailer liked his writing enough to petition the governor to get Abbott out. Things like this were possible long ago. Once released, Abbott was celebrated around town. He was taken to a dinner, where he thought that the waiter in a Greenwich Village restaurant looked at him funny. He stabbed the man to death and went right back to the big house forever. He hanged himself while living in the cell next to that of a friend of mine.

Modern convicts hate *Belly of the Beast*. Despite immortalizing them as countercultural icons of bravery, the book also describes their pleasure in homosexual sex with "kids." Prisoners are aware of this, are aware of the impression it makes, and disavow the book. It wasn't available in a single one of the jailhouse libraries I worked in or borrowed from. My father mailed me a paperback. But there are better books on the subject anyway. And you learn more from a day behind the wall than a treatise written about one.

My most valuable time inside was spent in four maximum-security prisons. For seven years I shared my meals, time, and air with men who could not live long enough to finish their terms. One guy I knew doing forty-five to life to atone for the murder of his grandparents discreetly notified me on the very day that he had completed half of his sentence. Half of a four-and-a-half-decade minimum meant over twenty years to go, but it was all downhill now! I saw a man complete a thirty-three-year term and later heard the interview he gave NPR; he had been the teenage getaway driver for a robbery that turned lethal while he waited at the wheel outside the store. Everyone got twenty-five to life. For some reason the actual shooters got out way before him, and he was a model inmate. He waited for parole board after parole board—each hit is two years, though if they give you only a one-year hit, you're going home after you see the board again in twelve months. Such things do not pass lightly; even on NPR you could tell he was somewhat off. The years had done their damage.

ALONG WITH MY OWN prison-time minimum of ten years, three months, and six days, I had five years of parole, called "post-release supervision" in the merciless euphemism of bureaucratese.

I violated it once, getting arrested for stealing a few jars of coffee when I relapsed. I was clean after the ninety days I served as punishment, so I finished parole with no other problems.

After the maxes, I did the rest of my time in three medium-security prisons, which were another world. I also spent a year in three different box facilities, also a separate realm . . . the SHUs of New York's DOC (Department of Corrections) system are hell's hell. The population of the state system dropped from 70,000 to 58,000 during my time in, reflecting the decline in crime that I've read controversially explained as the consequence of abortion being made available two decades ago.

If that was indeed the case, I spent years with people who were unintended, or at least unplanned. One of the things I learned never to mention, to avoid rubbing in the benefits I was born with (and wasted), was having a father. While Mother's Day was an annual card- and gift-making flurry, Father's Day was only noted by occasional grumbling regarding the "bitches teaching they seed to hate their pops." Just about all of the men, even the youngest possible (sixteen), were fathers, and of course they all technically had fathers. Sometimes they met each other as fellow prisoners for the first time inside; I witnessed this more than once. But the men, whether sons or fathers, did not function as fathers and had not been raised in traditional families. Along with my plural parents, I also learned not to talk about passports, piano lessons, and Paris.

THE TESTING I WAS put through revealed my limits: I wasn't a snitch, humility was a poor fit, and I feared physical confrontation, though not a battle of wits. Inside, I could count on probably being the smartest guy in the room and innocuous enough that anyone with a strong dislike for me was likely to be an indiscriminate bully. The cops never warmed to me the way they did to the upstate guys and toady porters, but they did consider me basically harmless. I met some of the worst people in the world but surprisingly also some of the best. Curing myself of moral relativism was a lesson I never learned at NYU, but the professors who did the instruction on the subject, supplemented by the books I read, are men you will meet in these pages. In part, this book is dedicated to them, my murderous mentors.

3

NEWJACK ISLAND

Rikers Island saps you. It's menacing, dull, dangerous, and viciously random; causality gets left in Queens, as violence strikes whoever happens to be in the wrong place at the wrong time. That description serves any joint, but unlike the eleven facilities I was to visit after my seven months on the island, Rikers demands its own chapter. Two facets of its nature single it out from the correctional facilities, transit hubs, and special housing units that make up the penitentiary landscape. It's not actually a prison but a jail. And it is most certainly a landmark in the underground culture of New York City.

Rikers is technically a county jail; it holds detainees at the county level, people who cannot make bail or are ineligible for it. Rikers "detains" them before they are convicted and rendered unto state custody. This means that most of its population is technically innocent, though admittedly not for long. The exceptions are the guys serving city "bullets," slang for sentences only a year long, and the most you can do is two consecutively, though city years are actually only eight months for these convicted prisoners. They are the ones who get the kitchen and graveyard jobs. For the rest of the accused, though usually not murderers, there is the possibility of bail. Unlike every other walled compound of which I've been a guest, Rikers was not mandatory. If I had had $150,000 I could have gone home until I was sentenced. My parents refused to pony up. There are men who spend years on the island, going to court for a five-minute appearance once a month, for lack of a hundred dollars to pay their bail. I always thought that a prison that only poor people have to stay in should have better food.

Rikers had been artificially enlarged with landfill, as I learned later, when I had access to *The Encyclopedia of New York City* as a library clerk upstate. Seagulls land on it for the generous portions of garbage, but no boats service it, as it has no port or piers. Even the NYPD speedboats that occasionally circle to fish hypothetical escapees out of the mighty currents in the East River are deployed from Queens. The only access is by a bridge leading from Queens to the island. It is colloquially known as the longest in the world, since some men spend their lives trying to cross it.

Since Rikers has been serving the city's criminal class for a century, it's had its share of celebrity tenants, including representatives of the druggy downtown scene of music and petty crime. Though rap is not my corner of pop culture, many of its stars have been welcomed to Rikers, as well as punk-rock talents over the years. Lil Wayne did a year on the island for a gun when I was already upstate. He became upset when his iPod was eventually confiscated, after first being allowed in as part of a plea bargain; he needed his beats to compose raps to. The ghosts of the past were never far. Herbert Huncke wrote a few short stories about his time on the island and how much he enjoyed the methadone; those stories are published in his collected works. Sid Vicious, detained for his murder trial after waking up next to dead Nancy Spungen, once came to C-95 to detox. That's the junkie's destination on the island, where I made sure to end up as well.

On my bus of detainees who weren't released from court, I was the only one who hadn't been to the island before, a fact I did not advertise. A cloud of misery floats over the many locked-down buildings on

Rikers. I knew enough to make sure I got placed in C-95, the famous
Five Building, known to junkies around the world, and a natural fit
for me. Even if I hadn't been dope sick or on a methadone program, I'd
have chosen the Five Building over the others. It's the jail on the island where you go to taper off methadone if your future is upstate.
Methadone had helped me after the madness of the summer's heroin
addiction, but now I had to get off it. It's not easy; William Burroughs
declined to mention it in his final publication, *Last Words*, but he died
on a maintenance program in Kansas.

If you have a misdemeanor, they verify your dose by calling your
program. The office that deals with that sort of thing has an evoca-
tive wall-size list of every methadone program in the city, with phone
numbers and counselor names. There are a lot of them; New York
has more addicts than any other American city. If you have a felony,
they detox you in expectation of your trip up the river. Your dose is
decreased by ten milligrams every three days until you hit forty, and
then you go down by five. I met a kind drug counselor who was able
to extend my detox by twenty days; it was a godsend.

The other buildings on the island have picturesque names. OBCC
is called "Oh Boy!" The "Beacon" is a red-topped building that looks
vaguely like a lighthouse; the "Three" (C-73), the "Four" (C-74), and
the "Six" (C-76) are the less prosaic others. The latter is for city inmates
serving a year or less and features young men working in bright candy-
cane uniforms; the prisoners wear archaic striped clothes that look like
Halloween costumes. There's also "Rosy," the Rose M. Singer, a facility that was never an option for me, as it is the building for women. I
visited a manic girlfriend there once before my own problems.

My time on the island was foreboding, scary, and lonely. I latched
on to those willing to tolerate a newjack and knew not to try buying
friends or pretend to be more of a gangster than I could convincingly
portray to specimens of the real thing. The island was gang-ridden to

the point of absurdity. I had to learn the prerogatives of Latin Kings, DDP (Dominicans Don't Play), the Ñetas, and most of all the Bloods, and right away.

Men were obsessed with the discovery of gang identification in everyday items, and many things were forbidden because of this mania. Even the cereal was claimed by particular gangs. Frosted Flakes were rumored to have been removed from the menu after the Bloods collected all the boxes of cereal, showing Tony the Tiger as rightfully theirs. After all, there he was, in his red kerchief. Then Rice Krispies vanished; obviously it was because Snap, Crackle, and Pop were respectively Latin King, Crip, and Blood. Cheap "Dada" sneakers, which used a crown as their symbol, were Latin King shoes, obviously. Today the jail just issues tan uniforms to everyone, letting you keep the underwear you came in wearing. Things were already bad back in 2003, when gang culture made most colors of clothing forbidden, as trademarks and shades became associated with affiliations. If Bloods claimed red and black, Crips used blue and purple, and Latin Kings wore yellow and black, you were left with green. I never had any truck with gangs.

Because I had mail coming to me, visits from my wife and parents, and people to call on the phone, gang banging did not appeal to me. Without those advantages, the surrogate family and general meaning to life that gang membership offers might have been more desirable. It is easy to not steal when one isn't hungry.

Being lonely is no easier.

One of the biggest problems on Rikers was the phone. It is a coveted and scarce resource, so obviously one to compete for. Dormitories had "slot time," daily periods toward the end of the day when certain people used certain phones. In the past, strife over the phones was bad enough to inspire a scar—the phone slice—going from ear to mouth. The phone slice was inflicted so frequently that the authorities devised a process allotting each user one daily six-minute phone call and one fifteen-minute call, each accessed by six private digits.

Obviously this gave rise to a system of pin-code extortion, in which the weak were forced to give their codes to the strong. The single benefit of this plan was that it gave the indigent a daily "debit" phone call to sell, each of which was worth seventy-five cents. A phone call was valued at an instant ramen soup, and that was something to those with nothing.

As a result of the business of selling calls, there were men on the island with accounts hundreds of dollars in the red, and if they went home and came back, that debt was waiting. The deficiency in this system was that force was often necessary to extort phone calls rather than buy them, which meant there was a potential for murder over an amount less than a dollar.

Gangs equated to violence, and there was one rare benefit of being massively out of place: no one ever asked me if I was "bangin'," so the one danger I could categorically avoid was being suspected of Crip affiliation. I remember the delight with which a sergeant once discovered me reading John Boyne's crime novel *Crippen*. At that time there was a wave of white kids from poor upstate towns who had become Crips upon entering the system. This caused beef with the reigning Bloods, and the white-shirted CO thought he had caught me at my Crip lessons. But alas, it was a work of fiction based on the first murder ever solved by telegraph. Dr. Crippen had escaped London after a dastardly deed but could not outrun the newly laid transatlantic telegraph cable. The sergeant returned the tome to me, disappointed.

In my stay on Rikers I had only four fights.

The first was with Barbero, the house "head cutter." He had kindly taken care of my shag, cutting my hair and trimming my eyebrows before the cops took me for more lineups. It might have helped; I wasn't picked once during the second round. Then the barber turned

on me, stealing some instant soup from me a week later. It was blatant disrespect, and a sign that being a white boy in this world would
mean frequent testing.

The bathroom scuffle I later had with the middle-aged Barbero was
not very conclusive. There was blood from my split lip, with no clear
victory, and only I got caught by the cops and moved upstairs to another dorm. However, fighting over a twenty-two-cent package of soup
proved to be the absolutely appropriate thing to do and useful to me
soon after. When I was transferred to another wing of the building a
month later, I overheard someone I barely recognized talking about me.

"Yo, that white boy love to fight, he fight for a soup!"

I was overjoyed. I didn't love to fight and didn't care about ramen
soup; I loved Latin and physics and nerdy science fiction. But my
paranoia had won the day in an absurd way; because I was afraid of
being considered a punk, I tried my twenty-five-year-old body out at
pugilism. I did not win, but I didn't have to, as long as I fought. I had
read similar accounts in all the prison memoirs I was gobbling up at
the time, trying to learn about the world I was slated for. But as a
young white prisoner in an American penal system, I could hardly be
expected to have only one quick test. I did everything I could to avoid
problems, but I made mistakes and had to pay for them by summoning all my meager reserves of courage. If you ever ask yourself what
you would do in such a position, I can assure you that you don't really
know until it happens. I've seen the toughest cats bitch up and run to
the cops for help, and the clearly outclassed go into battle with no
hope of winning but every intention of fighting for honor. I suppose I
fell somewhere in the middle.

My next test came soon enough. I managed to provoke a near
seven-foot-tall—maybe not a whole seven feet, but damn close—
African prisoner into a fight, despite previously having found common

ground and trying out my few phrases in Italian on him; he'd landed in Rome after fleeing his home country. The guy was serving the food with a ladle and managed to splash some of the gruel on my shirt, so after the meal I strolled over to him. I was holding two wrapped kosher trays of spaghetti and meatballs in my right hand, with which I was supposed to strike my death blow. I foolishly confronted him in front of his friends, thinking that asking him to be more careful with the slop was not unreasonable. Because of the audience, he informed me that he'd distribute it any way he pleased.

"Why do you have to be such a dick?" I asked. At the very moment I said the word "dick," he used his extraordinarily long reach, which seemed to come from up in the stratosphere, to punch me in the face. Now, in case you imagine such a thing to be a life-ender, it isn't. I was reading the *Iliad* at the time, for moral support, and I imagine Achilles and Patroclus exchanged such blows as a way of saying good morning. Of course I didn't respond with a chortle of mocking laughter and instead was knocked out of my slippers. But I rejoindered and had my moment of *aristeia* combat, managing to mush the two trays on him, almost reaching up to his face, and knocking us both over. It was not a dignified scene as we rolled around in kosher noodles. It didn't get any more serious than that, meaning no weapons and no friends jumping in.

The man who made sure I got a "fair one"—mano a mano rather than gang assault—was Doc Martin, a nickname of course, and one of GG Allin's old crew, a Murder Junkie associate. This made him Lower East Side punk-rock aristocracy, and the trip through Rikers is a familiar one for that set. GG himself was a legend, the most despicable man in a fairly despicable industry, which is saying something; the singer intravenously injected vodka as well as dope and speed and always interacted with his audience, whether punching women in the face at his concerts, or shitting onstage and eating it. It's on YouTube. GG Allin had been to prison and then died, and the Murder Junkies were left to continue going to prison.

Punk was antisocial enough that my teenage infatuation with it blossomed into many personal acquaintances in prison. By coincidence, the front man for Humyn Sewage, the band that opened for GG on the night of his last show before he overdosed, was another jailbird friend of mine. I met Spike Polite inside, and years later, after his release and after fifteen years down, I watched him perform in bars with stages for punk acts. Sewage was once a local hit band, and Spike was a punk's punk who appeared in the video for the one song MTV played by Jesse and the 8th Street Kidz. Spike was strung out on drugs and broke down when he brought home a guy in even worse shape. The guy was broke, too, and had also escaped from a Tennessee prison. At the time, Spike was living with a music professor who was obsessed with the band's "energy," which actually meant young boys and masochism. He had lots of photographs of skinny guys who thought they were the Sex Pistols. Spike needed the money. Spike and his new friend robbed and killed the professor. Spike didn't get too far, but the escapee was captured on a bus halfway across the nation. Even though Spike's role was secondary in the murder, he was given fifteen years.

Our mutual friend, Doc Martin, only had a single-digit bid ahead of him. He'd done a serious bid already, one long enough to send him to the maxes (to qualify for a max, you need at least a seven-year sentence, or really bad behavior). And fifteen years later, when I had to revisit the island for a winter due to the malfeasance in my third year of parole, Martin was there again.

His nickname was the product of adding "Doc" to his given name, the resultant handle referencing the favorite boots of punks and skins. He had a Jewish surname, at odds with the swastikas inked on his body. He once told me this was a consequence of adoption, but he also attended the Jewish services on Rikers with sincerity. And humor. One of the little artworks Doc gave me was a bas-relief carving of a Jew etched in a bar of soap and nicely faux-aged it with instant coffee. He titled his artistic meditation on anti-Semitic genocide "David Lifschitz." I couldn't take it upstate with me, but I wish I had. Doc was a talented artist and kind to me.

When we met, he forgave me for being new, ignorant, and soft, as long as I followed the advice I had asked of him. Doc was willing to let me pick his brain about state prison, how long I might be there, what it was going to be like for a white kid, etc. Part of the reason why I confronted the tall African was to avoid shaming Doc; he had taken a chance by associating with an untried newjack like me. He had let me handle this problem, told me I had done well even though no one would confuse my performance with a victory, and he suggested that I never confront anyone again in my shower slippers.

Being a well-liked and familiar convict, Doc Martin had been assigned a job by the guards on Hart Island, the next isle over in the archipelago between the Bronx, Queens, and Manhattan. Hart is where they bury the indigent, the bums, and nameless New Yorkers found dead every morning, as well as those who die on Rikers Island and aren't claimed by anyone; it's the city's Potter's Field. Washington Square Park once had that privilege, but now the burials are done far from the eyes of the rich and with prisoner labor. The *Encyclopedia of New York* later astounded me by claiming that a million people are buried there. The indigent dead are grimly and efficiently autopsied before being placed in cardboard coffins. Their internal organs, which are examined by a pathologist, are kept with their original host, though in a plastic bag. The bags are buried with the cadavers in the flimsy coffins.

One day Doc returned from grave digging in a foul mood and

went straight to the showers. To his misfortune, a bundle of "goon juice" had burst through a tipped coffin. Doc had been supporting the foot end, so it fell through the bottom and hit him in the face.

Unfortunately, it burst after being punctured by the screw in Doc's ocular orbit, which held his facial bones together after a motorcycle accident. The screw was under the skin, but just barely; Doc had once had me feel it. The cops bought Doc lunch from the real world after this atrocity, but the luxury of such food only raised memories that added to the litany of misfortune in his life. The last time I saw Doc in person, his pet rat had just died.

I ate many a meal with Doc and left Rikers right after him. The desk on which I filled out my initial paperwork at Downstate CF was covered in one of Doc's intricate, humorous drawings. I felt as if he had left it there for me, to bolster my spirits. And fifteen years later, I had to recognize him by the tattoo of a crucified skinhead on his arm and the old screw in his upper-orbital ridge, because his hair was now short and he was balding and his eyes were radically altered with yellow snake-eye contacts . . . but it was Doc nonetheless. Because Doc had known me as a young newjack it took him a minute to recognize the "oldhead" I'd become. I thanked him profusely for teaching me how to be a convict before I became one.

MUCH OF MY READING during my time on Rikers was meant to distance myself from my present reality. Life felt so hopeless, and the light at the end of the tunnel was impossibly far away, so I really preferred reading of the escapist variety rather than literary challenges. After all, literature inevitably reveals truths about our sordid lives, like the famous "naked lunch"—when you can finally see what's on your fork. That was pretty much the last thing anyone facing a chunk of hard time would want, so I reread all of William Gibson and lots of Philip

K. Dick and John le Carré. At the time of my sojourn there, the 1960s American science-fiction writer whom my father and I both idolized, Robert Sheckley, was in his last year of life. My father accidentally emailed him personally and ended up telling him about his young fan sadly incarcerated. The author sent me a signed typewritten manuscript and message of support, and died soon after.

Today it is one of my prize possessions.

However, I also read as research, and *Newjack*, by Ted Conover, proved useful. The author had gone through the correctional officer academy in Albany and become a prison guard at Sing Sing, all to secure the material for his book. A few years down the line, I found that I disagreed with some of the author's conclusions, for Conover saw only what he wanted to see: noble prisoners oppressed by mediocrity.

Newjack was written without any thought for the evil that Conover's subjects had wrought, and, as such, the book pathologically misplaced sympathies. However, I did not know this when I first read it and still thought that somewhere under lock and key, the master criminals, the Napoleons of crime and ultimate countercultural icons, were living under a rarefied criminal code of honor and courage. Little did I know that the disappointing population of Rikers represented the overall demographic well enough.

Prison was populated mostly by drug addicts, with the mentally ill thrown in (Ken Kesey's *One Flew Over the Cuckoo's Nest* was as helpful to me as the cavalcade of prison memoirs I plowed through), as well as a number of guys too violent to adhere to the social contract. Conover didn't get along well with the other COs, who probably smelled a rat in him, someone all too willing to be conned by the convicts. In *Newjack* he marvels at a murderer with a poem tattooed on him, not realizing that he revealed his incredibly low expectations of the prisoners by doing so. As a future jailhouse librarian, I would learn that poetry books were borrowed in a wave every Valentine's Day as the men plagiarized from them to mail verse to women in the free world. Prisoners use poetry as a means to an end, like anything else.

It was a good thing that I read *Newjack* while still on Rikers. Upstate I probably wouldn't have been able to; it's not banned, but a number of pages are supposed to have been redacted. That wasn't as bad as being totally banned, like Sun Tzu's *Art of War*, but it's hard to imagine a package-room officer taking the time to bowdlerize *Newjack*.

What's funny, and probably disappointing to its author, is that it isn't his scathing criticism of police brutality and the systematic destruction of the human soul that is forbidden for upstate prisoners to read. It is his description of the guards' locker rooms and the Sing Sing parking lot that is censored to prevent the information being somehow used to escape.

I NEVER MANAGED TO GET a comprehensive list of forbidden books from Albany, even as a journalist after my incarceration. Every package room had its own local standards, anyway. I received books in Russian and French at most jails until I hit one that simply couldn't trust Cyrillic. Apparently five Russian novels that my parents sent to me were routed to the central office in Albany for "translation." I wasn't made aware of that and never did get the books back, but after filing a grievance I at least managed to be compensated for them. I would love to have seen a copy of the DOC Index Librorum Prohibitorum, but I never had anything my parents sent rejected under normal circumstances. Even Albert Speer's *Spandau: The Secret Diaries*, his memoir of twenty years in a Berlin prison for Nazi war crimes, was allowed in, despite the big swastika on the cover. For a time, the magazine *Teenz* was forbidden as child pornography, but after a change in staff it was no longer deemed fodder for pedophilia. On Rikers the books had to be paperbacks, or the guards would rip the covers off. I was troubled by the sight of that destruction, but the guards had no qualms over ripping up books.

It was also at this time that I learned about the appeal of mass-market fiction: the books sold in airports and on bestseller lists that I'd avoided my entire life. To be polite I accepted loans of these books and read a handful of James Patterson novels. I wanted to understand why my peers swore by this schlock, and the experience proved useful in my later work at prison libraries. The writing itself was simple and formulaic. They could be finished in one afternoon; they were tall stacks of short chapters that kept the publisher's ink budget low. There was sex and violence, but I ultimately learned to wait a bit before returning the books, because my fellow inmates didn't believe that I really read them so quickly. I also tried the mass-market versions of genres I knew—Michael Crichton for science fiction, Sidney Sheldon for psychological suspense—but mass-market proved to be no guilty pleasure for me, being predictable, bloated with filler, and therefore horribly boring. I liked more difficult books best, not because they were great works but because they were challenging. And if I wanted fantasy, I preferred the high end.

Erewhon was worth revisiting, and an example of the sophistication possible in works of whimsy. After conquering the Gormenghast series, there's no going back to the shallow depths of Robert Jordan. And so on. . . .

Prison ultimately did make a good reader out of me, something I cannot imagine a modern American university education doing.

Each day on Rikers was just like the last, but we are infinitely adaptable creatures, and with time I grew to value my sedate and small life. I had no wish whatsoever to go upstate, if only because I feared the change. This was ridiculous, because the overwhelming consensus regarding quality of life on the island compared to upstate was for the latter. On Rikers entire months passed when I didn't go outside. Life was on pause on that hellish island, while everyone told me that upstate, things moved, and you lived, in however limited a way. It was true, as I eventually learned myself, but I also learned to fear surprises by then.

COURT TRIPS WERE a monthly horror. Sometimes they were scheduled just to make sure the buses didn't run too empty. We weren't allowed to know when we were going back to court, so I had to guess and be prepared to be awoken at four in the morning to breathe diesel for a few hours to make the five-mile trip, as our vehicle was delayed by endless stays in the court's truck traps where we sat shackled for hours. One of the most important things I could do to make the excursions less horrible was either not eat the day before or somehow poop in the middle of the night. The cells that held prisoners going to court only had a toilet out in the open right in the middle of them. Most people held it, while those who were thoroughly institutionalized shat in the middle of a crowd of thirty people with abandon.

The trips did provide an opportunity for prisoners to see men they had been separated from for a while. This included enemies; plenty of guys who had started as codefendants turned into witnesses at one another's trials. For this reason all the hard cases carried apples, which served as holsters for razors and scalpels, to court. We were all x-rayed and strip-searched, but our fruit wasn't, so the weapons turned the court holding cells into death chambers when the wrong prisoner got placed in the wrong cell, despite what his "separation order" might have said. Other men put into cells while still handcuffed were set upon, for whatever reasons, by those already uncuffed, and fought back by kicking and spitting.

The mayhem of the court trips led the authorities to take precautionary measures. If one had a documented history of having stabbed or slashed someone in the past, he was given a red ID. Some considered this a badge of pride, but it meant that the cutters' hands were locked into soft red mittens for the entire court trip. Watching a man attempting to eat a sandwich in tactical mittens was almost funny. Another problem was spitting. Most of the judges and DAs had been through the experience of finding someone guilty who then disagreed and expressed that sentiment with a gob spat at their faces. Any prisoner with a history of malicious expectoration was locked into a transparent plastic mask. Inevitably there were men in both mittens and masks, some of whom went to trials by jury wearing these get-ups. I'm sure their chances of getting a fair trial were not affected by the gear, but court decisions had long since decided that being placed in it wasn't grounds for an appeal.

I went to court in a cheap suit to look humble. I think the only effect it had was to make my court trips more uncomfortable. When after seven months I copped a plea and realized that I would never have to return to court, I experienced a great relief. Some men spent three years going back and forth, making this trip once a month. It was often speculated that the extreme discomfort of going to see your judge or even just paying a legal visit was incentive to get the men, presumed guilty by reason of their arrest and inability to be released on bail, to cop out to a sentence as soon as possible.

I stayed in C-95 for seven months, until I was transferred upstate. I copped a plea when it appeared that they were serious about going to trial, something I couldn't afford. Being convicted for even one armed robbery would mean a twenty-five-year sentence at a trial.

The advent of jury selection was the clue that it was time to take the deal. I didn't think court would end well, since I was eminently guilty.

My time on the island was not spent especially productively or wisely, but I survived. The day I was leaving, I saw a white kid my age being rushed to the infirmary. He had a gash across his face, a life-changing scar. I never learned who he was or what mistake he made, but I knew for certain that there but for the grace of God went I. My bail was too high to pay, and even though they could have gotten me out with property, my family seemed to feel it was a good lesson for me to experience this discomfort.

Somehow they convinced themselves that the island couldn't be that bad. The lawyer did tell them that going to court on bail, perhaps as a volunteer at a rehab program, would likely reduce the amount of time I would have to serve, but they weren't willing to risk their house in case I made a run for it. In truth, I think they simply didn't understand how easily I could have been the kid on the gurney. If you ever have to make the decision of bailing someone out or not, consider what you would pay for the person to not be scarred for life. Or how much it was worth to you for him not to be raped. Of course no one has the obligation to pay for the freedom of another, but the very possibility of doing so disappears irrevocably once the convicted is swallowed by the penal system. A place like Rikers Island, where teeth can go flying and mouths can be widened and assholes can be assaulted, is all the more evil because it's avoidable. For the lucky few, a sum of money put up for the duration of the trial can make the accused safe from these things, but that is not representative of most people's situations. There are definitely reasons not to bail someone out. But not many.

After the testing I had been through and everything I had to learn really quickly, I thought I was a little bit better prepared for the years upstate ahead of me. But there was always more to learn. You could write a book about the facets of incarcerated life that combine into the experience of knowing prison.

4.

KANGAROO COURT

After serving my time as a newjack on Rikers Island and a very
brief stay in a sorting facility called Downstate, I became a prisoner of Green Haven Correctional Facility in Stormville, New York,
and stayed one for four years. This big compound, surrounded by a
forty-foot wall and informally called "the last big house," was built
during the war and housed prisoners of war at first. Compared to the
majority of the state's facilities, it was quite old. In Green Haven's yard
I discovered and immersed myself in an arcane form of prison yard
tribalism called "the court system." Once this method of social organization was common but today is found only in a few other ancient
joints. I became a member of the "Irish court," one of fifteen such institutions in the yard, and remained one despite everything that happened as a result of being on the court for my whole time there. Not
one of the other eleven prisons I visited afterward had courts, which
was frankly a relief.

The court caused almost every problem I ever had in the "Have,"
as Green Haven was commonly shortened to. (Similarly, Comstock
became "the Stock," Auburn was "the Burn," and Wende CF near Buffalo became "Wendy's.") It also taught me most of what I needed to
know to make it as a convict for the rest of the bid, while simultaneously causing a daily anxiety spike that only let go of my little heart
once I returned to the safety of my cell.

Against the odds, I spent my decade down as a "stand-up guy." That is a category of convict that excludes rapists, fallen mobsters, informants, prisoners who have availed themselves of protective custody, the fanatically religious, child molesters, punks, and white Muslims. There are men on courts who are stand-up and then some: Mafia "made men," patched-in biker outlaws, old-timer yardfathers, and gangland shot-callers. These men are the yard aristocrats, the upper crust of this society. The rapos and rats are its hoi polloi, and the general population of stand-up guys its middle class.

They are generally white, but the term can be used as an adjective and compliment to describe anyone who doesn't tolerate insults or abuse while also not inflicting either. Stand-up prisoners do not look for trouble or prey on others; they are just deemed all right, "one of the guys." In other prisons, even this evaluation must be made on a case-by-case basis because the status of so many of the prisoners is unclear, but in Green Haven and every other joint with a court system, things are obvious. The stand-up guys are all members of courts, and everyone else "spins the yard." Anyone without a yard affiliation, no matter how tough or tatted up, has some black mark on his prison record. I didn't need anyone to explain that to me, and I saw no reason not to join a court myself. At the time.

The system of courts exists in only five of New York State's big old maxes: Green Haven, Auburn, Attica, Elmira, and Clinton. Not coincidentally, these are also the "lifer" prisons, walled-in compounds built to house men until their deaths. The administration has permitted this segregationist social system to survive. While the courts have the shortcoming of functioning as real estate for convicts to war over, they have the benefit of being territories the prisoners can care for.

A max prison yard is the size of a large, square baseball field, half enclosed by the exterior walls. These have gun towers built into them, which are only accessible from outside. The other two walls are made up of stone prison blocks, three tiers tall, each about sixty cells in length. There are fenced windows, but they open on the walkways in front of the cells, which themselves have three solid walls but no windows. This doesn't stop both contraband and information from flowing between the yard-facing blocks and the yard. One window I knew had its steel screen pulled back enough that a pack of Newports could slide through and a purple 30 mg pill of morphine would emerge. Razor blades were never passed that way, ensuring a pharmaceutical business that flourished for years.

Illumination in the yard is provided by powerful stadium lighting. Each prison has its own generator because of the power requirements. However, every now and then the power goes out, and experienced convicts immediately throw rocks at wherever they remember last seeing a cop making a round. The cops run, which they rarely do, and head into their booths, "bubbles" with space heaters. Things turned savage just like that, triggered only by darkness.

My first impression of the yard was a confusing jumble of sweating, muscular men. It looked like a fantasy from a certain kind of men's magazine, and felt like a labyrinth of danger, but within a month I had the whole place mapped and could read it like a tabloid. It would have been death not to. But only an idiot would have missed tension in the yard. The atmosphere thickens with dread, and the potential for violence becomes palpable. Silence is the most terrifying sign of all, as it means the threat is so close to breaking out that the prisoners are not making noise in hopes of not drawing attention to themselves, like the little mammals we once were in the age of dinosaurs. The whole show is ostensibly being monitored by men in towers through binoculars, but their level of attention varies. I once witnessed a grueling fifteen-minute-long duel between a knifeman and his victim, who broke his own glasses and used the arms as ice pick–like weapons to poke into his assailant's face. Maybe the cops were letting it play out for some reason of their own, but someone was probably just taking a nap. The man who sacrificed his glasses won.

Typically, though, when fistfights are spotted from the towers, an order to break them up goes out over the loudspeaker. If it is a gang assault or weapons are in play, the terrifying profile of a marksman with an AR-15 assault rifle appears on the tower. This is the response to continued violence despite an order to cease. A shot in the air means everyone must lay facedown immediately and remain so until ordered otherwise. In my ten years I never heard a second firing. Everyone knows that after the first warning shot, the guards have the legal right to kill. Even a rubber bullet to the head can end a life, and real ammunition is more commonly used today. The supposed non-lethality of rubber slugs made the outnumbered and nervous correctional officers trigger-happy.

THERE ARE NEUTRAL PARTS of the yard. The thin walkway that takes you all the way around every one of the fifteen courts in the yard is a thoroughfare that is unclaimable, though if you make the circuit enough times you will feel a thick, unwelcome gaze that causes you to keep your eyes straight and your pace brisk. At its very middle is a soggy patch of grass or cracked concrete, typically left for meetings between members of different courts or for the courtless to have a little room to talk to themselves. One prison had a pole at the center of its yard, left over from a forgotten effort to induce the murderers to play volleyball. A madman named Loco, who eventually received a further conviction for stalking the singer Jewel with daily missives spanning desperate affection and venomous derision, spent his days kung fu fighting this pole. When he finally defeated it, the cops did not punish him. They had spent years watching his struggle with the thing and respected the effort. However, when Loco accepted a pack of cigarettes one cold March to strip down and slide through the muddy slush in the dirty, unkept Switzerland at the yard's center, the cops marched right over, restrained him, and took him to the mental health office. I ran into him in Brooklyn recently, but he claimed not to remember the incident.

The other neutral parts of the yard are the steel benches set in front of televisions, which are housed in little shelters to preserve them from the weather. There are typically three televisions per yard; one for sports, one for weekend movies and basic cable, and one playing Spanish programming. This doesn't mean the benches are safe; a friend of mine was knocked unconscious from behind while watching *The Apprentice*. But at least the TV areas don't belong to anyone. Clinton-Dannemora, where two prisoners infamously escaped from in 2015, additionally features woodburning stoves, lending a medieval air. Men up in "Little Siberia" cook meals outdoors on them through bitter upstate winters. The sight of a snowy hill in a yard enclosed by siege-resistant walls and dotted with glowing fires was both beautiful and grimly terrifying when I saw it while passing through in transit.

The rest of the yard is partitioned into areas "belonging" to subsets of prisoners. A yard can have fifteen rectangular paddies, some on grass, others on concrete, with a picnic table or two. These courts are right next to each other and are not separated by fences or walls, but the invisible borders are taken seriously, lethally seriously. In theory the courts are for exercise. They each have weight-lifting setups, with identical amounts of equipment issued by the welders of the prison metal shop so that no favoritism can cause discord. There were dumbbells and barbells, lat-pull machines and squat racks. Each court also had a buried armory, a secret spot known only to the inner circle, where digging a foot down (which is below metal-detector capability) would lead you to a bag of oiled flathead screwdrivers, ice picks, and blades of various kinds. Every spring the yard would close for a day or two while cops with handheld metal detectors and shovels would search the yard for knives churned up by the winter. In preparation for this, we would "seed" the yard with paper clips stolen by the box by guys with "white collar" jobs. The constant ringing of the devices and occasional discovery of paper clips infuriated the guards unlucky enough to bid yard detail that day, but seemed very funny to us.

THE IRISH COURT WAS COMPOSED of forty convicts who didn't look like marchers at the Saint Paddy's Day parade. It was a tolerant court, even letting me become one of the crew. There we exercised; celebrated birthdays with little snacks we brought outside; played cards, chess, and even Scrabble for cigarettes; and endlessly lied to one another about our criminal exploits. In theory we also had each other's back. Being a member of the Irish court for a few years at the outset of my bid made me acceptable as a stand-up guy for the rest of my time. I should never have had to show my papers again if not for a vile incident in my fourth and final max. Presenting one's documents was not like those tense moments in spy movies when the Stasi gets on the train and announces, "Everyone vill now show papers, please." Bringing out your rap sheet and any other paperwork (such as a newspaper article recounting your misdeeds or a misbehavior hearing disposition specifying *involuntary* protective custody) to present to the court captain or other authority to look over was a rite of passage for getting on a court. Everyone acted as if they were embarrassed to infringe on your privacy while also wanting to know what the new guy did. Having your paperwork OK'd involved demonstrating that the reason for your incarceration was not creepy; sex cases invalidated one automatically, while violence against women was evaluated case by case. It was an old and storied jailhouse custom, which I successfully navigated because my record was so short.

However, I once watched an interesting confrontation between two criminal codes get worked out in the yard when a bona fide Genovese crime family made man was transferred to us from the Feds. Unfortunately he came with a rape case. In theory as a man with a "button," he couldn't be touched without lethal consequences at the hands of his criminal associates. Everyone who has seen *Goodfellas* knows that a capo has to authorize anything physical. However, even though the case that put him away for a decade was supposedly a frame job, almost a century of precedent forbade having anyone with a rape case on the one white court in the yard. The Italians all wanted to kiss his ring, while everyone else wanted him gone. The matter was solved with a phone call to the "skipper in Canarsie." A delegation went over to the phones, and the mafioso authority in Brooklyn told our court captains, Danny the Bookie and Jimmy the Wig, that they didn't have the power to make the guy do anything . . . so he should voluntarily not come on the court. The made man wasn't too happy about this, but everyone saved face.

Sometimes just showing your papers was insufficient. Guys coming in with fresh numbers who were suspected of something questionable committed on an earlier trip to prison were asked for their entire criminal rap sheet, while the men who might have snitched in court had to present their trial minutes. Even then there were some who slipped through the cracks, but the backlash that a man faced when someone from a past prison turned up to report that he'd been in PC (protective custody) or a sex offender program was at best hu-miliating and at worst deadly. But the court system shows how des-perately men wanted to be a part of something, anything, in the lonely, crowded world inside.

Including myself.

I WAS BROUGHT ON the court on my first day in prison by a Chechen criminal named Alex, who had done time in Germany and Israel, as well as in Russia and the United States. He was a terrifying man. I'll never forget the lesson he learned from Palestinian Arab prisoners in the Holy Land. The best place to stab a man, he told me, was the asshole. If you were lucky, sepsis would finish your job for you, but at the very least your enemy would think of you every time he took a shit.

Alex had ulterior motives, of course, for sponsoring me. He didn't care one fig for the court. He had no need for the nominal protection it offered, being tougher than anyone on it. And he had no use for the society of the court members, speaking English only well enough to hold someone up. Alex didn't work out, just made sure to always carry a knife. So he put me on the court with the intention of cashing in on the favor; he explained that not everyone can just join a court, but that some have to pay for the privilege. This was patently untrue, but I was saved from the friendly extortion that was to come by his ever-ready knife: within weeks of placing me on the Irish court and vouching for my criminal and violent prowess, known to him, he claimed, from Rikers and by my reputation in the Russian commu-nity (all bullshit), Alex was caught with the knife, got a year in the box, and I never saw him again. The Chechen hadn't actually both-ered to read my documents, trusting in his knowledge of my sort. I was the Russian version of a type: upper middle class, educated Jew, brought to prison by drug addiction. There was another such specimen already on the court named Billy Barovick. He's a drug counselor today, after serving a sentence for drugs, steroids, and a gun. Being a downtown Manhattan kid, he had his own issues fitting in, so naturally he wanted to have nothing to do with me.

The purpose of the courts was providing a place to work out. The captains were official figures who signed off on a register that the yard cops had, noting the amounts of weight-lifting supplies issued to each court. Of course, if a blade happened to be found on a court, these captains were also the ones asked about it. But it's so easy to toss an ice pick onto an empty court as everyone goes in for the night that the cops usually just collected them in the morning and threw the frame-job weapons away. They did so early, as the yard opened at eight, and the weight lifters would run to their courts and "hold down" the weights they needed for whatever brutal routine they had planned for the day.

EACH OF THE FIFTEEN courts had the same setup of dumbbells and barbells. The weights were gross constructions melted together in the welding shop, so whatever poundage they were meant to represent was always an estimate. The lightest dumbbells were 35 pounds. That is not a beginner's weight; real gyms start at little 2.5-pound dumbbells and go up by that increment. We had hand-tooled leather slings that allowed a long barbell to have small dumbbells suspended from it. Since we could not be trusted with equipment of lighter weight, which was too easy to wield as hand weaponry, the smallest jump in weight we could make was an increment of 70 pounds. The lightest barbell was 135 pounds, and the least one could add to it was a 35-pound weight on each end, swinging with the wind and your failing pectorals. The gains required to manage this system were almost superhuman, but with the whole yard watching and the testosterone thick in the air, you wound up pushing much more steel than you ever thought you could.

I went from being frustrated by the enormous increments to wishing for real 45-pound plates so that I could squeeze out a proper 315-pound bench press. At the age of thirty, weighing 190 pounds and having trained for six years, I managed three plates for one real rep. That was the acme of my bodybuilding career.

I was no tough guy, but my peers forgave that because I was scrupulous about the exercise and funny. The six years I spent as a bodybuilder left me wearing a suit of muscle but was compromised by three herniated discs in my lower back. I worked out on a six-day schedule, dividing my body into chest, legs, back, triceps, biceps, and shoulders. I jogged five miles on the seventh day and did abs every day.

I was always looking for mentions of prison yard courts in books on the subject, since the system and its physical components were so obviously obsolete and arcane. While the courts were not brought up in Jack Henry Abbott's *In the Belly of the Beast*, I finally found a discussion of them in *Mob Star: The Story of John Gotti*, by Jerry Capeci. In it I read about a certain Gambino big shot, which is how I learned that I'd spent four years working out on John Gotti's weights. Gotti had done some state time in the late 1970s and spent it in Green Haven. He was captain of the very court I exercised on before it was called "Irish." In reality it wasn't even that; the court took all the mutts who were white, even if only culturally; we had a few Latino bikers. An interesting fact that also turned up in *Mob Star* was that the court Gotti had presided over was twice as large. I asked around, and it turned out that at some point in our checkered past there was a pair of motherless junkies in charge. Nothing was sacred to these men, and Gotti was gone by then, off to orchestrate the assassination of Big Paul Castellano. The heroin-besotted captains sold off half the court to the influx of Dominicans, who didn't have a place of their own yet. They were a new feature in the prison system but did have plenty of smack. That was why our court was so small! Junkies were still in charge when I was there, too.

The courts were vaguely divided according to race, language, and origin. Each had its expectations; the Christian court was the only one that didn't require papers. Instead it demanded tolerance for everyone. As a result, when there was a yard-wide beef that the courts had to settle, the Christian court was not invited to send someone to the palaver. The courts were selective, like clubs or gangs. If you took anybody, you had nobody.

The three Latino courts were run in Spanish. That did not imply that the Latin King court, Dominican court, and Rat Hunter court had matching goals. There were black courts, like that of the Bloods, the Brooklyn court, and the West Indian court. These were closed to whites, except for the rare gang-affiliated ones. The Muslim court was run by blacks, though its members were of various races. The Asian court was twice the size of any other and took Chinese, Korean, Vietnamese, and Thai prisoners. The Italians had Albanian wannabes and Westies, but mostly wanted for their prospects' names to at least end in vowels. It was the only other court I ever spent time on except for my own. The territory of a court was recognized as sacrosanct. In four years I only walked onto the Irish, Italian, and West Indian courts, and the latter was to borrow their deadlift bar. The invisible fencing worked better than any real barrier I've seen.

COURTS HAD BIRTHDAY PARTIES, when food items were brought out. I used to have a Sunday breakfast with a fellow Russian and Mike (Maciej) the Polack, in which we each supplied our Slavic food from packages sent from home. Black bread, pickles, smoked sprats from cans, and raw tomatoes and onions were a weekly treat. It gave us a little feeling of being home, even if the vodka was missing.

But it wasn't all fun and games, like a cotillion with free weights. Once you joined, you had obligations, much like medieval knights had to go out in the field of battle for their liege lord, whether he was right or wrong. This might make it seem as if the term "court" is just a gussied-up euphemism for "gang," and in fact I believed this whenever I was asked to put myself at risk, and otherwise when we had birthday parties or squatting competitions. In any case, since the court was a resource, a piece of property in the yard that had value, it needed to be protected. Gangs of men fought one another in court wars; for this reason, I always thought there was a tacit promotion of the atavism of courts by the staff. In fact, this ultimately divisive system demonstrated the authority's fear of Attica-type unity among the prisoners. Violence was the ugliest feature of the court system, but also its bedrock. Nothing in prison was yours unless you held it down. The first time I held a blade in my shaking hand and the first time I taped magazines around my trembling torso, it was to defend the court. The use of magazines for armor is ubiquitous inside. I quickly learned that. As much as I enjoyed *The New Yorker*, David Remnick didn't spend nearly enough on paper. Though overpriced, my subscription to the glossy issues of *National Geographic* instantly became worth every penny.

The term "court wars" may have you imagining defending one's court, together with one's court brothers, against marauding forces of Bloods or Crips looking to take away what's yours. It never really happens that way. Our biggest standoff sure didn't. It started with love. Mack the plumber, who had a sunburst tattooed to ornament his belly button, was in love with a pimply girl, a rookie cop. She didn't mind the attention and found a use for all that pent-up testosterone. After ten years down with no female contact, he gave her his full attention. As a result he did something truly stupid for her, and I found myself with a scalpel in my clenched fist while Mack cut himself with his. We had to defend the court against half the yard after the woman opened up some kid's cell for Mack the plumber and his friend (who just happened to be our court captain) to run in there and beat up the sleeping inmate. The victim was black, of course, which is why the other courts felt so strongly about the incident. I was shocked, because it seemed that we were obviously in the wrong. The reason we were told why it was OK to play hit man at this woman's orders was that this convict, whose windows faced on the outdoor smoking section of the visiting room, was masturbating while gazing at our wives, sisters, and mothers while visiting. Then the explanation switched to his having exposed himself to a female cop. I doubted he had "pulled out on the bitch" and knew that there was a locked gate and catwalk between him and the window within sight of lady visitors . . . and if he had managed to rub one out at the sight of the very large and often elderly women who typically came to visit, God bless him. It was a crock of shit.

But both the guys were court members in good standing. One was the captain, for God's sake, and we couldn't just let them be swallowed by the angry mob. So we explained that we would dispense justice ourselves. However, things only got menacing for the rest of the court for harboring these two. We were surrounded by angry black prisoners who didn't like the idea of white convicts beating black ones on behalf of our captors. It didn't help when the cops tried making a show of force by posting up in front of our court to stop any attack from happening. Now we really looked like we were in league with them. I dutifully taped the periodicals over my torso and accepted a scalpel from the stash. A terrible two hours passed until the bell rang and we all went in without bloodshed.

Except for Mack's hand, cut by his own scalpel, which we bandaged with a sock.

In the end, the problem was solved with a bundle of heroin worth a few hundred bucks. Our Croesus, who had a $400,000 inheritance, bought it and "spread the love," paying off the angriest of our opponents with full bags of dope, "New Yorkers" worth fifty bucks each. The bribe was accepted, he became the new captain, and it was back to business as usual. This was early in my bid, and for me a precedent was set. Being on the court came with privileges but also problems. They didn't have to be my problems in the least.

ONE OF THE SIMPLEST and yet most pernicious ways courts had of complicating my life as a prisoner was by interfering with my freedom of association. I had to socialize with men I didn't want to because we were on the same court. I earned the enmity of one head case by gently, carefully declining the privilege when he decided I should be his best friend. He was an odd duck from Long Island— tall, very good-looking, and in possession of an enormous penis, which he blatantly showed off by showering naked in the yard and sunning himself dry. He was also serving thirty-three years to life for "two bodies," as he always put it. The devil is in the details, of course. He was a patricide and had hunted his father's girlfriend down to where she hid behind a washing machine and finished her off with a baseball bat. This was a real horror story, though his mother and grandparents—his maternal grandparents—still came to visit.

He explained himself with a strange tale of needing to slay his post-divorce father to save his mother from a murder plot, which sounded like fantasy to everyone. He wasn't too clever or popular, but after he turned against me he did recognize that I was vulnerable because I was out of place. For years he schemed against me, with the goal of having me expelled from the court. Eventually that was his own fate, through means unconnected to me, but his strange hatred lived on.

When my wife left a loving message with a local radio station that served our joint, he told the whole yard that with my atrocious vanity and powers of deception I had obviously written to the radio station myself with the false message from my wife, whom he knew well from staring at her in the visiting room. Nevertheless, he pointed me out to his mother as one of his closest friends, and she was obscenely nice to me when we met on the visiting floor.

And so it went. The court was always a hotbed of trouble, and I frequently considered leaving voluntarily, though my pride always stopped me. I had only read about the kind of behavior I witnessed in Frans de Waal's books on chimpanzee society.

Apes vied for status and fruit; we had heroin instead of apples and pears. So why did I stay? I needed a place to work out and told myself that I put up with the court tension, extortion attempts, and mornings with madmen because of the weights, but it was actually pride, genuine foolish vanity that I paid for with endless stress. I wanted to wear the mantle of a stand-up guy, even if it was duplicitous of me. Even when I was censured for being too close to Chino, a Mexican friend, I defended my decision and continued to come to the court when I should have told them to fuck themselves.

AFTER YEARS OF ACCEPTANCE, though, my status was called into question by an enemy more formidable than a double murderer or Genovese capo: the law. I had reached my fourth and final max and was in my seventh year of incarceration. I went out to the (severely limited) yard and met the local white community. It was a drill I knew well by then—meeting the local stand-up guys and yardfathers, establishing whom we know in common, like dogs sniffing each other's ends. This time, however, something went wrong. I did what I was supposed to do, paid my respects, but a few days later I felt a ubiquitous cold shoulder. In the hallways the guys were avoiding eye contact so as to not have to nod a greeting. Outside, only the men who would talk to anyone would say more than a few words to me. I'd seen this happen to others who had sinned, guys who backed down from a fight or snitched or had some aspect of their past revealed. I was being "creeped out" and I didn't know why. Now I understood why alpha chimpanzees that had been dethroned soon died from a lack of will to live. We are social animals, and ostracism is hard on the psyche, even if you're right and they're wrong, even if you know you've done nothing wrong. And not knowing why something extreme is happening to you in prison is agony.

I finally managed to get an answer out of a cabdriver killer. He told me at a time and in a place where no one else could see him talk to me.

"It's your case, man!"

Armed robbery? That was a strange transgression in the company of killers. But that wasn't it. What happened was that a cop had told a pet inmate of his that I was some kind of terrible child molester—the lowest thing one can be.

Clearing this up was simple enough, as I had all my paperwork and promptly brought it out to show the guys. About half a year later I was locked between two gates with the very cop who had done this awful thing. I asked him why he had said that about me but never got past a denial. To this day I don't know if the cop really thought I was a "Chester" (rhymes with . . .) or just didn't like the looks of me. If that jail had a court system in the yard, I would have at least been beaten up over the misunderstanding. And I never did get to the bottom of it. The incident chills me to this day.

COURT LIFE WAS ULTIMATELY the best way to initiate my jailhouse education. Its tribal system remains poorly documented and will probably disappear in the next wave of penal reform. Other than the chimp study, the only books that helped me navigate those treacherous waters were ones about the psychopathology of criminals and other sociopaths. I found some gems dating from the juvenile delinquency epidemic of the early sixties in old editions on dusty jailhouse shelves. As they were concerned with rumbles and zip guns, they served only as period artifacts. The nonsense that I lived through in the courts was the natural consequence of human frailty and hunger, the wages of addiction, and the stress of competition for limited resources. But the stand-up guys held their heads high and really did try their best to live up to an ideal. It was all we had, so we respected it. I know I did; when lifting John Gotti's weights, no less would do.

5

BLACK IS BEAUTIFUL

But some of my best friends are black!" That old chestnut rang through my head, over and over, during the entirety of my sentence. My race mattered even half-a-dozen prisons down the list of my ports of call, even when I was a known entity, whether as a person or at least by reputation. Every white prisoner was viewed with suspicion by the non-white majority upon arriving at a new joint. The content of my character did not take precedence over the hue of my pelt. I had witnessed the astounding phenomenon of Barack Obama's election, and even that unprecedented event had no bearing on the tense realities of race hatred inside, which resembled much more the world described in Eldridge Cleaver's *Soul on Ice* than the years 2003 to 2014, which I spent sharing the fate of those in the black-majority pocket universe that is the American Incarcerated Nation. At every new prison—and I passed through twelve of them—I was suspect. All of us, the one-fourth of New York State prisoners who were white, were suspect. Every pale face was assumed to be a racist until proven otherwise.

It didn't help that we shared a skin tone with the preponderance of our captors, or that there really were self-proclaimed white supremacists among us, bristling with swastika tattoos. The fact that many of these Nazis were Hispanic or came with other asterisks was an irrelevant nuance. No one relishes being a prisoner, and taking responsibility for that condition is a sign of maturity, a trait convicts are not well-known for. Looking for a reason for your fate other than your own fault is tempting; I read Albert Camus's *The Fall* in hopes of finding it to be a condition shared by all mankind. According to French existentialism, it is only for people like Jean Genet (whose *Thief's Journal* I liked much better than *The Blacks*) and myself, more so.

The black prisoners, whose demographic slice inside greatly exceeded their actual population in the real world, believed so many young black men found themselves in prison because the penal system was modern-day slavery. This ideology made things rough on a gringo like myself, suddenly a member of a despised minority.

I myself toyed with the idea of calling myself a political prisoner, a hostage in the war on drugs, but ultimately the responsibility was my own. However, I was not accustomed to being the target of a wave of hate directed at my hereditary identity. Whenever I was a newjack at a facility or just moved into a new cellblock, there was an immediate, unspoken accusation of racism from the hostile majority. White prisoners just came with a presumption of guilt, and the responsibility of disproving it was on us. Otherwise we were just more "racist-ass crackers," lumped in with the "farm-boy guards," "guinea gangsters," the majority of unincarcerated Americans, and the Aryan Nation. It was a strange position for a liberal New York Jew to find himself in, but as it was repeated over and over, I came to understand that this hatred was the status quo.

Nothing changed when Obama was elected, however much of a banner day it was inside, and I doubt much has changed since.

The world I had lived my first twenty-five years in was a starkly different one. I went to inner-city schools that had kids of every conceivable race in them. As an immigrant child, I was poor; there were black kids whose clothing inspired dreadful envy in me. Later I traveled across America, including driving through the South, with hardly any money. I often had to rely on the kindness of strangers, and Americans of every race gave a damn. Before coming to prison, I had never heard the N-word used in earnest.

Inside, it was perhaps the most commonly used word of all. The vile history and transgressive nature of those notorious syllables caused them to be spoken by both black gangsters and white racists with the same frequency and even intention. The white prisoners used the word both to come off as tough guys as well as pejoratively. What complicated matters was that some white prisoners had been in so long and absorbed the majority black culture so thoroughly that they could get away with saying "That's my n—— over there" and not imply ownership. Nevertheless, there was an old joke about this: "What does every white convict do after saying 'n——'?" The punch line was a long, careful look around, to see if any of the brothers had heard you say it.

I HEARD THE WORD more over those ten years than I will for the rest of my life. But avoided using it myself. Not because I'm such a virtuous person, but because it felt cheap to say something to one person that I'd be afraid to say to another. In prison I trusted in my nature, in the content of my character and its perception by others, enough to not avoid using the word when it felt socially advantageous, whether quoting someone or mouthing the words to a song, and to avoid it otherwise. Especially since it was just about always "otherwise." For this I was respected; my fellow prisoners decided I did not have objectionable racial hang-ups.

Segregation was still very much the order of the day when I began my bid in 2003. For example, breaking bread with a man was not understood as a metaphor or an abstraction to take lightly. As it was clear that I was new, I was immediately told by the old guard of white prisoners that if I ate with the blacks or Spanish, I couldn't expect to come back to white society. The same applied to whom I worked out with and whom I walked the yard with. There were exceptions to all these rules, and it really just mattered who *you* were, but the invisible lines between the races were respected by everyone.

After all, the whites barely made a third of the population, so it wasn't as if they were setting the rules. On holidays blacks made meals that were carefully portioned out to all the members of their race in good standing on a tier, the Hispanic and white cells being politely skipped. I felt a sting the first time I was singled out for my race and unequally treated, but it felt normal soon enough, when the white guys in the yard sent me soap and shower shoes and cigarettes just because I was new and stand-up and white.

SHOWING A PREFERENCE FOR the company of races other than your own would soon draw attention, but there were always exceptions. Four years into my bid I thought I had enough clout to run one through. I had gotten close with Chino, a Mexican friend, and wanted to exercise with him. By then I had broken all the other rules anyway, but in private. Working out with Chino in the yard was public, and I fell right into an enemy's gambit. I had come in conflict with the strictures of a racialist society and was accused of insufficient loyalty. A creep wanted me off the Irish court because I seemingly preferred the company of a Mexican. I had to make an impassioned defense of my right to befriend whomever I wanted, while remaining a stand-up white man. I made my speech with a knife in my pocket, a knife everyone knew was there, and the little clique that stood against me ceased their campaign. Just like I ceased mine to work out with Chino.

In prison the racial anger that my black peers lived and breathed was a revelation. I thought the idea that one could be born wrong was the very definition of racism and something we all opposed, black and white. But I was misinformed.

I had a decent grasp of civil rights–era history and wasn't prepared to find an antebellum world of Uncle Toms and modern-day slavery. I was also inside in 2008, when the remarkable event of the election of Obama occurred, and heard him called a "house nigger" by the more militant black convicts. Prisoners are mostly uninterested in politics, feeling it to have little to do with their lives. The minority of prisoners who are into politics usually favor the most extreme forms of demagoguery. As a result, Louis Farrakhan is a revered figure inside, and Al Sharpton is spoken well of, while Obama was always muttered about as being "too white." In 2008 I was literally the only person to check his book *Dreams from My Father* out of the jailhouse library. The well-intentioned assistant librarian actually thanked me for taking it out and thereby proving her right.

Apparently the head librarian had wanted to get the cheaper paperback, but the assistant argued that such an important book would be so popular as to require the sturdier hardcover binding. I read it and was astounded. Obama was an actual writer, a thinking intellectual politician! The book was subtle, smart, and very interesting. I deeply hoped he would be elected.

The night of the election, everyone had his radio on, and when the news was announced, there was a huge commotion of banging and shouting. The cops were furious, ostensibly at the disturbance, but really because our guy won, their guy lost. But was he really our guy? In the morning I went to breakfast, floating on a cloud of victory. It felt as if the skies had opened after eight years of Bush storm clouds. Sitting in front of me were two young black kids. They talked about the election, too. Perhaps it was said for my benefit, but one said to the other that now it was their turn to have slaves. Later on Michelle Obama had a garden in the White House, staffed with many white volunteers, and I heard the same thing: the white gardeners were the first of the Caucasian slaves, the beginning of white slavery that Barack Obama would enforce.

That atmosphere of angry resentment that I learned about in prison was easy to see in the language. Words like "cracker," "honky," and "peckerwood" weren't just ways to set your prose in the counter-cultural 1960s. I grew used to being addressed as "white boy," knowing that this particular term wasn't meant maliciously. However, Abdul Majid never called me that.

It was a coincidence that Majid was my neighbor for a year early on in my incarceration. The joint was a max, where almost everyone was serving double-digit sentences. The exceptions were the men with histories of escape who could not be trusted to the chain-link fences of mediums, or those who were too violent for them. But it was more common to have a neighbor like mine, whose sentence was simply life. He was also a CMC inmate, which means "centrally monitored case." This was not a result of his extreme behavior or gravity of his crime, but of his influence with other prisoners. While Majid was not the only jailhouse celebrity I met, he was the sole man calling himself a political prisoner with whom I agreed regarding the title. So did the state; it certainly had no intention of ever releasing Majid, who had long been reconciled to dying behind bars.

He'd been locked up since 1982 and was half of "the Queens Two" of the Black Liberation Army (BLA) fame. They had killed one cop and injured another after their van was stopped in the borough on suspicion of burglary. The trial was decried as railroading, with the defense asserting that the police had allegedly "hypnotized" a witness. Majid was a cop-killing revolutionary. He was a key member of the BLA and formerly a Black Panther. He became my friend; he valued my education, because it made it possible for us to have geopolitical conversations and solve the problems of history through the steel wall that kept us apart. Majid was tall and bespectacled. The decades had added a slump to his back, some gray to his hair, and a shuffle to his step, but his mind was as sharp as ever. He kept it well nourished with fiery revolutionary radio programs that occasionally mentioned him and his partner, Bashir Hameed. The two codefendants were never allowed to be in the same prison.

Every day his mail was full of newsletters from other freedom fighters, Marxists, animal liberation activists, and various malcontents. He would pass on these materials to me, and I would politely take and review everything. Majid never pointed out when he'd been mentioned, but I found the notices myself and told him so. Everyone else on the tier of barred cells could hear us, so the recognition must have pleased him, but he never showed it. I had clues as to what a big deal he was, like the time Tupac came up and Majid reminisced about holding him on his knee. I told him about my own night spent smoking crack with Gil Scott-Heron, but Majid knew him, too. He had known all the authors of black liberation classics, whose books I brought into the cell to have a better handle on our discussions. Huey Newton was a disappointment to him, while Bobby Seale he was proud of, although I found his book *A Lonely Rage* simplistic.

Majid had spent thirty years of incarceration married to a devoted New York City schoolteacher. She had been a black Hebrew Israelite and bore him a son from their conjugal visits. Majid was very proud that the boy was spending a year of his college education in Africa. Sadly his wife died early of cancer. He was not allowed to attend the funeral, especially since it was held in Harlem.

The possibility of an armed breakout in the capital of black America was too much for the authorities. He took it gracefully.

Abdul Majid acquired that name upon taking his shahada and converting to Islam. He was convicted as Anthony LaBorde. He never explained any of this to me while we lived next to each other, keeping our conversations to history, politics, and philosophy. He wore a kufi and a beard, and his pants were pegged high so that they would not touch his shoes. His forehead had a mark on it from touching it to the floor in prayer. When Majid was locked up for something once, he asked me to bring him a rock from the yard. Apparently he needed it for the ritual. Islam had come to define him when politics was no longer viable, and he had no time for the extremism of Nation of Islam or the other offshoots. He was simply a Sunni Muslim.

What Majid was too humble to tell me was that he was also the security chief for the prison's Muslim community. It took me years of absorbing context to understand the implications of that. Because of who he was and what he was in for, Majid immediately had a position in every prison he was sent to. The hierarchy of prison Islam, known as "Prislam" by its opponents, had several ranks. Head of security was the most responsible, prominent, and dangerous post. Majid had been a man of action out in the world and was not a jailhouse convert, so he was a natural for it. Treasurers were known for their sobriety and accounting abilities. They held on to funds to pay for the debts of Muslims in trouble and to fund events and celebrations. The most knowledgeable Muslim prisoner was appointed as the imam, not to be confused with the official imam. Religious clerics paid by New York State hold a position with the same name but do not get the same respect, since they cash checks from the same people as the "pigs." The dozen imams I met doing this work over my decade were all foreigners, hailing from the subcontinent or North Africa; I practiced my French with one particularly affable Algerian. There were enough Middle Eastern prisoners born and raised under the crescent that they had a congregation as well. Islam was well represented inside; the food was halal, Ramadan was observed, and the *ummah* even included kitabis who memorized the entire Koran. But they played absolutely no role in the functioning of Prislam. Piety was not the highest qualification.

There were white Muslims. The Albanians, Kosovars, and Bosnians didn't have it held against them, but the other converts were all men who were no longer stand-up, no longer welcome in the white community. Many were sex offenders, who had little choice between Islam and protective custody if they didn't want to be mistreated. Others were men who had signed into PC because of a debt or a beef they were afraid of. Upon release in another prison's yard, they were prime targets for conversion, because they had been revealed as soft and not stand-up. Once they turned Muslim, there was no going back.

Jailhouse Islam is not just another faith. It is a way of life, an organization for self-defense, and the faith prisoners adopted as the fiercest expression of their blackness. There is an active effort to convert new members and a strong cultural bias for black men. Muslim prisoners professed to believe that the Allah of the Koran was the one true God and Muhammad was his prophet. Islam has long been the fastest-growing religion in the American prison system.

This fact was not lost on the authorities, as was made clear during the events of September 11.

I had arrived three years after the terrorist attack, but the consequences inside were still a matter of great controversy and the subject of many conversations. Even though all the DOC facilities were nowhere near the blast zone and no threats had been made concerning the prison system, the authorities in Albany had a large population of malcontent Muslims under their watch when an attack on the country in the name of Islam was perpetrated. That September the prisons were all locked down, which halted all internal movement. No more Friday Jumah services, no phones for a while, no access to television in the yard. The prisoners were kept in their cells, wondering why they were being punished for the twin towers. Then the transfers began. Muslim prisoners who had influence in their communities were packed up in the evening and put on buses in the morning. They were sent clear across the state, with the hopes that they would lose whatever local power they had accrued. For those who resisted this unorthodox procedure, there was another solution. "Administrative segregation" was a way of putting someone in the box for an unspecified length of time without the justification of any particular incident. A few of the Muslim firebrands ended up "ad-seg'd" after September 11.

Obviously all of them were black. The guys who were thus shuffled around acquired a lot of anti-system cred.

Majid was released into Green Haven about the time I got there in 2004. It was all an overreaction to an unprecedented event. Even though the world of Islam in jail is radical, it is in the black nationalist sense rather than posing any threat of jihad.

Nevertheless, the societal shake-up that September 11 initiated brought some things out into the open. In prison this was already clear thanks to the racial segregation, self-imposed and otherwise, but the sudden sensitivity to threat and treatment of the black Muslims proved that the history of slavery had not passed through America lightly.

The prisoners I knew weren't innocent of the crimes they were convicted of, and often embellished them as part of the convict's bravado, but they still resented their personal condition and the appearance of so many young black men ruled by corps of white guards with a very different cultural background. The Red State rural scene of hunting, pickup trucks, country music, and dip (chewing tobacco) was out of sync with the world the prisoners came from. The men from the hard streets of Brooklyn frankly despised the pale-faced farm boys doing their job, some meaner than others, but just men doing a job in the end.

Majid had four years of university education under his belt and read all day, but his ideology led him to believe strange things as well. For example, he once argued that pork was such terrible slave food that it had no nutritional value. There were much stranger things that men in the Nation of Islam and other groups believed in. I read Alex Haley's *Autobiography of Malcolm X*.

Haley had been editor of the US Army newspaper, *Stars and Stripes*, and had also written *Roots*, which in its televised form had a great effect on the nation in its day. I liked the book, despite feeling that I was not its appropriate recipient. Its introduction to the Nation of Islam was eye-opening. Malcolm X finishes the journey described in his autobiography by traveling to Mecca, witnessing white Muslims making the hajj just like every other race, and leaving the Nation and orbit of Elijah Muhammad in order to convert to orthodox Sunni Islam.

AS THE YEARS PASSED, I got to know the world of black supremacist organizations better. Nation of Islam (NOI), which is not recognized as a form of Islam by some Sunni and Shiite bodies, was a cultish offshoot from the faith, created by anger as well as better-intentioned elements. But this being prison, there was always a more extreme group, and in this case it was the Nation of Gods and Earths, which was founded by a man called Clarence 13X, who left NOI in 1964. The group was informally known as the "Five Percenters" or "Godbodies." For years they were considered a gang by the prison administration. However, a 2004 court decision allowed them to evolve into a legitimate faith, with holidays and fundraisers and all the other trappings allowed to a formal religion. This nation was composed of Gods, who were the men, and earths, or ladies' auxiliary. They only permitted original man into their ranks, though twenty-five years of study enabled Caucasians to cleanse themselves of their whiteness. Intense study of the supreme mathematics and supreme alphabet, a mix of numerology and the 120 NOI lessons by Five Percenter "scientists," is necessary for the auto-apotheosis of becoming a God body. Prison was full of Gods.

There were other organizations that I couldn't find as much to read about. I learned a lot from Leonard Barrett's *Rastafarians*, a faith that so many prisoners adopted. Rastafarians insist that they are the true Jews, real elders of Zion, while frauds like myself were pretenders. I knew a lot of Rastas, and they were generally cool, but cultural derision for homosexuality, or "battiboys," was viciously powerful. I knew one of their gang members, a "Lion" named Hitman, who grew his hair to enable it to hold a matching black leather compartment that held the drugs he dealt in the yard and a weaponized razor. When the cops approached to search him, he would scream that his hair is protected by his right to practice his religion, and it could not be touched.

A number of black prisoners wore fezzes, like Turkish pashas. They were allowed to wear this headgear, just like Jews wore yarmulkes and Muslims had kufis and Rastafarians their huge knitted "crowns," as symbols of their respective faiths. Members of the black Moorish Science Temple of America considered themselves to be Moors from North Africa. They also believed that their ancestors had not been brought to America as slaves but were part of a Moorish presence in the New World that predated Columbus. This meant that the United States was built on Moorish lands and stolen from them.

In this turbulent, roiling world of black identities and black nationalism and black supremacy, where I found myself part of a despised minority, I had the tone-deafness to tell an Indian guy from

Guyana named Nigel a racist joke, in one of the most frightening and stupidest episodes of my incarceration. He did not laugh and gave me a cold look, and I hoped that was that.

But by the end of the day I was getting stared at by groups of black men. In the next few days, I found that men with whom I normally made small talk were avoiding me. Some of the white guys, the ones with black friends, were keeping their distance from me in the yard as well. Privately one of them told me I should watch my back.

Nigel had recently converted and used my joke to score points in the community he had just joined. I sought him out to apologize for giving offense and explain that I was just trying to be funny, and had failed. He didn't want to talk to me. I felt a hit was being planned and started skipping nighttime yard. My fear was visceral.

AFTER A FEW DAYS it suddenly all ended. The cold shoulders warmed up, the stares melted into nods, and no one avoided me. If anything, Nigel seemed chastened. I had not mentioned any of this to Majid, and was actually deathly afraid that he would find out.

We were talking, comparing the afternoon I once spent with Amiri Baraka in the Hamptons to his experience with the poet, when he changed the subject.

"By the way, you don't need to worry about nothing. I told them you weren't like that, just your sense of humor."

So he had known the whole time. In fact, as Muslim head of security, it was to him that my transgression was reported. Maybe he let me sweat for a few days to teach me a lesson about my loose mouth, but he wouldn't let anything happen to me, especially not for some neophyte to score points. Much like in Trinidad, the Indian population's racism against the black population of Guyana was well-known; I suspected that Nigel's outrage at my joke was purely mercenary.

Besides, Majid had spent two years living next to me and chatting the evenings away. He really believed what he said when he vouched for me. Thank God for that, and thank God for him. I was much more careful for the rest of my bid, as I couldn't count on having a friend of his stature to remove my foot from my mouth next time.

UPON MY RELEASE, having shared the small world where black men represent the greater part of the population and set the cultural norms for everyone else, I had come to know its language and rules. I became familiar with the codes, tenets, taboos, and tokens of American blackness. There is a face black men wear for white society, and then there is who they are at home. Having been a lodger in that house of pain, I learned intimately what I had known only abstractly.

Black people are just like all people. Some are good and some are not. Treating people as if they have racial characteristics rather than individual ones is the very definition of racism. My friendship with Abdul Majid allowed me to become acquainted with a complicated mind, one encompassing both noble traits and flaws. He was not an avatar of a movement, not a saint of black liberation, but nor was he just the cop-killing enemy of law-abiding America. He was just a man, and an occasionally great man, who was black, and it was a privilege to spend two years with him in the cell next door.

When I got my transfer papers and packed up, I had time to give him a wink and say, "Black is beautiful." He answered, "You know it, baby," and I never saw him again.

6.

STRANGERS IN A
STRANGE LAND

ad I gone to prison in California, I would have a lot more to say
about Mexicans, as well as Vietnamese. In the Michigan system
there are Somalis, and Minnesota features Hmong inmates. A Russian convict I knew told me that the prisons of Latvia are full of Nigerian nationals. Florida is incarcerated diversity; all of Latin America
is represented in places like Dade County. Hawaiian prisons are full
of Samoans. Massachusetts has Southies and Kennedys. The Midwest prison populations are split between white "peckerwoods" and
Mexicans who themselves are divided between deportable *paisas*
born south of the border and Chicanos whose native language is English. The federal system sweeps up many international criminals
hailing from other lands or committing crimes between them, but not
all. In general any prison inevitably has a smorgasbord of prisoners from around the world like the New York State system does. In
2007, 10 percent of the people incarcerated by New York State were
foreign born.

Did I count as one of these strangers in a strange land, an *auslander* swept into the maw of American incarceration? The strongest
evidence against me was linguistic. I conducted my visits and phone
calls in another language, and it wasn't Spanish. The cops who listened in on our phone calls were often chosen because they spoke a
particular language, but there was nothing they could do with me. I

was also seen reading in the incomprehensible Cyrillic alphabet as well as in French. Once a year I read something short and easy in French to keep up my ability to do so; Camus was an obvious choice, and I could manage Georges Simenon without a dictionary. These outlandish behaviors marked me as a stranger, and it got stranger.

By speaking Russian to a gay Uzbek who looked like Bruce Lee, or a Han Chinese, I engendered a rumor that I spoke Chinese. The enormous Russophone population of Asians was unknown to the prisoners. My interlocutor was an identity thief who spoke little English. My ability to communicate with him, by which I learned a lot about credit cards, made me a suspicious figure. This was all beyond the American pale, and my cosmopolitan air developed into a full-blown stench by an act of blatant translation committed in the yard for everyone to see. I was witnessed helping a French killer communicate to a Russian mobster by translating for both of them without a *soupçon* of English in between. Nobody thought of me as a native-born American after that. Years later a cop I suspect of acting with a promotion in mind actually reported my use of a yard telephone in Russian. I was just talking to my mother when I was surrounded. The cops came and terminated my phone call. I was taken to an office and interrogated. The result was that it was officially recorded that English was not my only language. Being apprehended and revealed as bilingual was the closest I ever felt to the KGB sleeper agents I read about in John le Carré novels.

The fantasy of Cold War operatives seeded in the suburbs, speaking KGB-taught English, was exciting for me. I read *Tinker, Tailor, Soldier, Spy* and *The Spy Who Came in from the Cold* and others in the genre. I looked for more of the same in Tom Clancy books but didn't find it. Instead Len Deighton's *Ipcress File* and Graham Greene's *Our Man in Havana* and *The Comedians* filled my need to read about being out of place with a purpose. I loved *The Day of the Jackal* and

Six Days of the Condor and put them on the list of movies I wanted to watch when I got out. A friend of mine lent me his treasured copy of the scripts of Patrick McGoohan's 1969 masterpiece of a television series, *The Prisoner*. When I finally got to see it, the seventeen episodes became my favorite television of all time and space; the titular prisoner, unlike me, was courageous enough to refuse to try to assimilate. I didn't have that luxury of choice, but the espionage books did teach me how to fit in with élan.

I spoke perfect English, my second tongue, without an accent, and instead made mistakes in written Russian. Growing up on an American diet had canceled whatever genetic inheritance should have made me "look Russian," even though I grew a beard. Whenever I disclosed my identity, I was told that I didn't look the part. I pretended to know the rules of baseball. For fun I permitted myself jokes about pitching touchdowns and deliberately called football "rugby"; "ruggers" would have been misheard dangerously, as every word that came out of a white mouth was examined for evidence of racism. I once saw a misunderstood anglicism that a jailhouse friend, a frat boy gone to seed, deployed disastrously. He said that someone on the basketball court next door to our makeshift tennis court had their "knickers in a knot." "Knickers," a word unfamiliar in the States, was too close for comfort. It did not go over well.

I kept the joke of my ignorance of American sports running for years precisely because I really was ignorant of American sports and preferred not to explain why. After all, I had been born in New York City's Beth Israel hospital and had no excuse for my poor assimilation except for my parents' snobbish elitism. The reason why I first ate peanut butter and jelly at the age of twenty and had no idea what Cap'n Crunch was or who the Brady Bunch were was not one I wanted to share with my fellow prisoners. Telling them that I came from a family that considered itself to be culturally superior to the society that reared me was an insult cloaked in condescension. Besides, it was rarely that much of an issue. In the end I looked and spoke enough like an American to pass for a real one. I came with an asterisk, though, thanks to the extra tongues in my mouth, used not just for speaking godless un-American languages but also eating disgusting foreign foods.

Nevertheless, the Nigerian, Korean, Israeli, Serb, Indian, and other expatriates I knew were fellow strangers in a strange land, sharing my crushing out-of-placeness. But I was born an American citizen; they cowered at their just-about guaranteed deportation only with each other.

I had always made a habit of reading the literature of other cultures, especially those beyond the anglophone preserve, and in prison I allowed chance meetings to direct my choices. A Czech friend, in for drunkenly assaulting the love of his life, sent me down a Bohemian path beyond the Franz Kafka I already knew, loved, and practically lived. His sense of humor was in congruence with what I found in Bohumil Hrabal and Jaroslav Hašek; *I Served the King of England* and *The Good Soldier Švejk* were companions that kept me in good humor, as their protagonists took misery and injustice with such aplomb. When Švejk is sent to jail, he is quite happy with the boards he has to sleep on, since it could have been the cold stone floor. The Czech wife beater and I told each other our stories in a mix of tongues; the only Russian my friend knew was "давай чясы," or "give me your watch," remembered from a long-ago robbery he suffered at the hands of Red Army men in Prague. The Latino contingent sent me to Mario Vargas Llosa and Carlos Fuentes and Gabriel García Márquez; Jorge Luis Borges was already familiar and, like Kafka, seemed to be the author of some of the absurdities of my condition. Unfortunately I never met a hispanophone prisoner with whom I could talk literature. Mario Puzo's *Godfather* and *Omerta,* the classic Mafia books, gave me some background on the ideal platonic form of the gangster that my Italian American friends were shooting for. But reading books to understand men, especially strange men from strange lands, is ultimately secondary to reading men themselves. Those "readings" remain with me today, better preserved in my mere human memory than all the anthropology and history and ethnography I consumed.

I practiced my spoken French with a murderer whom my wife had encountered at a family event and declared demonically attractive. Alexandre Charbit was serving twenty years flat for stabbing his wife to death, and there was a lot of blood. Alex didn't try to flee, because he believed he hadn't committed a crime. The police disagreed. The jury found him guilty, and the judge showed mercy in sentencing him to less than the standard twenty-five years to life for murder. I met him when he had less than half his time in.

He had enough identities for a dozen killers. The man was a Parisian Jew with Mexican citizenship, as well as having a wife and veterinary practice in Monterrey. His roots were Sephardic; Alex's grandparents had come to France from Morocco. However, his shoulder carried a Confederate flag tattoo, which I saw in the shower. Alex had picked it up along with his fluent English and an undergraduate degree from a Texas college. The tattoo was a relic of time spent with a "motorcycle club" in Texas.

But he was no Dixie rebel; despite flying the stars and bars, inside he ran with the Mexicans. Alexandre suspected that he had a better chance of finding acceptance with other foreigners than with the xenophobic white prisoners hailing from the lower middle class and below. Nevertheless, among the Spanish speakers he was known as "Vampyro" because of his pallor. That nickname was probably uncomfortable for a professional veterinarian, but he made it work.

Mexican justice would have been kinder to him; I read about it in several biographies of William Burroughs, like *Gentleman Junkie* and the book of interviews that Victor Bockris published. Burroughs was sent out of the country eleven days after shooting his wife between the eyes. He called it an accident, but an American prosecutor would have gotten a murder conviction out of this atrocious game of William Tell. Of course, this was in the forties, when white foreigners were given the benefit of the doubt in such cases. Nevertheless, the pastiche *Autobiography of Joseph Stalin* recounted how the Soviet assassin who killed Leon Trotsky with an ice pick, the Spaniard Ramón Mercader, served twenty years in Mexican prison for the crime. He remained silent and did his time, from 1940 to 1960, and upon his release immediately went to the USSR, receiving a hero's welcome, an apartment in Moscow, and a pension. I mentioned this to Alex, who scoffed that the Soviet Union could not bribe away the conviction for political reasons. The American State Department made sure of it. His own case would have been easily dealt with had it happened in Mexico with the deployment of his family resources. A few thousand dollars would have made it all go away, he considered.

Alex kindly humored my schoolboy French and gave me Simenon novels and *Paris Match* to read and was always quick with a joke about dropping the soap. Although he didn't seem like anything one would find in an American prison, he was actually the second francophone Sephardic Jew I met inside. The other, Pinky, had a missing finger of that name and a *nom de famille* identical to the capital of Burkina Faso. You can look it up if you want to know the truly preposterous name for a smirking little French career criminal. Alex and Pinky both looked like characters in *Casablanca*, darkly handsome, world-weary, and cynical. In the company of Alex, I felt as if I were back in the real world, though he and Pinky might as well have been Martians in the wider world of prison.

My good friend Idiabe, on the other hand, blended in better. He was dark, dreadlocked, and very heavily muscled. He may have superficially fit in with the crowd but was no less a stranger in a strange land. Known as "Africa" to most of the prisoners, he began his road to the big house in Biafra.

Today the conflict there has receded from memory to become another minor Cold War proxy war, but Biafra was once more than a crisis; it was a cause with activists and agitators and mercenaries all its own. The regional Biafran regime wanted to break away from greater Nigeria. Its independence was denied with the terrible tool of intentional famine. Idiabe's family was involved in the conflict: hunger was his first memory, but men with guns whispering conspiracies with his father was a close second. His family was on the losing side. They first fled to Egypt, but London was where Africa spent his youth, where he grew up with other Biafran refugees. He assimilated to the English youthquake well, becoming a mod suedehead fighting in street skirmishes with chav skins at football matches. The Royal Marines were next, and the Falklands War came right after. Being a veteran of a second forgotten conflict gave him the funds to search out a new life to live.

Idiabe landed in New York, a young ex-soldier traumatized by two very specifically twentieth-century conflicts, and got a degree in civil engineering from Columbia University. He began a career with a city job and soon acquired a Jewish wife and child. He was happy, but not for long. As he explained, a burglar had come in through the fire escape and stole his computer, which held all of his work data—engineering plans with which he had been trusted, his first big project—just as Idiabe was coming home. He reverted to the lessons of his youth, the cordite and death and man-tracking. He followed the thief, catching the man, but did not call the police. The burglar did not survive the encounter. When the police arrived, Idiabe went quietly. In the absence of a criminal record and considering the circumstances, he was given fifteen years to serve.

Idiabe read my *New Yorker* and *Harper's* and *Atlantic Monthly* magazines. I brought him rubber-banded stacks of periodicals through a few different prisons while we both aged over ten years of incarceration. Others knew him as the volunteer teacher who taught calculus in the yard when Bard College demurred. He was responsible for the math proficiency of many jailed kids whom no one ever bothered to teach the use of numbers beyond multiplication tables. It was impressive to see him sitting outside, poring over textbooks with gang members. But he was hardly a gentle giant; he really had hunted and killed a junkie burglar.

One day a prisoner resembling Mark David Chapman showed up. It was mostly the glasses. I had just read a book about John Lennon and thought it was funny to pretend his killer had joined us. The man was shorter than Chapman and could not have been housed with us in any case. The real ender of John Lennon's life is held in an upstate correctional facility's APP Unit, where prisoners who cannot be kept with the regular population because of celebrity or notoriety are housed; Tupac did his time for rape there.

One afternoon, Idiabe, faux-Chapman, and I were out in the yard of Napanoch, an "honor max." This old jail looked like a castle and offered privileges like a real gym, movie theater, and the bodybuilding supplement creatine sold in commissary. We had inmate organization-hosted dinners with bison burgers and Scotch bonnet peppers, care of the Native Americans and CAU (Caribbean African Unity), respectively. The prison also had a forty-foot-tall wall and gun towers stocked with AR-15s, of course.

I should have paid more attention to Idiabe's musical tastes; he had once been a mod, after all. Because I could never resist a joke, I spread the rumor that Chapman was among us the same day I noticed his miniature lookalike. I added some context to the drop of poison I released into the rumor mill, to make sure it spread: "Chapman's here, can you believe it? Killed the Beatles. How could they bring a guy like that here? A scumbag who gunned down John Lennon back in 1980. Shot him up at the Dakota, Mark David Chapman. Yeah, little guy, with the glasses. Mustache. Yoko Ono. The poor Beatles, over *Catcher in the Rye*, too. Yup. Like Son of Sam, killed the Beatles, serial killer. Fucking terrible."

The news spread fast, and my joke came to a head only two weeks after I released it. I was chatting with Africa in our lovely "Rapo Park," a corner of the yard with chess boards and sex offenders. I noticed that he had stopped hearing what I was saying and was staring over my shoulder. When I turned my head, I realized that he was staring at the pretender to the king of celebrity-slayers. Staring hard. That moment I saw the bloody future and was about to tell him about my stupid joke, but it was already too late. He marched over and got in the man's face, the seashell woven into his dreadlocks shaking in fury. He was shirtless, and the muscles and veins of his Apollonian torso were at attention, ready to rip the man in half. Africa began interrogating not-Chapman as to his motives: "Why? Why did you kill John Lennon, you shit of a dog?"

"No, no, it wasn't me," the baffled defendant insisted. "I didn't do it!"

"Do not lie to my face! You have made a confession. You . . ."

Clearly the man had been explaining that he didn't kill the Beatle a lot recently. But this was different, and it was intense. That dangling seashell in front of him may have felt like an omen of his imminent demise. The man's fear of an enraged Idiabe overcame other taboos, and elicited the words one never hears in prison: "No, it wasn't me. I didn't kill anyone, I'm here for rape!"

Because Idiabe had been convicted on an "aggravated felony," his green card could not save him from eventual deportation. As Biafran citizenship is no longer a meaningful concept and the United Kingdom wouldn't take him, he was sent back to a Nigeria he barely knew. In a conversation a week before his flight "home," he told me he would have preferred the Falklands. Still, he left me a Lagos phone number. He gave me a pack of cigarettes right before leaving, having quit in expectation of Nigerian poverty. Today he's back on the continent where his nickname wouldn't make as much sense. Perhaps they call him America.

Trying to understand his predicament led me to read accounts of those who are not just incarcerated but incarcerated in foreign lands. It was a continuation of old habits; as a free man I'd read Solzhenitsyn, Boethius, and, the most frightening of all, *The Violent Man*, a science-fiction author's description of incarceration in China for Western missionaries. A. E. Van Vogt usually wrote about future supermen, but his description of Maoist prison scared me thoroughly. Every morning, the inmates knelt in a ditch while their guards pissed on them. Another such powerful narrative was *Shantaram*, by Gregory David Roberts, which depicted the years spent by an Australian druggie in an Indian prison. His having to come to terms with a coexistence with insects—eating, drinking, and bathing in them, even hosting them in a variety of orifices—left me with immense gratitude for my own sanitary circumstances. In Russian accounts of incarceration were studies in buggery and degradation. Third-world journals, like what I read of Latin American prisons, were exercises in starvation and brutality. Everywhere was worse than where I was. Maybe Iceland has some sweet prisons, but I don't think anyone spends long enough in them to write tomes complaining about the poor-quality prison lox.

Inside, I read Arthur Koestler and Primo Levi and *Papillon* and Elie Wiesel and Varlam Shalamov. While there are obvious differences in these memoirs, there are also unexpected similarities. Prison definitely has distinct local characteristics, but in truth it is more

alike across borders, cultures, and even centuries than different. In
The House of the Dead, Dostoyevsky's account of a two-year sentence, a fellow convict sells the great author a handmade chess
set. The man in the cell next to mine, meanwhile, was using papier-
mâché to craft a chess set to sell to me. Across two centuries, two
continents, and two radically different societies, the condition of
incarceration nevertheless resonates with patterns as old as chains
and walls.

Perhaps my reading of this genre (which exists as television, too,
in the form of *Locked Up Abroad*) is what left me with less fear of
the big house than is healthy. I am an American citizen, so I knew
that even in the worst-case scenario, it would be Attica. That may
sound strange to a normal person with a normal fear of Attica, but it
is still a Western, democratic, humanist, capitalist institution and not
the Maoist urine baths or Indian weevils or Russian sodomy or Latin
American sodomy or Stalinist death. I would live, and I would get
out, and I wouldn't be deported. But no matter how out of place I
sometimes felt, I was neither the first nor the last to find myself in this
predicament.

Jim was the son of a prominent Korean art critic, raised as an intellectual with a detour into addiction. He lived in a very posh West-
chester town with some very down-market habits. We were almost
doppelgängers. His father was big in Korea; mine in Russia. Both men
are cultural critics, and both of us sons have inherited our fathers'
tastes and talents while struggling to escape their tall shadows. Drugs
were tempting to us, a shortcut to the contentment that true success promises (though whether it delivers is another story). Jim's weak-
ness for heroin cost him twenty years when his purse-snatching victim
had the misfortune to clutch her bag ardently. He tried to take her
purse, and she held on . . . to the death. Jim was caught and admitted
the theft, but he was mortified by the news coverage. The murder he

was accused of was, he insisted, an accident. He had acknowledged his crime and the addiction that motivated it but denied that he punched his victim in the face after knocking her to the floor. For some reason, the media added that bit of nastiness to the reporting. The reason could have been because he had actually done it, but I could not imagine the slim, thoughtful Korean boy decking an old lady.

One fine morning Jim arrived at the prison I was being held in after moving from our former spot, where there was enough of a Korean population that he didn't have to bother mingling with anyone else. This was not the case at the second facility, and I was glad to have the company of a smart friend. However, he arrived badly dopesick, struggling through withdrawal. Our previous prison had a paralysis ward and plenty of powerful meds for low prices, and a couple of 30 mg morphine pills a day for a few years had left Jim readdicted. Understanding his situation was no challenge. Jim's sister sent him books, but the habit he had built up was crushing. The possibility of spending one's days reading the best of the world's literature while flying on morphia sulphate is just about the best way to make the reality of prison subside. It's exactly how to push regret and sorrow under your bed, but there's a price. I saw withdrawal eating away at him and sympathized with this clever kid. He was the one from whom I learned of Alan Moore and Neil Gaiman, and who convinced me to read Haruki Murakami again. I ended up tackling *1Q84* eventually, thanks to him.

There was dope for sale in the yard—fifty bucks for a bag of it. I had a carton of cigarettes under my bed, worth exactly what a bag of dope cost. It was everything I had saved up over the course of a year, but I lent it to him so he could feel human for a night. Jim was soon feeling normal and then some. But he was called down for a urine test the next morning and was sent to the box that afternoon. Somebody had watched it go down and dropped a slip. I never got the crate back, and naturally his friends called me the cause of the problem on many levels. Some merely resented my role in his downfall, while others suspected I set him up.

I actually did see him again. When we were both placed in Coxsackie correctional facility a year later, we would pass each other in the corridors, but he only nodded to me and never came out to the yard to meet. I had written off the debt long ago but I valued his company. Perhaps he associated me with the demons responsible for his problems.

The other foreigners I came to know from my years buried alive with them were no less out of the ordinary. Some had been criminals or prisoners in their native lands as well as in this one. Others committed their crimes across borders. These strangers could certainly each have come with his own manual, but the truth is that these men were books, bound in varying shades of human leather and as interesting to me as anything I read. They made my small, dark world a larger and more interesting place. I'd like to think that I served the same role for many others. The protagonist of Robert Heinlein's novel *Stranger in a Strange Land* did exactly that. I don't claim for myself or for anyone else I met the mantle of Heinlein's supernatural messiah. That character enlarged the experience of others. He made the small scope of human experience wider. And so did we.

7

FROZEN CHOSEN

There were more Jews inside than I thought I'd find. According to the New York State statistics for 2013, about 7 percent of its prisoners were of the Jewish faith.

Given that the proportion of white prisoners is about a fourth of the total, combining these two facts would lead one to the mistaken impression that one out of every four pale faces on ice was named something like David Berkowitz. In fact, almost all that Hebrew 7 percent are minority prisoners who call themselves Jews for ulterior motives. In truth, the only demographic contingent with fewer representatives than Ashkenazi Jews in New York State prison is Asians. The 7 percent solution (the name of a lovely mystery I read that featured Sherlock Holmes and Sigmund Freud solving a murder while indulging in their narcotic habits and not a book that has anything to do with this chapter) is clarified by identifying the missing variable in this statistical fluke. Jews can receive kosher food, which is widely considered a desirable diet.

Inmates registering as Jewish in order to participate in these meals account for most of the Jewish population. The rabbis employed by the state had a polite euphemism for this crowd, something I learned after serving as a clerk for four of them in various facilities. Orthodox Judaism does not permit one to simply decide that one is Jewish; either you are born of a Jewish mother or you go through a demanding and lengthy conversion process, which was strategically unavailable to prisoners, not least of all because of the necessity of immersion in a mikvah bath. "Self-declared" was the rabbinical term for those who were not really Jews. These words were jotted discreetly in a corner—in Hebrew letters, Yiddish words, and pencil—on the paperwork that arrived with a transferred inmate describing his religious affiliation. The rabbis knew not to make an issue out of this, but being Orthodox they had to know who was halachically Jewish to count the members of a minyan. The pretenders doing it for the kosher food called themselves "paper Jews," to make sure no one mistook them for actual Jews. This chapter is devoted to the real thing: Jews on ice, the Frozen Chosen, such as myself.

THE JEWS I KNEW in prison were an interesting sampling of the tribe. They were a mix of those who were destined for prison and others for whom incarceration was the result of one bad afternoon. The Jews gone bad who were just passing through on short bids were universally drug addicts. There is a correlation between the storied Jewish yearning for ecstatic and mystical experience, and the path of chemical-dependent intronauts. I had noticed this earlier at venues where people took drugs to feed their heads rather than their bodies. Jews flocked to Grateful Dead shows, followed Phish, and dominated the trance-techno scene. Many of the druggy books I studied, like Alexander Shulgin's *PiHKAL* and *TiHKAL*, which were explorations of psychedelic compounds and MDMA, were written by Jews. The author of those bibles of psychopharmacology actually named the psychedelic compounds he discovered using Hebrew letters derived through Gematria, the numerological study of the Torah.

Having also seen the devout pray themselves right out of their own heads at the Western Wall in Jerusalem, I thought there was something in Judaism that welcomed seekers. Marc Chagall painted Hasidic Jews taking flight from the dark ghettos of Eastern Europe on wings of prayer, study, and insight. The hippies I knew in high school who invited me to their seders just took LSD. However, call that the nice side of the street. Taking ayahuasca for the psychedelic experience leaves one with fewer inhibitions about heading down other recreational avenues, like trying heroin for kicks. Crossing over to the other side of the street is when Jews get hooked. Narcotics are illegal and as a result put many of the Jews I met behind bars. They were usually not in for too long, but often repeatedly.

Sonny, an Orthodox Jew and heroin addict, knew every rabbi in the system thanks to his many short trips to prison. They would even help him with packages of kosher food. The *landsmen* I encountered doing serious stretches were a stranger bunch. Those with sentences of more than a decade were often quite memorable people. An actor who'd killed twice became my friend despite being forty years older than me. His sentence was then twenty-five to life after having served about fifteen for the first murder. I happen to know that he was recently denied parole, despite being seventy. Another was a master mechanic for Mercedes-Benz, said to be taking the weight for his kid, serving a sentence for his killer son. One prison had a crew of Sephardic Israeli ecstasy smugglers. They suffered terribly from lack of hummus.

Brooklyn sent up Jewish wiseguys every now and then, but the most exotic were the several murderous Hasidic Jews. Having broken man's laws, they concentrated on honoring God's, and all went through massive difficulties to keep kosher in an environment not suited for it. One Lubavitcher was serving fifty to life. Phil Drelich had killed two people, weighed more than 350 pounds, and kept the Sabbath while working on his appeal, thirty years after his crime. Before leading us in prayer, he tied a ceremonial belt around himself, separating his clean upper half from his soiled nethers. He actually required two such belts joined together to encompass his massive belly, but all that fat was purely kosher. None of the men who kept scrupulously kosher saw any contradiction between their current piety and their criminal pasts.

WHAT'S MISSING BETWEEN the skid-bid junkies and Torah-observant murderers is what most people imagine when they think of Jewish convicts. But white-collar criminals just didn't go to maximum security; those guys wind up in the feds with other nonviolent types. Toward the end of my sentence, when I reached a much less intense medium-security prison, I did meet corrupt stockbrokers, pilfering bankers, thieving agents, and one really crooked dentist. I even played all-Jewish tennis doubles with these tarnished men. But for the most part, I was in the wrong type of prison to learn insider trading or where to get Caribbean MDs. The one Jewish doctor I knew in a state max was an abortion provider who was in for murder, after turning down a malpractice plea deal. And the state-provided Jewish doctor who treated me almost killed me the moment we met. After waiting forever for my appointment, I went into the spartan office and sat down.

"OK," he said, "you're Mr. Genis, and I see you are HIV positive."

My heart dropped into my shoes and my vision went blurry. "What? How? When did this happen? Oh my God . . ."

The doctor looked down at his paperwork and changed his tune. "Ah, I see, you're HIV negative, not positive. Yes, well, moving along . . ."

That kind of bedside manner could have put him on the tennis court with the other bad Jews, in my opinion, because he nearly killed me with fright.

The Jews I had to figure out, and quickly if I was to join their number, were not just big machers who got pinched but heavies, guys who had taken lives. These were high-status kosher tough guys calling the shots, and because I was neither very tough nor kosher, I hit the books about the people of the Book.

While every facet of incarceration can be better understood by reading, this exercise gets complicated when the subject is Jews in the joint. On the one hand, Jews have such a limited history of notorious criminality that its luminaries can easily be listed: Meyer Lansky, Dutch Schultz, Bugsy Siegel, Bernie Madoff, Leon Trotsky. Jews make no memorable cameos in the pantheon of jailhouse memoirs and movies. On the other hand, there is the Holocaust, where millions of Jews were incarcerated in "dedicated facilities."

The literature of Jewish incarceration must include the bleak works of Primo Levi. I read *The Drowned and the Saved* with the same horror that I absorbed Elie Wiesel's *Night*. The emotional impact of life in the Nazi camps was at its worst for me when the characters' impotence was demonstrated. Jews sometimes wound up in places like Dachau with relatives and friends and were made into bestial competitors for scarce resources, totally unable to help one another. Limiting resources prevents prisoners from uniting against their true enemy, something I saw in action every day when there were only so many chicken legs or telephones, which we struggled over. But this was not a lesson specific in any way to the condition of Jews inside. In fact, while I did learn from my reading that things could be worse, I had trouble identifying with the Jews in the camps. To me their defining feature was their innocence, which made their pain sacred. My travails were deserved, so I did not come any closer to a comprehension of my own state as a Jew in confinement through the study of Holocaust literature.

I did, however, befriend the ex-husband of Wiesel's female relative.

He was doing twenty-five to life for ordering a murder for ten thousand bucks. Fascinated by his proximity to genius, I asked what the great Wiesel was like. To my dismay, my friend admitted that while he had a weekly Sabbath dinner with the writer, he had never managed to read his books and therefore avoided the subject. They talked about baseball instead.

Unfortunately, my friend was an example of a rare creature that is hard to find even in prison: a Jew who is also an idiot. But he had a good heart; it was too bad that his sister had the misfortune to marry a junkie. My friend forgave his addicted brother-in-law when he stole his Cadillac, but when the man started beating on his sister, he had him whacked. Wiesel never visited him inside.

When I reached Rikers Island, I was still frightened of black Muslims and the Aryan Nation, thanks to television, and so I registered my religion as "none." Somehow the facility rabbi noticed me, called me in, and fixed this oversight. It was the first of many kindnesses I received from the Jews involved with the New York State prison system. It would have been Clinton or Attica otherwise, twelve hours away. But in exchange I was expected to participate in the program beyond eating through its excellent bounties. For four years I attended every ceremony and ritual, prayed kaddishes and davened, watched Hanukkah candles melt. Despite immigrating to America as part of a family of oppressed Soviet Jews, despite a trip to Israel with my father, despite my nose, it was the first time in my life I was a Jew.

The guys on the court in the yard didn't quite believe me. How could a Jew lift weights? Where was my yarmulke? Or my horns? Very few members of the kosher program were welcome on the courts. The Aryans knew they were supposed to hate them, even if they weren't quite sure why. The Muslims with any geopolitical awareness considered Jews an enemy. Among them "Arafat," "Qadaffi," "Jihad," "Bin Ladin," and "Osama" were popular nicknames. The Nation of Islam had a policy set by Farrakhan against us "bloodsuckers" and "termites." And then there were the black Jews. The black Hebrew Israelites—the extravagantly dressed men who harangue passersby in Times Square—are notoriously opposed to us "pretenders." They attended Jewish services to disrupt them and claimed that they were the only real Jews in the room. The rabbis feared and hated this group so much that in some prisons it was the Muslim imam who was their chaplain rather than a rabbi.

The rabbis were, on the whole, quite ignorant of the world in which they worked. I had a Jamaican neighbor in Green Haven who called himself "Hitler" and was merely looking to borrow the infamy and did not share his predilection to genocide. He was actually a nice guy who didn't mind sharing his expert cooking with *Juden* like myself, but his moniker still caused trouble.

One day the facility rabbi paid me a visit in my new cell, which was only a few gates down from Hitler's. At that very moment, Hitler's friend was trying to get his attention by calling his name, a gambit that wasn't working because Hitler slept in the afternoon wearing his headphones to keep the dubstep going. The rabbi stoically tolerated the first few times he heard my neighbor being called, but the tension escalated as the man shouted, "Hitler! Hitler! Hitler! Wake up, Hitler! Blood clot, Hitler! Hitler! Hitler!"

The prisoner was probably calling out to him about preparing dumplings, which took planning, because you had to soak macaroni for a day in advance before rolling it into balls. Hitler's were the best in the joint; I ate a few every time he cooked them. But the rabbi, by now immensely angry, was convinced the calls were directed at him, and I could tell the situation was about to get ugly.

"I don't have to tolerate this," the rabbi announced. "I'm getting an officer."

I begged him not to and told him it had nothing to do with him, that it was just someone calling his friend by his nickname. This mollified the rabbi, who almost believed me, but when he went to take a peek at who the ersatz Hitler was, things only got worse. The sight of a small dreadlocked Jamaican sleeping with headphones enraged him. This couldn't be "Hitler." The rabbi decided I was covering for the bastards, and I received a stare accusing me of base calumny. At least Jamaican Hitler wasn't prosecuted for a hate crime. When he woke I couldn't make him understand what the problem was; he offered to send the rabbi dumplings. I let the matter die away, never succeeding in clearing up the episode for anyone.

Meanwhile I was shocked to hear that the Jews weren't including me in their count for their minyan, which requires ten Chosen or nine and one Torah. I had muddied the waters with someone I wasn't sure about; I didn't want to seem "too Jewish," and it got back to the Judaic extremists. The Hasids who ran the show proved to be just as unsure about me.

What makes a Jew a Jew, anyway? By Orthodox standards, I was lacking. My Jewish blood came from the patrilineal side. That is enough, however, to make me one of the tribe, according to Israel's Law of Return. I invoked a rather different code when disputing with the incarcerated Hasids. According to the Nazi Nuremberg laws parsing racial purity, which governed the Third Reich, one Jewish grandparent was enough to qualify as Jewish. I told the fanatics that if I was Jewish enough to die for it, then I was enough of a Jew to count for a minyan. I took to reading the voluminous books on how to be a proper Jew. If reading the literature of the Shoah did not help me, perhaps the Talmud could.

I learned enough to realize I knew hardly anything, and I took a course by mail in the rules of kashruth. I earned a certificate that technically qualified me to be a mashgiach, the ritual expert in charge of overseeing a kosher kitchen. I could pray in Hebrew and swear in Yiddish. But there was no compromising with my persecutors. It ultimately didn't matter how much effort I put into being a Jew. My mother was a blond shiksa, and these were people who thought the letter of the law was more important than its essence. The very concept of the "Shabbas goy," who took care of lights and ovens and such on Saturdays, seemed preposterous to me, because either God was either easily fooled or the laws of kashruth were unimportant in essence. Following the 613 rules was said to be required of a Jew, and yet I did not feel myself any more Jewish by keeping to them.

Since I was to be a Jew now, I had to explore the question of what this meant beyond never cutting my cabbage heads but peeling them leaf by leaf. This was necessary to avoid consuming an insect hiding in between them. I stopped looking for the answer in books of Jewish law. It turned out that the more useful sources were by secular, Anglophone Jewish novelists.

Philip Roth, Saul Bellow, and Joseph Heller explained much of myself to me. It was in *Portnoy's Complaint*, *Herzog*, and *Good as Gold* that I found evidence proving I was a Jew after all. The intellectual egotism I knew well in my father and better in myself was common to us. We were oversexed, simultaneously needy, and a bit predatory. I was of a gabby culture no matter how much I wished I was the strong, silent type, and I loved an argument while fearing an actual fight, just like the Jews in the brilliant literature that came out of Judaic America. The characters I found there were funny, chubby, horny, and hirsute. Roth's clever, insecure protagonists *were* me. "Too Jewish," Jackie Mason might have said, but it was right for me. Portnoy's complaints were familiar, even if I am a Soviet Jew, from another culture and another continent. There is something universally shared by Jews; I've often wished to go back to Israel to witness a society in which we are not the "other." I suspect the distinction matters, but the unique genetics forged by generations of Diaspora still makes for a population blessed with something that is distinctly our own. Another characteristic I found familiar was our disbelief. We are blasphemous; don't many of us have trouble believing that God appeared as a burning shrub? Hard to imagine the creator of everything caring whether you write about him as "God" or "G-d." Turned out that we were a stiff-necked, stubborn people, and cynicism expressed with sarcasm was ironically just another of our traits.

For ten years the Jews hammered away at my atheism. I wanted to believe in God to please them more than anything; they were just so decent. An organization called Reaching Out sent a monthly newsletter and offered all kinds of help on a personal basis. Rabbi Spritzer, its helmsman, was a force of nature who could get Hanukkah candles lit at a distance. He mailed out siddurs and tallits to congregations in American prisons (county jails, state and federal prisons, and military brigs) and those posted on navy ships and army bases. The rabbi interceded on behalf of tarnished Jews looking to be better by keeping to the rules, calling wardens, and subsidizing sukkahs. He even sent sealed kosher foods to indigent Jews.

I corresponded with him for a decade, and our letters ran the gamut of what was possible in this context. The rabbi used to enjoy mentioning Matisyahu, the reggae-rapping Hasidic singer, until I received the glum letter informing me that he had moved away from Crown Heights. The implication was that he was no longer keeping to Orthodox rules, as 770 Eastern Parkway was the vector where godliness and Chassidus intersected.

This building, which exists in a further seventeen replicas around the world, is ground zero for a Messianic cult that some critics claim has left the world of Judaism, following to the same logic that is used to argue that Mormons aren't Christians.

Breaking with precedent, the Chabad-Lubavitchers had not selected a successor rabbi after the 1994 death of the Rebbe Menachem Mendel Schneerson. According to the Messianic brand of Chabad, the Rebbe was revealed to be the Messiah after his tragic passing more than twenty-five years ago. Even though Schneerson is buried in Queens, the polite way to speak about this matter with those still faithful is to assert that the Messiah has remained "concealed" since then. If you wanted a nod of approval from Rabbi Spritzer, you finished your letter with "I want Moshiach now!" Presenting enough exhortations to the Rebbe to reveal himself was considered a possible formula for the end-times to begin. And yet I sent a letter to the Rebbe.

I first noticed the possibility of writing to the Rebbe in the correspondence printed by Rabbi Spritzer between himself and other incarcerated Jews in the back pages of the Reaching Out publication. Several of my own letters were later selected for inclusion, but before they were considered I had to demonstrate where I stood spiritually.

I asked about the possibility of posthumous communication with the Rebbe and was explained the procedure. I was to pen a respectful letter to Rabbi Schneerson, including a question. This letter would be placed, randomly, into one of the many volumes of the Rebbe's collected correspondence, and whichever of his letters it landed on was then photocopied and mailed back to me. I had asked when my family would forgive me and got back something about atoms. After a few dozen such letters exchanged over the early years of my incarceration, Rabbi Spritzer started asking me how many real Jews were in each of the congregations I rotated through. I never held that question against him, as he needed to know how many Passover boxes,

Hanukkah candles, etc., to send, and I hoped he didn't blame me for padding the count.

The holidays meant a little extra attention for us incarcerated Jews. Reaching Out and Aleph, a similar Chabad organization based in Miami, were not the only ones sending help. When I was in Catskill Mountain prisons (aka Borscht Belt hotels) they dispatched food for Rosh Hashanah; we even got the head of a fish, traditionally served to symbolize the New Year. The New York Board of Rabbis sent each of us hamantaschen every Purim and an annual Passover box. For ten years I anticipated the annual gift. This treasure box held a dreidel, canned fish, chocolate coins, a Haggadah, and macaroons, which I found to be sickeningly sweet but could trade for more tuna and gefilte fish.

Gefilte fish was a friend for years. Not only did I collect and savor the little tins that arrived for Passover, but I looted the long-expired commercially sized cans from the prison kitchens. I consumed industrial portions (128 ounces? Do cans come that big? The other guys used them as stools) of entire schools of gefilte fish in gallons of stinky jelly. Thanks to the Borscht Belt hotels, we also received donations of long slabs of fish loaf, fence-post-sized and -shaped portions of gefilte done in a different style. It was nicely sweet and savory at once. I was grateful to the Israeli kitchen worker and ecstasy smuggler who slipped me footlong sections to eat in my cell. However, it was with disappointment that I also witnessed the precious gefilte fish wasted. Many of the men who finagled themselves onto the kosher rolls were not Jewish and had no affection or even tolerance for the dish and simply couldn't believe it was eaten as it was, cold and covered in slime. I watched as it was boiled and steamed, mashed into rice, braised in tomato sauce, and even battered and deep-fried. Mostly, though, it was traded off, and mostly to me.

My friends from Eastern Europe and Russia were amazed by how many prisoners claimed to be Jewish for access to better eating. Long accustomed to people changing their names and claiming an Armenian nose to hide their Jewishness, they viewed America as the only nation on earth where people pretended to be Jewish, apart from those trying to become citizens of Israel. But food is truly the stuff of life to prisoners. On Rikers the kosher alternatives were double-sealed trays that were hard to imagine satisfying a grown eater, let alone a Jew, but things got better. When I got to Downstate, the sorting facility, I met with Rabbi Leser. This great man asked me, "So, do you think you might need kosher food? The company of Jews?" Eleven days later I was in nearby Green Haven, the only joint in the system with a hot kosher kitchen. Without his intervention, it would have been Clinton on the Canadian border.

The food was good. I ate the work of Ronnie the Rapo and Little Josh for four years. Slabs of cod fillets cooked in butter, Nathan's-type beef hot dogs, macaroni glued together with mozzarella cheese . . . and the holidays! We had our celebratory chickens for Rosh Hashanah, dairy periods, eggplant Parms, and cakes galore. This splendor was all kosher; I knew how long one must wait between meat meals and milk, and our guys were always ready with the food the moment that we could halachically eat it. The ovens were burned free of leavened bread every Passover, and we built a sukkah to eat outside in every year. Getting into this *frum* paradise was a challenge I only later realized I had sidestepped; there were men on the regular cold kosher diet that was available statewide, scheming on how to get in. They put in transfers for years, tried to convince outsiders to advocate for their need for kosher food and religious observance. Real Jews did wind up in Green Haven, guys who never took four steps without a yarmulke for their entire lives, even while committing crimes, and, luckily, ate at the same tables I did. Hasidic Jews all gathered there, funneled by the Orthodox rabbis around the state.

Orthodox is the maximally conservative type of Jew one can be before crossing into sect territory (Bobovers, Lubavitchers, Satmar, etc.). They make themselves a bargain because Orthodox rabbis can minister to the needs of Reform and Conservative Jews as well, though not the other way around. The rabbi of Coxsackie correctional facility was a woman, and therefore unacceptable to the Orthodox, who have set ideas about the roles of the genders. The other rabbis were careful to keep their opinions to themselves, but they did reserve a lowercase "r" in referring to her. If she noticed that she was "rabbi" in their correspondence, she pretended not to.

She was a large, jovial woman who constantly sipped diet drinks and had very few actual Jews to serve. Her prison was considered a disciplinary one, where few Jews landed. Once she learned of my education, she gave me a historical novel to read. *The Red Tent* is about the interaction of biblical women in the privacy of the shelter in which they menstruated collectively. I read it because without the context, I wouldn't have. I always welcomed novelty, though I got exactly what I expected with that masterpiece of feminist revisionism. Years later, when I mentioned the book to a group of Lubavitcher wives, they were no less surprised than they would have been had I brought up my reading of *Mein Kampf.*

Every year the Passover seder was an experience. *The New York Times* covered one such occasion with a photograph of most of the Jews in our hot kosher program. In the foreground was Brian Marmulstein, a biker who once stole a bag of fifty hot dogs, hiding them in his underwear and passing them out to everyone in the yard who wasn't grossed out. The Passover I spent under the lady rabbi was supposed to be a strictly give-out-the-grape-juice operation, as the only Chosen present was me. Everyone else was black. However, I gave the men the option of leaving and then started to read from the Haggadah. It seemed no one had ever gone through the ceremony with them. The opportunity to expose these men to something novel was mine; I ran the seder as it was supposed to go. The guys asked the four questions in earnest, ate the ritual foods, and drank their four cups of juice in an approximation of the ceremony. They all thanked me, for they had thoroughly enjoyed themselves. A few days later the rabbi asked if there had been any trouble with the distribution of the bitter herbs and maror, and was pleasantly surprised to hear that the ceremony had been a success.

The grape juice that was a feature of both the holidays and our weekly kiddushes proved to be a desirable commodity. To understand why, consider the old joke: "What did the drunk say when offered grapes?" "'No thanks, don't take it in pills.'"

There are many occasions in Jewish ceremony that call for wine. Because of the prison rule forbidding alcohol, big plastic bottles of sickly sweet purple grape juice was our Manischewitz. The Purim tradition of getting drunk enough to be unable to tell Haman from Mordechai was hinted at by the Chabad volunteers who were sent to the incarcerated congregations on holidays but left for us to improvise. The copious amounts of grape available turned out to be just the thing to build on in the quest to defeat sobriety.

One of the many characters I came to know over the years was John the Jew, who was actually a Catholic Pole but wore the moniker well. A dedicated burglar, John was on his third bid when we met. He knew to register as Jewish, ask for the kosher diet, and put on a credible show whenever the rabbi was looking; prison had made a passable Jew out of him. He'd even absorbed enough Yiddish to talk about "meshuggener shvartzes." John got high on drugs when flush with funds, but what he reliably enjoyed was a drink.

John brewed the bottles of kosher grape juice into hooch, either using bread as a catalyst or brewer's yeast when he could get it. Pill bottles of yeast were worth several packs of Newports, because you could make a lot of jail wine with them. There was a removable wall panel in the 150-year-old joint we lived behind where John kept a private wine cellar and still, in which a batch was always bubbling. John left that prison by being unexpectedly dragged away to the box after failing a urine test, so unless someone else discovered the space behind the panel, there is still a vinegar-grade portion of wine in there now.

The receptacle in which the grape juice was usually fermented was a washed-out milk bag. Our cow juice came in 2.5-gallon bags made of extra-sturdy plastic with built-in spouts. They had nozzles that would release their contents according to pressure, so they worked just as well as vents. The milk bags regulated themselves automatically and were therefore the finest casks available, but other less handy vessels were also used.

Fermentation creates an unstoppable flow of gas, so malodorous explosions of unvented hooch were a hazard of the trade. Brewers using simple garbage bags had to "burp" them daily, as an explosion of fermented fruit juice left a stink so powerful that detection by the authorities was inevitable.

When I was let in on the secret vintner, I couldn't just drink for free but was given the unpleasant task of filtering the yeasty sludge out from the fermented liquid. My first time doing this nasty work was also my first drink in a half-dozen years. I managed to not fail or get the operation busted but also ended up much more drunk than I expected. Half a decade of enforced prohibition takes away whatever tolerance you think you had. After delivering the plastic bottles of filtered hooch to the prison's movie theater as instructed, I made a thorough ass of myself. I handed out the dozen bottles to the predetermined recipients, sat down to enjoy the film, and drank more. Inspired by a cockney X-Man on the screen, I carried on a monologue in a British accent until I threw up. At the time

I thought I was quite funny, but upon discovering the Technicolor vomit in the toilet, the cops decided someone had been stabbed, and every single movie patron had to lift his shirt to demonstrate a lack of punctures.

I filtered the fermented grape juice much more slowly the next go-around.

WITH TIME I LEARNED that makers of hooch across the state system valued the kosher juice more than any other. Some went through the rigmarole of formally changing their religion, only permitted once a year (and not at all for those in solitary, where too many "converts" were also looking for a kosher diet to add variety to their dismally dull lives), for access to the juice. Unlike John, I ultimately experienced the act of feigning Jewish belief as a blow to my integrity. Having been an atheist for as long as I had been an anything left me poorly prepared for life as a Jew. However much I tried to compensate with thick volumes of Martin Buber, out-of-fashion Sholem Aleichem novels, and the brilliant Hayim Nahman Bialik, developing a sense of Yiddishkeit was a struggle with the faith included. Being Jewish was more than liking gefilte fish, but at best my impression of Jewry was one of a people with an abstract relationship to God. At worst, if we are to abandon all objectivity, it is atheistic. To put it simply, Jews seemed too cosmopolitan and too clever to believe in a god, let alone the dictatorial, primitive, and terrifying God of Abraham. Jews question things.

Would an Einstein, or Proust, or even Adam Sandler really blindly send his son to sacrificial death at a mountaintop at God's commands rather than to an Ivy or at least a good state university?

Rabbi Spritzer was clear on one thing: A Jew is a Jew, even if he calls himself an atheist. The Hasidic Jews, aware of the Jewish propensity to worship Phish or the Comintern in place of Hashem, simply choose to believe a little harder, to make up for the rest of us.

By the same mechanism, my friend Rubin prayed for me.

I met him early on; he was a member of both the kosher program and the yard court I was on. He'd been doing time for most of his life; he was then serving a sentence for a second killing. He had done his first for murdering a girlfriend, back when bids were shorter. He was now serving twenty-five to life for ending the life of his good friend, who met death at the point of an antique SS dagger. Nevertheless, Rubin did his best to be a good Jew. He took apart the sandwiches I made him, eating the cheese halves separately from the flesh. The former actor had abstained from mixing meat and milk, but not narcotics. If he had eaten meat at breakfast, he'd chase his morphine with black coffee. The drugs served no less than faith and art in helping his seeker's soul soar above the drabness his violence had condemned him to. He introduced me to Lenny Bruce, Arshile Gorky, and *The Prisoner*, through books and conversation; a decade was to pass before I saw the latter in Technicolor. He started including me in his prayers even before I got him an album of Philip Guston paintings, caring enough for me to pray for my health and happiness. It was touching to witness him earnestly compose the necessary Hebrew. I was grateful, just not convinced.

I stopped speaking to Rubin on three separate occasions, the third time being the last. In me he found a friend who was inappropriately young, a rare intellectual, and a convict still hopeful. For my company he'd do anything—including threatening me with a can top (our face-cutters of choice) for wasting "our" time. His jealousy went a long way toward proving to me that friendship and love are just levels within the same emotional spectrum, which features resentment and hatred on the other end. I value my memories of Rubin's kindness; he taught me how to be a decent prisoner and a Jew at the same time. He was the only person who prayed for me, even if he also scared me a bit.

Years later I read what the judge said at his sentencing, having found the account on the internet: "Just because Mr. Rubin kills the people closest to him doesn't mean he merits any leniency." Maybe I got off easy.

JEWS IN PRISON DIDN'T have it substantially better or worse than everyone else—just some extra food. There was no wink between the Jewish crook and his lawyer who freed anyone. However, it took going to prison for me to understand that I am a Jew. I read and studied, ate kosher and lit candles, and still am not sure what it finally *means* that I am a Jew, only that I'm definitely of the Chosen People. It took a trip up the river for me to understand what a big deal that was. At times I thanked my stars, and at others the deal was not always a good one. But I had made my bargain with god, God, and G-d. Gefilte fish only sweetened the deal.

8

SEVEN THIRTY

In prison vernacular "seven thirty" is not just a notation of the current time but a way of saying someone is crazy. Describing a convict as "fourteen sixty" indicates that he's twice as nuts as the average incarcerated loon. "Seven thirty" is code for "mentally ill" because a form titled #7.30 is filled out when an officer notices psychiatric issues in an inmate and requests a psych referral. This document follows a prisoner for the rest of his time as a ward of the state to alert those who might have to deal with its subject and his loose wrapping. Then the jailhouse status transcends its context. It proceeds to jump the barrier, almost like quantum tunneling gets an electron through lead, and determines features of one's parole supervision in the free world. It's not cool to get a 7.30.

There are other terms to describe psychological illness. MO ("mental observation") has been adopted to mean the same thing as a "bug out" or "nut" or "head case." The nomenclature is so varied because it describes so wide a range of pathologies of the men in prison. It wasn't always this way, and the transformation of the correctional system into a warehouse where the mentally ill are kept safely far from society occurred because of political upheavals. The big state asylums that dotted the nation closed down in the 1960s, thanks to patient abuse scandals, overuse of lobotomy and Thorazine, as well as Ken Kesey's *One Flew Over the Cuckoo's Nest*. Reading that work was no less helpful to understanding my world than jailhouse memoirs. However, once the asylums closed down, their residents failed to get cured. Before the late 1960s the homeless were a very small population consisting mainly of Bowery winos, the truly down and out, and the fiercely independent. Luc Sante described this demographic very well in *Low Life*. What came after the bureaucratic changes was a nightmare. Very quickly the population exploded into one composed of men who could not take care of themselves beyond self-medicating with street drugs.

This massive failure of social engineering left the lowest rung of society's safety net, the correctional system, to deal with an army of "bugs." Almost a hundred new prisons were built in New York State after the 1970s in response to the rise in poverty, reactions to urban unrest, tough-on-crime policies, the crack epidemic and the violence that came with it, including the influx of guns.

Reading old accounts of the prison system gives you a different perspective on what it's evolved into. Of course the unnatural stressors of incarceration have always created Birdmen of Alcatraz and less picturesque lunatics, but also the hordes of shuffling, stinking men unable to hack even the lax American discipline required of modern convicts. Jack Henry Abbot's *In the Belly of the Beast*, which describes New York State prison in the 1960s, features a lot of truly bad and violent men, as well as a few unlucky ones who weren't really tough enough and became victims, but no madmen—no convicts who thought they were someone or somewhere else, or who believed their food was being poisoned or that Hollywood starlets were communicating with them through television. I saw examples of all this and more, men who clearly belonged in a place where their mental illness could be treated, but because they had broken the law as well, their punishment took precedence over their well-being. Finding someone unfit to stand trial only happens in movies. After the violence of crack days, the law hardened again, undoing the reform-minded initiatives of the 1960s and throwing away the key. Non compos mentis doesn't fly anymore, and no one without a celebrity lawyer has been found innocent by reason of insanity for a long time. Today pretty much everyone is fit to have their day in court.

As the overwhelmed psychiatric staff in a prison could tell you, that does not mean it's true. The most extreme example I witnessed of untreated mental illness was a man afflicted with coprophagia, and I don't mean poor Pop who was tricked into eating the worst of sandwiches. If you know your Greek roots, you'll have already identified this as the compulsion to eat shit. He'd been given dozens of tickets (misbehavior reports for "unhygienic acts") and was seemingly kept on a diet of pure antibiotics because of his "hobby." The coprophage was a dapper little black guy in his fifties whom the cops kept catching loitering by toilets, where he would beg prisoners not to flush. I was caught off guard and complied, only to be dressed down by the officers, who asked, "You think you did him a favor? You want to be responsible for when he drops dead?"

I did not and flushed from then on, earning the man's stink eye. This inmate was serving years for some crime and was considered fit to do so. Perhaps he had refused therapy, but beyond the antibiotics, I saw no evidence of any treatment he received for his grotesque condition.

Only five minutes of observation of any prison, from Rikers to a max, will demonstrate that today's incarceration is as much for the mad as the bad. Perhaps the largest portion of the prison population considered part of the spectrum of mental illness is the addicted. If you accept the disease model of addiction, then contemporary prison appears to be mostly for ill people, with a sprinkling of those who kill people. Of course, while society officially accepts that addiction is a mental health issue, complete with genetic predisposition, susceptible populations, methods of treatment, and insurance coverage, based on our reaction we really feel it is a failing of morals and punish addiction most harshly.

I myself served ninety days in solitary for a relapse while incarcerated. If they weren't so to begin with, the multidecade terms America routinely hands out surely drive plenty of the men nuts. However, lest you find yourself overcome with sympathy for these neglected sufferers, remember their victims. Drug addiction causes almost all property crime in this wealthy nation and often bleeds into violent crime when it is encountered. Robberies like mine are straightforward results of addiction.

Meanwhile it is the crimes of the mentally ill that are often the most heinous: murders involving torture, rape, and sadism, violence committed for pleasure and molestation without a hint of empathy. The families of their victims and their survivors are not consoled by a diagnosis of mental illness in the men who touched their lives to introduce horror and pain to them. This equation resolves into the preponderance of crime being caused by mental illness, whether addiction or the schizophrenia, etc., that motivates the gruesome antics beyond property felonies.

The question of responsibility is not one we can expect to easily solve; simply figuring out what to do with the criminally insane is enough of a challenge. The line for psych meds is long in every jail, but because of the potential for abuse, some of the drugs that might pacify chaotic minds accustomed to violent solutions to problems real and imagined are forbidden. The calming chemicals of the benzodiazepine family, like Xanax, Valium, and Klonopin, are simply not used. Now and then someone with a private lawyer, one not assigned by the state, can get a prescription court-ordered.

Similar struggles are fought over painkillers, which are trafficked in a healthy black market in the yard. For regular inmates, pretty much any pain up to that accompanying cancer is treated with aspirin. However, there are doctors who are free with the morphine in the special hospice wards, where prisoners are transferred to die. The old convicts waiting for their parole-in-a-coffin are not allowed to smoke but are awash in OxyContin and other opiates. Because the convicts getting opiates in prison hospices don't have access to the yard, jobs as orderlies and porters in the four death units (those offering palliative care) around the state are very much in demand. Sneaking the seniors cigarettes to trade for pills is common. I saw such a porter get drafted out to another jail after years on the job; he was sent back on the next bus and admitted to the hospital himself so he could detox. The prisoner orderly had acquired an enormous morphine habit over his years of taking care of dying convicts and trading tobacco for pills.

DURING THE TEN YEARS I served, I worked a wide variety of jobs. Almost all of them were the jailhouse equivalent of white-collar work, but my two years serving as a porter/tutor in a maximum-security prison's bug unit was a plum position I was given in a nod to my compassion. I'm not sure how Dr. Hanson decided I had an especially strong sense of it, but later on I did realize that compassion is a quality prisoners are particularly poor in. Hanson was a kindly shrink with a Scandinavian heritage and a shock of white hair. His greatest fear was of drugs finding their way in and upsetting his charges' fragile brain chemistries, which he supervised with medications. I had seen the outcome of such things myself. A "bug" just released from the box had to stand in line behind Gordo, a cheerful fat Boricua. The mentally ill man had just celebrated his release from solitary by smoking a joint outside. The back of Gordo's head had apparently offered intolerable insult, because the bug swung his fist at it, flooring the innocent man. The cops couldn't believe in the randomness of this episode, so both of them got tickets for fighting. When Hanson saw the results of the men's urinalysis, he got Gordo off and the other bug transferred.

My job was a strange amalgam. I served the guys their meals, which came up from the kitchen in big rolling cases, but I also facilitated groups in which issues I never expected to discuss came up. For two years I took care of a crew of honest-to-God monsters and grew to love them. The ward was in Green Haven, a max where everyone is locked in a cell overnight. However, most of these guys had a history of hurting themselves when left alone. A fellow named Pork Chop took his eye out with a plastic spoon once. Another guy tried to castrate himself, and rhythmically bashing one's head against a wall was a common sight.

I got to know and care about a felonious pig farmer. He was a fat, awkward ginger with a bad case; along with a friend of similar qualities, he attempted to kidnap a young girl in his pickup truck. The other guy got way more time, but even with a lesser sentence prison was very hard on my rural charge. He even converted to Islam at one point, hoping to improve his conditions, but things were still stressful enough for him that he kept harming himself and wound up living in Hanson's special unit. After I had gotten close with him, one day he gave me all his heavy metal tapes "to hold on to." That night he tried cutting his wrists and was rescued and eventually returned to the dorm, but the experience was hard on me. To this day I blame myself for not having acted on the bad feeling I got when he gave me the box of tapes. He did say he'd be wanting them back and in all actuality had not cut deep enough to put himself in danger of dying, but I might have been able to prevent the episode. The other guys said it took multiple mops to get all the blood off the floor.

I spoke with him after he got out of the hospital. Once we established that he didn't in fact want to die (though he did want his Dokken tapes back), I asked why he had cut himself. He showed me places in his leg where he had stuck needles and pins.

There was enough metal still in there that a magnet stuck to him. Cutting and poking himself felt good to the red-bearded farmer. I'd heard of this behavior before, but it's hard to process in someone you think you know. I'd also read about self-harm in James Frey's *A Million Little Pieces*, and it made sense as a way of getting yourself to feel something, anything at all, even if it was pain. But then the book was revealed to be a fraud, something I already suspected when Frey reported that he had a root canal without anesthesia (my wife works in the field and explained that this isn't possible), and I lost confidence in any lessons I had drawn from it.

THE MEN WERE AN EXTRAORDINARY collection of aberrations. The most friendly, good-natured kid had molested his sister, traumatizing her for life. Jackson, who wouldn't brush his teeth, had pushed a woman under the subway, earning him twenty-five to life. It was a case I remembered from the papers, involving a homeless man downtown. Curious as to how atrocities like this happen, I fed Jackson extra trays to earn his trust and tolerated the reek from his mouth. Finally I asked him why he had done it.

"Had to, Danny."

"But why?"

"It was her or me."

And that's how delusions kill.

TO WORK IN THIS PLACE I also had to suspend my judgment of sex offenders. An older wife killer named Larry, who had worked there for

a decade by the time I showed up, taught me how to do this gracefully. He had killed his wife during a spat, buried her, told the police
she left him, and felt so bad about it a few months later that he turned
himself in. Still got twenty-five to life. Larry never judged the guys for
their pasts but evaluated them on their current behavior. That worked
for the dorm, and we worked well together. It was more difficult
when I ran into one of the guys outside their unit, but that happened
rarely.

Rob was such a helpful, seemingly well-adjusted guy that I could
never understand why he was there. I understood that all wasn't well
with him one day when we met as he was picking up a parcel sent
from his family in the package room. This happened rarely, as few
people were in touch with the special-needs guys from Hanson's program. The inmate who was smooth and charming up in the dorm was
now rocking back and forth like a perpetual motion device. I tried
calming Rob with our usual banter, but he couldn't keep up. Every
passing prisoner or guard was someone who was after him; he was
scared to death. I waited with him until he got his package; the cops
left it for last because they misinterpreted his discomfort as attitude.
They also told me to clear out after getting my own, but I knew Rob
needed my help to get this mundane bit of protocol achieved without
a problem. I wouldn't leave until he got his food from home, too, and
suggested they call Dr. Hanson to confirm that. Rob was on a heavy
dose of psychotropic meds, as were all the guys, and even though I
had not been dispatched to help him, I was in a position to. But only
to a point.

In my hubris I had once questioned whether they needed to be so
zonked, but it turned out the professionals knew better.

In group we once focused on Harold, who was a pimply teenager,
discussing why it was wrong to make your sister blow you to let her
play Xbox. He was reported to the police by his own parents, who

also came to visit him every other weekend. They didn't bring his sister, but she wrote. Another fellow had a second set of pupils floating over his original pair. He moved around slowly and carefully, carrying porn on him at all times. He would look at the images even as he ate; he had molested a boy, and this was his way of fighting homosexual urges. There was a silent Mexican who had raped a baby before throwing the evidence off a roof. He was not allowed to go to the yard, because the Mexican gangs had a kill-on-sight contract on him. Guys like this didn't get much out of group, but no one tried too hard with them, as it was clear they were never going to be released back into the world.

DOC HANSON ASKED ME from the very beginning whether I would be able to treat sex offenders as I would any other inmates. Now, stand-up guys are supposed to hate rapos and molesters, but I always thought this was a tactic to minimize their own crimes by finding others guilty of even worse atrocities. Sex offenders were told by every facet of Western society that one should not sexualize children, that one should not have sex with women against their will. There is no vagueness on this point, and the guys themselves knew it was wrong and were ridden with guilt. But they simply could not stop themselves. Did they belong in prison, or a mental hospital? Probably the latter, but the families of the abused children, or those of the raped women, did not want to see these men cured. Like the cops and inmates, they wanted them punished.

Dr. Hanson's program for these sick prisoners was a compromise between the two impulses, and I was drafted in to help in that effort. Being a little crazy myself, I did my best and then some. I arranged for the cleaning crews but also helped the guys grow a vegetable garden. We grew so many tomatoes that once I bagged up forty portions of a few tomatoes each and gave them out to any inmate who passed by. The cops were furious, especially because they couldn't lock me up for this—I was giving away the fruit, not selling it. Finally one of them could stand this small kindness no longer and stomped all my bagged tomatoes into mush. Then he made me clean it up. I did it with a smile while whistling. Doc Hanson couldn't interfere, but he ruffled my hair and said some things that modesty prevents me from repeating here.

I repainted the walls of the place for our annual inspection and also taught the men how to exercise on our weekly trips to the gym. Leading them through weight-training routines was a comical sight and greatly irritated the gym rats who wanted to use the equipment they felt was for them and not for "retards," but I stood up for my guys' right to exercise for one hour out of the week, and they loved me for that. I also taught them everything, from multiplication tables to how to address envelopes to basic facts about our world. Most of all they appreciated my geography and history lessons. I ignored the colorful scholastic materials and instead drew elaborate maps on the chalkboard to explain the breadth of the British Empire or how America split during the Civil War or the extent to which the Nazis conquered their *Festung Europa*. The men were fascinated by the effort put in on their behalf and studied the maps intently, sometimes correcting my work from the encyclopedia. Doc Hanson wasn't as keen on the huge swastika he found in the middle of Europe on his chalkboard, showing Axis occupation during the WWII segment, but I had to tell him to blame Hitler for his successful blitzkrieg.

EVERY COMMISSARY DAY the guys were paid a few dollars for their participation in the program. They could buy one coffee and one pack of tobacco, which they would proceed to drink and smoke all in one afternoon until they altered their mental state with caffeine and nicotine. Then they would argue and scheme and steal for the rest of the stuff that was bought by the few guys who had a little extra. There was loan sharking and "juggling," in which you borrowed an item and paid back two.

On my serving shifts I handed out the food as fairly as I knew how, leaving extra trays of desirable items for the evening shift. Anything extra I handed out. The monthly day when liver was served for dinner was always fun; no one but me ate the lovely beef liver, which shimmered greenly. I was saved a five-pound portion, which was meant as a joke but appreciated by me. The guys watched me devour about half of it with fascination. On chicken leg day I was careful to stash two trays behind the chalkboard, to keep peace between the shifts. However, there was no friendship between my shift and the two black porters who came after me, who were as cruel as the orderlies in *Cuckoo's Nest*. They hated the guys and would deliberately throw away extra food rather than share it. On days when the meal was something everyone liked, they would steal the food and serve only half portions: half a chicken leg per "retard." I tried to not get involved, but one day the situation came to a head when I found out they were serving the men raw zucchini. I asked the p.m. staff whether they ate raw squash, and they said no, but figured the mentally ill wouldn't care. This was painful to witness, and I went to complain to the prison staff. It was then that I learned that the guys had been snitching on the p.m. team on my behalf for a while now, but to no avail. They were not considered trustworthy and were presumed to be making the abuses up. My contribution caused a few changes and many personal resentments against me. The p.m. staff dropped a note to the security staff that I was in grave physical danger and had to be moved out for my own safety.

Doc Hanson knew all about the difference in how I was treating the guys compared to how the second shift was. But there was nothing that could be done about it. They were black, while Larry and I were white. Firing them would have caused a race riot.

And so the criminally insane suffered every day after 4:00 p.m., and waited patiently to get a double breakfast from Larry and me. Hanson did, however, vouch to the deputy of security that I wasn't in any danger and didn't need to be transferred out.

The guys put on as good a face as possible on things during the day, but at night it was nature, red in tooth and claw, as they started waking up with semen on their faces. Every morning a fresh victim would find himself stuck to his pillow, or with an eye glued shut, or with male goo in his mouth. Whoever the culprit was, he was stealthy, secret, and silent. Many suspects were proposed; Larry and I had our own theories, until Harold simply told me who the perp/perv was.

"I seen him. It was Jimmy. Whacked off right in that guy's mouth as he snored," he reported. Larry and I were floored.

I'd have believed any other candidate but Jimmy. Oh, he was angry and jealous enough to take his revenge served warm, and Harold the informant had in fact been the very first victim sprayed. But Jimmy? He had only one leg, and it was amputated high. The middle-aged Hispanic Jimmy I knew rolled around in a wheelchair all day, asking for shots of coffee and cigarettes. He'd had a crutch once, but it was taken away after he swung it at someone. Jimmy's leg had been cut off so far up that pants fell off him. He had been a unipod since childhood.

I had trouble imagining it, but I should have remembered my own childhood reading.

C. S. Lewis's Narnia books were an early blow to my system and may have induced Anglophilia in my prepubescent cortex. How wonderful to pass through the back of a wardrobe into a fantasy realm? Or to voyage with Prince Caspian on the good ship *Dawn Treader* until the sea turned sweet? One of the stops the vessel made was on the island of the Monopods, invisible beings who hopped around on their single great foot. They were no less dexterous than bipedal men, having been single-footed all their lives. Ironically, at the time I was reading Lewis's Space trilogy, *Out of the Silent Planet*, *Perelandra*, and *That Hideous Strength*, on Christ in the solar system.

I ARGUED THAT BLAMING Jimmy for the cum shots was preposterous. The rattle of him prowling around in his chair would have woken the dead, even with the powerful psych meds that kept his victims asleep. I couldn't picture him maneuvering his way to someone's bed and then masturbating accurately enough to ejaculate right in someone's shut eyes or open mouth. But then I saw . . . everything.

One afternoon a cop was called away from the dorm and left half a cigarette burning. I'd been immobile in the day room, reading an *Atlantic Monthly* for so long that Jimmy forgot I was there. Everyone else typically fidgeted constantly, so being motionless was almost like being invisible. Jimmy certainly didn't see me as he came right out of the wheelchair and hopped across the room with utter grace and silence, returning effortlessly while puffing on the cop's Parliament.

Jimmy was never proven to be the cum-shot killer, but I had witnessed enough. No wheelchair was required. He was perfectly capable of silently hopping over to a guy's bed and whacking over him, especially since every guy creamed had denied him a cigarette or committed some similar offense against him.

I ran into Jimmy a half decade later and told him I knew what he had done back in Green Haven's special unit. He denied it at first, humbly gesturing to his handicap, but eventually couldn't resist telling me that the bastards deserved it, that they were greedy and no good anyway. Since there is always a deeper circle to this inferno, I might as well disclose that Jimmy was HIV positive. And aimed for the eyes.

TO BETTER UNDERSTAND HOW this degree of mental illness affects a person, I read much of the literature that explores it. Many of the works I consulted dealt with neurotic malaises that poorly corresponded with the real-life examples with whom I was eating my meals. Robert Musil's *Man Without Qualities* meandered over the gradual erosion of a sense of self, while *The Brothers Karamazov* explored murderous rages and how one can come to them quite rationally. *Crime and Punishment* provided the best justification for murder ever penned, and anyone who is convinced by its conclusion, and Raskolnikov's inability to live with the crime, is too easily cajoled. I read de Sade to try to understand if there was truly any aesthetic to evil, and followed that up with Michel Houellebecq's *Elementary Particles*. The French author made an argument for the humanity and even nobility of perversion. Antonin Artaud tried to do the same for cruelty, and the foibles of Alfred Jarry's *Ubu Roi* made a mocking sense of madness and evil that was delightful to read about but utterly unnerving when it was housed in the cell next to yours. The truth is that these sophisticated interrogations of psychosis provided little illumination regarding the mentally ill men around me. These were men who cut off the ears of their kidnapped victims rather than their own.

One Flew Over the Cuckoo's Nest was a more accurate look into the world in which I was living, with its simpleminded obsessions, petty cruelties of the orderlies, and horror for the person with moments of lucidity interspersed with his blessed madness. I also read Robert Stone's *Prime Green*, an account of Kesey as a cult leader on the bus Furthur, driven by Neal Cassady with sounds by the Grateful Dead.

Kesey did not come away from his getting to know mental illness unscathed. I'd like to think that I did, though the very compassion that Doc Hanson prized in me was also the obstacle to my experiencing the "naked lunch," that lucid moment when you can really see what's on your fork. I could visualize all my fellow prisoners' smiling faces but not one of their howling victims. That is an unbalanced state, just as Kesey's was after writing his brilliant novel. Mental illness is truly something to be wary of. Nietzsche warned me of staring into the abyss, and in response I read *Ecce Homo*. Those men knew they weren't going home. They knew they had done terrible things. But their problems were the procurement of coffee and cigarettes, not spasms of guilty self-loathing. That is the enticement of the condition. The freedom from responsibility for one's actions is seductive, despite its high price. The mentally ill can worry about Top rolling tobacco rather than the atrocities they committed.

Dr. Hanson eventually retired, but before he did he became my conduit for communicating with my wards after I transferred out of that prison. I sent a letter back to let them know I'd landed in a fine place with a great gym, etc. I did my best to remember their names: Rob, Smoky, Harold, and so forth, but the letter I got in response was signed by each and every one of the guys—thirty names in all. It officially came from Hanson, but he'd obviously taken the opportunity to offer one of his "normal life" lessons, teaching them what it meant to participate in ordinary society. That day he taught them how to write a letter to a friend, even if they didn't get any letters and didn't have too many friends. Hanson was a compassionate optimist who had long ago made his peace with the cruelty of reality. The letter was sweet and naive, blustering in parts and humble in others. It left me in tears.

9

THE VELVET MAFIA

first learned of the Velvet Mafia, fabulous and deadly, years before encountering some semblance of the notorious cabal in prison. Gay criminals are a feature of every prison movie, often in conjunction with queues of muscled men and shower rape. New York's fascinating intersection of crime, queer, and bohemian life is well documented in films like *Midnight Cowboy* and *Cruising*, which are inevitably set downtown and always after dark. It is the same phantasmagoric wicked play world in which drugs are trafficked.

But the actual Velvet Mafia always seemed to be somewhere else— just around the corner, metaphorically speaking. In New York it was rumored that nocturnal London clubland was ruled by a fierce family of homosexual criminals, cockney pimps, narcotic traffickers, and brutal sodomists, likely modeled on the Kray twins. While a traveler to London, desperate to score some first-grade ecstasy, I was asked about the Velvet Mafia's stranglehold on New York after dark by the same kid who sold me aspirin. It appeared they had heard the same things about the Rainbow Apple that I had about swinging London. The details were always too vague to pin down but cohesive enough to form a consistent impression. This gay mafia was reportedly a loosely connected network of drug-dealing nightclub impresarios who were HIV positive and quite ready to make you so as well, if you dared disobey them. When I came to prison, I met homosexual prisoners and befriended a few. I was finally in a position to answer the question: Did a gay mob actually exist? And just how gay was prison, anyway?

Over the course of my decade upstate I got to know homosexual prisoners of every type. Before prison, homosexual sex was an abstract concept for me; now it was taking place in the double-bunked cell next to mine or in the last shower stall of the communal bathhouse called the "car wash" or under a certain stairwell that everyone took care to approach very loudly. Locations for trysts were hard to find and generally respected; you had to know where it went on in order to avoid walking in on one.

To most accurately convey the unique facet of the already outré world in which I had arrived, I will use here the language that its protagonists do. It may not conform to the carefully correct standards of contemporary America, but it's a verbatim expression of how the men who do the things described here talk about them. The cognitive dissonance between those who use long-initialism descriptors (like LGBTQ+) as well as personal pronouns (like "they" in the singular) and incarcerated men getting each other off in the shower while lathered in Corcraft soap is sharply, well, dissonant.

I began with the wrong books, the Classic Greek corpus, in using literature to enhance the accuracy of my understanding of this new world of gay life in prison. Back in my middle-class existence, gay friends were just a fact of life, but that wasn't so inside. The ancient Greeks had very contrary beliefs about homosexuality compared to modern thought, so what I learned from the classics also didn't help. Sappho's poetry was especially useless. I thought the less inclusive mid-twentieth-century past would help, so I reread William Burroughs's *Queer*, but the dry and effete musings of a man who truly believed the brain was the primary erogenous zone elucidated little. The men groaning under the stairs were not getting fucked in the cerebellum. I read in *The Beat Hotel*, by Barry Miles, that during the period in which Burroughs's sex life was wholly comprised of orgasms bought from boy prostitutes in Tangiers, he was known as "the Invisible Man" by the Moroccan locals for his bloodless demeanor. In Miles's biography of Burroughs, *Gentleman Junkie*, I learned that when he was desperately in love with the young Allen Ginsberg, Burroughs dreamed of a "mind-meld" that would fuse the intellects of the lovers. Ginsberg declined the possibility of doing so by announcing that he "didn't want [Burroughs's] ugly old cock." That dry and sterile depiction of homosexuality, much like Oscar Wilde's coy hints at love that dares not speak its name, presented gay relationships in almost platonic terms. In the case of both authors, when lust did rear its head, it was in the context of a relationship between the old and the young. The Romanticism of the nineteenth century could not be said to apply. I soon turned to Jean Genet to figure out the Velvet Mafia.

Genet—French counterculture star, criminal, playwright, and committed sodomite—really enjoyed the sex in prison. His *Thief's Journal* featured men like the ones with whom I shared the showers: tough bastards who sucked an occasional dick, and God help you if you called them on it. The simpering poofs from Edwardian drawing rooms and beatnik cold-water flats had nothing in common with the brawny sailors from the port of Marseille or the various prisoners of the Francophone world. *Papillon* confirmed the accuracy of Genet's depiction of the ubiquity of gay sex in his underworld. I read Edmund White's brilliant *Genet: A Biography*, to see how much of his subject's accounts were fantasy. Some were. Genet depicted sex between men in much the same way as he did crime: it was exciting, euphoric, manly, countercultural, and transgressive . . . not in the hippie sense, however. Genet made homosexuality feel rebellious in the sense of its being a great big "fuck you" to conventional society. I cannot imagine Jean Genet being a supporter of a cause like gay marriage for that reason, just as none of the convicts I met had any particular interest or love for the cause. When that question was current, about ten years ago, I got into fierce arguments by defending the right to gay marriage and was surprised that some of my opponents were men who I knew enjoyed the occasional shower screw. I gathered that these guys didn't want the normalization of homosexuality. They had embraced it out of derision for everything else. A certain stripe of homosexual prisoner sees himself as the ultimate outlaw. Since good is bad and bad is good inside, nobody messed with the outlaws.

In a perverse correlation, the circumstances of prisoners' sex lives determined the amount of respect they got. For example, the straight prisoner who had committed a sex crime made him fair game for nonconsensual sex, and had it the worst. While it was widely acknowledged that a child molester or serial rapist could be treated that way, this was hardly true: anyone weak was vulnerable to predation. "Faggot" was the accepted term for such persons; even other gays called them that. The connotation of the term spanned from friendly banter to vicious hatred. Things were more complicated for those without life-defining details like rape convictions. Plenty of men who had gay sex in prison would kill you for putting it that way; it was only "gay" if they were bottoms, even "power bottoms."

The prisoners who were openly gay did not have an especially hard time. Though their status was below that of regular joes and far below that of stand-up guys and gang members, in my time in prison I never saw gay convicts truly oppressed or abused. At one joint they even had a table of their own in the yard, and it was beautifully decorated.

Whatever nonconsensual sex was going on was usually initiated with bribes and sweet talk. Almost exclusively it was intergenerational and interracial. The one time I saw it become an incident was when a young white kid stabbed an older black man after an overture had been made. This was rare, however. Prison rape appears on-screen much more often than it does in reality.

Despite the free use of the word "faggot" in prison vernacular, the only convicts who were dedicatedly homophobic were the bullies, insecure tough guys who didn't want to sit next to someone openly gay in the mess hall, and the new Muslim converts, who found the part in the Koran about throwing homosexuals off mountains. As for the rest of us, prisoners were surprisingly tolerant.

THE CONCEPT OF "GAY FOR THE STAY" was already on the wane, and yet there were enough men taking part in this age-old convict practice for me to get to know one and ask him how he rationalized it. Irish had a child and a devoted wife, who appeared for conjugal visits every three months. He also regularly had sex with willing gay prisoners. He was not a young man but devoted hours of every day to jogging and abdominal exercises. His beautiful torso was not sculpted to impress his wife. Irish had a friend who worked in the clinic who would check out the health of his prospective boyfriends. HIV infection rates are much higher among prisoners than in the general population, including a substantial number of men who do not know their status. The civilian male nurse was gay himself and performed this service for Irish, one that made a mockery of all the confidentiality procedures in place.

I saw Irish in tears once. He was moping around the gate to the clinic, where he had just learned that a new boy in the joint, a boy who was cute, young, and susceptible to Irish's advances, turned out to be HIV positive. Condoms cannot be used for gay sex among the inmates because they are strictly contraband inside; you go to the box immediately for possession of one. While they can be used for having straight sex with staff, such acts are not just against the rules but legally prosecutable. By law a convict does not have the power to give sexual consent, just like a minor, since staff members have authority over him. Nevertheless it happens and rubbers find their way in. Condoms are also the perfect vehicle for "boofing": wrapping something up and concealing it in one's rectum. Even an ounce of marijuana, properly packed and tamped down, feels like nothing at all once it is past the anal opening and in the rectum. The insertion process is unpleasant, which is why professional smugglers bring a smear of Vaseline on their earlobe to the visiting room, where a package will be handed over and immediately boofed. I'm not spreading hearsay; I know from experience.

Because condoms are hard to come by for these various reasons, bread bags are a popular commodity. They have to be wrapped around one's member in a certain way, but, apparently, they can work. When I first began my bid, the sight of entire loaves of sliced bread in the trash perplexed me, but I eventually figured out that what I was seeing was evidence of the theft of a bread bag, and not the bread itself, despite the archetypal literary crime of Jean Valjean from *Les Misérables*.

Irish explained to me that when he had started bidding, thirty years earlier, sex with men was more acceptable. He discovered then that lips are lips and butts are butts. He was always the "top." And would cut you if you called him a "homo." Jack Abbott's memoir is despised by modern prisoners for this very anachronism. Career criminals and experienced prisoners used to have sex with "fish" a lot more up till the 1980s. But prison culture has since changed. Abbott describes a world in which part of being a hard man was buggering the soft ones. In one chapter of *In the Belly of the Beast*, Abbott explains how much he enjoys shooting heroin by reminiscing about having turned down "a kid" the other fellows had procured for him to sodomize as a birthday present. He wanted to do the birthday dope instead. That time. It was clear that at other times he had made different choices, and perhaps at some point early on he had been that kid. Many modern convicts considered this gay behavior, but Abbot and others of his time certainly did not.

THE SEXUALITY OF PRISONERS is never truly extinguished. Men like Jack Abbot and Irish, who compartmentalized their lives into what is done inside and what isn't, were the opposite approach of that taken by the "shemales," transgender prisoners. Many were tall, and all were phenomenally brave to walk around the hypermacho world of prison looking *fabulous*. In some ways, those prisoners who had had boobs put in before their convictions were guaranteed an easier time inside. There was a "lizard," as the older guys put it, named Juwanna in my first joint. If you add an interrogative inflection to the pronunciation of her name, you'll get it. As a resident of a male prison, she charged a stamp to see her rack. It was a bargain, to get a glimpse of so much silicone. Her bust was oversized, defiant of gravity, and worth the postage. But she was no beauty, and way over six feet tall without heels. The Muslim prisoners would make a big show of leaving the showers when she entered, even though there were separate stalls. Juwanna helped me with my hair; I learned how to braid the ponytail I grew by watching her nimble, long black fingers twist it through the bars separating us. But her exotic nature made sure things were never simple for Juwanna. One night it was a guy's birthday, and part of the fun was sending a naive newjack over to her to ask how much a blow job for a white guy would cost. The newbie believed the guy in question was indulging on his birthday, even though had he gone through with it, he would never have been treated the same in the yard. Times have changed since Abbott's day. So we all watched the newjack amble over to her, negotiate, and return to our table.

"She said white guys are less work, three packs."

Everyone howled. The kid was disappointed at his wasted time, effort, and embarrassment since no head happened that night. But he soon grew to be no less transactional than the rest of the shysters. The guy had a sister at loose ends, or just a loose sister. He rented her for romantic visits to another guy on our court with an inheritance, our fat cat with the $400K—just handholding and smooching in visiting rooms, when she wasn't snoozing off benzos in the children's area. She asked him for a few grand so that she could move closer to the prison, got it, and never returned. I met her actual husband years later when I was shackled to him in transit.

Another segment of the prison population consisted of men living as women. This meant that they grew their hair long and styled it. They used Kool-Aid as blush and lipstick, retailored their clothing to make it as tight as possible, padded the regions that needed padding, and made sure to never allow any facial hair to grow. One I got to know—Gigi—painfully plucked out her beard and mustache. Men fought with knives for the right to comb her hair. However, she had eyes for me, and when she once winked across a hallway at me, I blushed. Gigi was pretty.

Prisoners haven't yet heard of "preferred pronouns," as many are still working and nouns and verbs, but we have, so let's use them. Inside, she had her choice of sneakers and narcotics, as well as men who fought for the chance to watch her sleep. But back in the free world, Gigi was a hardworking working girl. She looked me up after we were both paroled and sent me "enticing" pictures. I wanted to write a story about the downtown strip joint she worked at, where Wall Streeters went for the big finale, the "gun show" at the end. As much as Gigi wanted to be a pretty girl, it was her nine-inch cock that paid the bills. Gigi declined my professional interest, and I turned down hers.

But comely Gigi and buxom Juwanna were the exceptions. Most of the trans women were not gorgeous. I remember one called Kitty, also over six feet tall, who was friends with old man Katz, so old that he'd visited Europe by ocean liner. Katz had also been a personal friend of Manuel Noriega as a fugitive in Panama. He had attempted suicide after getting lured from his refuge in Panama by the FBI and sentenced to a murder bid . . . at the age of seventy-five. Katz was rumored to be gay himself, though past the age of confirmation. He and Kitty would make a grand entrance at the door of the kosher kitchen, announcing, "It's us, Kitty Katz!" and the old man inevitably blushed in delight.

Upstate I evolved from keeping a tolerant distance to having a gay best friend. In the beginning, before I had a name and a reputation, I could hardly afford to strike up friendships with homosexuals. Even relative neutrality had its hazards: I saw one nerdy white kid express support for civil union back in 2005 or so and get tortured for it. The poor guy didn't realize it was actually 1960 in there, and the black Muslim prisoners were relentless in their intolerance of homosexuality. However, I also saw the karmic cost of oppressing gay prisoners. Early on, an old-timer advised me never to bully. I soon learned why, when a nasty piece of work called "Murder One" kept taunting a quiet gay convict, only to find himself being viciously beaten by his victim. Plenty of homosexuals in prison, having grown up gay in group homes and juvenile detention, were forced to learn how to fight with skill. Engaging in physical combat with a gay opponent was a guaranteed loss; if you won, you did not win any points for beating up a "mook." And losing to a "lizard" was even worse.

In the beginning I did my best to make it clear that I invited no attention from my gay prison-mates, but as my name accredited years like a tree grows rings, I allowed myself more latitude, and my status and experience made me less vulnerable. About seven years in

I found myself working in a library with a man in well-preserved middle age who was not too far from myself in background. He had worked in media, even as a stringer for the E! channel, but had fallen on hard times after emptying his husband's bank account while impersonating him. He got the divorce papers while doing his bid.

Having learned how he had floundered in the real world and heard the set of stories he told his latest middle-class prison partner, I realized that this man was a pathological liar at a level I'd never encountered before. However, he was still an intelligent, sophisticated, and sensitive friend over a period of years. I'd never known a homosexual this well, so the question of the difference in our sexuality came up. From an early interest in my uncle's *Hustler* collection, I'd known that I was straight. Later pickup attempts from other men had never angered me. I took them with pleasure, regarding the passes as flattery. So it was without any prejudice that I wondered how such different traits can excite one human but not another.

Becoming friends with a gay man made me wish to learn more about this life outside of the context of prison. I read gay authors from Sappho to Wilde to Jayne County. If Genet had made homosexuality seem macho, Sedaris made it feel ordinary. In his accounts in his essays about things like his vain attempts to impress boyfriends and the cozy intimacy of a long relationship, I came to learn the simple truth that men who love their own sex simply love each other just like men who love women. *Amazing Disgrace*, *Rancid Pansies*, and *Cooking with Fernet Branca* by James Hamilton-Paterson also made gay life feel all too similar to my own. Picnics, fumbling, jealousy, lust, dieting, and longing . . . It was all so familiar, just with a different pronoun. The violence and other behaviors surrounding gay sex in prison were very much a function of the situation.

When Genet and Burroughs returned from covering the Democratic Convention in Chicago (the one that yippies infiltrated to nominate "Pigasus"), the Frenchman was asked what he'd thought. He said that the policemen had nice legs. I wondered if Sedaris would have, only to learn that my cynicism was misplaced (he would, I've been informed).

TOWARD THE END OF MY BID, I landed in the prison where you're sent if you say that you're gay and out when passing through the sorting prison at Downstate. Groveland was a remarkably beautiful facility, with a tree-lined alley, dorms built in brick houses, and a tennis court. I got a job in the library and watched as the bushes were cut down and a camera installed to watch "homo hill." Trysting locations were the cheese in a constant cat-and-mouse game. The cops were looking to bust prisoners breaking the rule against "unhygienic acts," while the guys were trying to get off.

The day I caught Dirty Tommy in the act was one I cannot excise from my memory. Tommy had introduced himself by asking for books on AIDS to "deal with his condition." He came to the library often but didn't appear to read much. I finally figured out what the score was when I caught the rhythmic movement with my peripheral vision. I gave the two young men plenty of time.

I had a long talk with Tommy; I told him that it was disrespectful, that by giving someone a hand job in such close proximity to me he was basically including me, and that wasn't something to which I'd consented. I said that he was taking advantage of the fact that I wouldn't tell on him, and making my workplace a hazardous one by doing risky things ("spreading disease" was how the less enlightened librarians put it). I spoke to Tommy earnestly. He agreed to everything, made me promise not to tell a certain JR, and whacked off some

other guy under the table two weeks later. I learned to work crowded
weekends and avoid the quiet Tuesdays during which Tommy plied his
trade.

"RENT BOYS" WERE A FEATURE of all the tales I read where the criminal
intersected with the gay. However, many of the men who had decades
of prison time under their belts must have experimented with gay sex
at some point. I noticed that questions of experience with such matters were simply not asked. I was never propositioned inside, although
after the bars closed on the west end of Fourteenth Street in Manhattan, I had guys sing at me, "We're chicks, with dicks, some pussy on
a stick?" It was all in good fun, much like how Genet described. Despite how experimental I was with chemicals, I never tried it.

I also lived with a tattoo artist for a year and never got a tattoo.
That's how I know it wasn't for me. I know I'm not even bi-curious. I
had a decade of opportunity to try but never experimented, even
though sexual deprivation hits twentysomethings hard. I guess I will
never be an associate of the Velvet Mafia. In prison I only heard more
rumors of the HIV positive cabal, without ever actually meeting a
member. But through my friendships with men who were gay, and
reading the literature that deals with loving one's own sex, I came to
what can be best termed as an absence of an epiphany. Just as the
Velvet Mafia is an exaggerated chimera composed of overheard
grunts, the homosexuality of prison life reaches the real world as a
baroque, inflated, and perverted version of its much more mundane
reality. I wouldn't even be able to count how many homosexuals I met
inside, as I never knew who actually was one. It really didn't matter.
Perhaps that is the epiphany: it just doesn't matter all that much who
you have sex with.

10.

INFERNAL GREYHOUND

Department of Corrections buses are externally no different from their original incarnations. Seen on the New York State Thruway, they appear to be the cheap public transport they once were, with no Mad Max–style cages and gun turrets welded to their roofs. You have to really know what you are looking for to notice the police-car lights that can be made to spin in blue and red above the cab (called "turning on the Christmas tree" in cop-speak) or the welded gun cage crammed into the back, where the seats for carsick passengers were once located, across from the toilet. Perhaps the biggest difference is that the Greyhounds have accumulated enough mileage that they can no longer be insured for civilian passenger use, though it seems that 500,000 miles on the odometer is just fine for prisoner transport.

If you drive this state's main arteries, you've probably been right next to one of these people-movers without any idea of the chained-up misery a few feet away from your air-conditioned or heated unchained comfort. Seen from the outside, one might expect comfortable, plush seats to be behind the enormous tinted windows and raised seating, high above sedans and even SUVs. But the soft cushions were ripped out long ago—they're too easy to stash things in and too soft for the asses of the scumbags they carry—and replaced with hard plastic. But the DOC simply couldn't do anything about the nice windows on the old Greyhounds, the tinted square yards of glass an unfortunate relic of their former lives. The smaller DOC vans that can carry only a third of the cargo that the big Greyhounds can are a more accurate reflection of how the prison system believes its charges should be shuttled about. They have no windows at all, only narrow slits right under the ceiling. These serve as portholes in the miniature transport vehicles built for the purpose of moving prisoners short distances and can only be seen out of while standing. Standing is strictly forbidden during transit.

The buses run across the state of New York, four days a week, on four-hundred-mile trips from downstate to Canada. They likewise run four hundred miles west to east, from Lake George to Buffalo, but never cross the state line in either direction. Every bus had a specially licensed driver-guard, a white-shirted sergeant to supervise, and a cop armed with a Glock in the inside cage, each of them making close to three figures every sixty minutes. The cops on board were given "hazard pay" while in transit, even though the extreme shackling that the standard protocol required made us into inanimate objects and therefore not at all hazardous. The conditions were absurdly painful for us cargo, but comfortable, safe, and lucrative for our escorts, so it was hardly surprising that every trip required an inordinate amount of time. Each trip took a minimum of twelve hours—twice as much time to cross distances that New Yorkers consider manageable for commuting to a weekend country house.

The overtime was achieved in part by hiding the buses, which would pull into gas stations with enough room behind them for a DOC Greyhound to park discreetly at a suitable distance from any other vehicle. It would then take an hour just for the driver to take a leak while sixty prisoners sat baking or freezing in the locked vehicle. Somehow it then took another hour to hand out sandwiches, and then yet another hour would pass just for the hell of it. The old vehicles plodded along at only forty miles an hour or so, gumming up the right lane of every highway they disgraced; I saw a state trooper flip us the bird once, presumably for slowing down traffic with our languor. It could also have been evidence of the rumored hatred between New York's law enforcement officers and the corrections corps. Our correctional officers considered themselves to be cops and even successfully lobbied for the right to carry concealed firearms, but police officers and state troopers did not agree that their function was law enforcement or that they should be allowed a gun to accompany their equally questionable badges. There had been conflicts between the groups that included violence, though usually at least one of the parties was off duty and alcohol was a factor.

The rationale for the hazard pay was the possibility of violent escape and was also applied when prisoners had to go to a hospital for treatment. The theoretical increase in proximity to freedom didn't only justify paying an escort a good deal more money, it also meant guns were brought into play. Firearms are a very carefully controlled element of incarceration. Most civilians imagine that prison guards control their wards with the threat of deploying a sidearm, just as a cop's authority doesn't come just from his badge but his holster. In fact, guns are not even allowed inside the walls of any institution. The battered Glock wielded by the cop on our transit bus was the closest view I had of a gun in ten years.

Every prison has its armory, where the rifles for the towers are stored, and where pistols are issued to COs on escort duty for transport, hospital visits, court appearances, and funeral trips. This facility is always outside the prison walls or, in the case of medium-security joints, on the other side of the barbed wire fencing. Armories have their own security protocols, and the baroque dance involved in keeping prisoners as far as possible from triggers during the required stops during bus transport to pick up and drop off weaponry adds time to every trip. Any stop a bus makes at a prison, even if dropping off a single passenger, requires leaving the firearms at the armory and then retrieving them afterward. Again, the overtime possibilities are tremendous.

The rigmarole around the guns was a sight to see. The pistol issued to the cop posted in the back cage of the bus did not travel with the man himself. First every transit prisoner was shackled and seated. Then the officer, as yet unarmed, briskly passed down the aisle to enter his cage, locking himself inside and unlocking a steel slot that opened to the outside of the bus. The cruddy, dented automatic was then passed by another officer to him through it. The handgun was treated as reverently as if it were the Holy Grail, and the bullets carefully counted. The reason for this involved ritual was the possibility of a prisoner's overpowering the guard in the bus aisle and snatching his sidearm. The likelihood of this occurring was not too strong, given that our hands were cuffed together and shackled to our waists, with each man's leg shackled to that of another. Once the transfer of the weapon was completed, the caged officer could shoot whomever needed shooting in the back of the head.

The role that firearms played in my own life was minimal. I have never shot a gun, although I was once allowed to fire a .22 caliber rifle at a target when I attended Camp Billings as a ten-year-old. But guns are the great equalizer of force, as I read in Richard Burton's disdainful analysis in his high-Victorian *Book of the Sword*. I had the great Dover reprint of this eccentric book by the swordsman scholar. A projectile weapon can ignobly kill at a distance, meaning without danger to oneself, and was therefore, Burton argued, not an honorable weapon. Shank-wielding convicts felt the same way.

From Will and Ariel Durant's eleven volumes of *The Story of Civilization*, which I relished as the best of history books, I had learned that, earlier, crossbowmen captured during the fourteenth-century

Hundred Years' War were immediately executed rather than held prisoner, as they upended not just feudal hierarchy but the meritocratic balance of combat. Archers were bad enough, killing at such a distance that they were safe themselves, but crossbowmen were creatures that could defeat a noble with neither skill nor breeding, making them terrifying agents of chaos. Its ultimate expression came in Herman Kahn's *On Thermonuclear War*, an echo of Carl von Clausewitz, when an idiot could not just kill from a position of safety, but end civilization. Stanley Kubrick illustrated this memorably in *Dr. Strangelove*. I understood the power of a firearm instinctively when I painted a water gun with a girlfriend's black nail polish to use as a weapon on my first desperate attempt at robbery. While I was not convincing enough to achieve my ends with my squirt gun, when I was myself arrested, the combination of "Get on the ground, motherfucker" and the chrome metal shooter in the cop's hands froze my blood.

THE FIRST TIME I saw a cop shoot a round in the air from a tower was memorable. Judging by the assault weapon's profile, each tower overlooking the prison yard was manned by a rifleman with an AR-15. The towers are parts of the walls of all older prisons; the freestanding watchtowers that are depicted on Gulag memoirs exist in medium-security prisons that are fenced in with barbed wire. The walls of the old maxes are thirty feet high and stretch down under the ground halfway to hell. There is never any access possible to them from inside the joint, so they must be entered from outside. The rifles could not even be accidentally dropped into the yard because of chicken wire fencing jerry-rigged later for this very purpose, though lunch does reach the cops on tower duty via a pail on a pulley. One of the most frequently reinforced lessons of the twentieth century was that the possession of weapons can upend the balance of power with frightening

ease and speed. The threat of just one bullet can divert a plane of innocent people to Cuba, and a box cutter can lead to the destruction
of the twin towers. A firearm in the hands of a prisoner whose parole
date is beyond his life expectancy would likely result in a hostage
crisis.

The Attica riot, the true end of the 1960s in America, concluded
with the political embarrassment of too many dead bodies—civilian
hostages as well as unarmed (at least with firearms) prisoners riddled
with bullets. The convicts had put the guards into the standard green
prison uniforms, and the gambit proved successful when the shooting
started. The point being made was that the prisoners' lives were worth-
less, and the evidence was the casualties of "friendly fire." The wanton
murders committed that day caused a scandal, and of course it was the
prisoners who were blamed. But they didn't have any guns, and the
Attica armory, like every other such facility, was outside its walls.

The sacrifices of those men resulted in a (steadily eroding) reform
package, care of governor Nelson B. Rockefeller, which included edu-
cational opportunities, enhanced communication with families, conjugal visits, and more. New York State prisoners still celebrate the
anniversary of the riots—the only holiday exclusive to them. Every
September 13 convicts go to the mess hall wearing the state green
uniforms, take trays of food, and refuse to eat. The unwanted food
doesn't go to scavengers; instead, the wealthier prisoners make sure
to feed the indigent in private. The cops used to change the menu to
pizza that day, to tempt the weak and break the show of unity. So
much time has passed now that young inmates are often ignorant of
the uprising, but "Attica Day" was still observed by at least half of
the max prisoners during my time in, some forty years after the gun-
less rebellion. If Attica could be taken by threatening hostages with
shivs and shanks, the possible damage a convict with a gun could do
is what drives the armory protocol and Glock procedure.

Transit was always much longer than it needed to be, but it was painful for several other reasons as well. The proximity to freedom that it hazarded, while denying one the real thing right outside the plate-glass window, was tantalizing. Meanwhile moving to a new joint meant the promise of change, which all prisoners inevitably learned to fear. This threat was exacerbated by the vicious and dangerous orientation process of every new destination. Prisons often made examples right at the gates to show us who was boss. I've seen teeth scattered on the floor of an intake hall in response to a perceived lack of respect.

Wheelchair-bound prisoners were moved with their chairs locked into the back of the van, shackled into them. The rest of us had one leg shackled to another prisoner's. The chain between our ankles was short enough to make even a few steps torturous. With an intelligent partner you could navigate a customized gait that would preserve your leg skin though still bruise it. But getting partnered with a newjack meant a bloody ankle; climbing steps thus encumbered was especially hard. Any attempt at a running escape with this hindrance was impossible; it would require a three-legged skip, the joined limbs acting in unison. When I read Kurt Vonnegut's story "Harrison Bergeron," about limiting the motion of the graceful, I thought that even that great fabulist had not imagined what the Department of Corrections could.

The next piece of hardware ruining your trip was a torso chain. You had to have a well-defined waist for it to neither drop under your rear nor ride up and constrict your breathing. On me it inevitably did one or the other. The handcuffs that kept your fingers inches apart and your wrists bloody were fairly standard-issue cuffs, locked in front, like those used by cops and dominatrices. However, a black steel box joined the bracelets to the waist chain, immobilizing your wrists in a contraption that was gruesomely painful. The black box didn't just cause bloody chafing, it also kept your hands in a good position to whack off but little else. That meant that getting food from your hands to your mouth involved a yoga maneuver that was hard on guys with even moderately sized bellies.

After twelve solid hours the shackling arrangement also destroyed your upper back but demolished your lower.

NEITHER PRISON KEEPERS NOR prisoners like situations without precedent, and both try to prepare for every eventuality. One-armed men? I knew two inside, the first being a fellow called "Bum," who told lurid stories about women who lusted for what he could do with his stump. These single amputees got the waist chain in every circumstance, with a single cuff attached to it.

Wise prisoners expecting a draft-out made sure not to eat the night before their bus ride. The daylong spans were enough to necessitate bathroom visits, and the Greyhounds still had their original toilets in the rear, though with the door torn off and the seat pared down to a porcelain bowl. Taking a leak in one was bad enough; your partner still had a leg shackled to you but could at least turn his back. God help you if it was anything more than a piss.

I was once on a north-south peregrination when I saw a hefty fellow get himself into a jam. The prisoner was no newjack but probably wound up on the draft without any foreknowledge, as the schedule of prisoners' movements was generally kept a secret to prevent your calling in an ambush. The possibility of a super-criminal arranging to be freed from a DOC bus in transit is pure celluloid fantasy, but some cops play along.

Typically the guards would show up one morning with draft bags and order you to pack up. Then you'd be locked in your cell until early the next morning, when the bus left. Your friends would call your mother to inform her of the change of venue. Your property would inevitably be reduced by a draft, as everything you possessed had to fit into a maximum of four large white plastic sacks. You were no longer allowed to pay to transport more of them, as had once been the case. Before this regulation was installed, I saw a lifer travel with seventeen draft bags; transfer from one prison to another was an expensive operation for him. Since the current limit of four bags was a challenge for anyone who had already put some time in, drafts were Christmas for the unlucky transfer's neighbors. I myself inherited clothes and books and porn and food and cooking equipment from guys who needed all four bags just for their absolute vital possessions.

Experienced prisoners, however, usually know about their draft in advance, and what most prisoners do as soon as they are about twenty-four to thirty-six hours away from the Greyhounds is cease eating. The person I saw who hadn't taken this precaution was put into a dreadful position.

He probably just couldn't hold it any longer; it is hard to imagine anyone making the conscious choice to defecate on a DOC bus. The throne is dirty and the privacy is nonexistent, but it is the man to whom you are shackled that makes the proposition so gruesome. I watched the big guy who had to go struggle with his bowels for hours until finally raising the white flag. He and his partner shuffled down the aisle to the facilities, knowing enough not to bother asking the cop to separate them. The men mitigated their discomfort with the forced intimacy by facing opposite from each other and standing as far apart as the leg shackles allowed. Without a door between them, the man not on the toilet stood and had to look through the cage directly at the gunman posted there. His partner's relieving himself came and went with the utmost rapidity, but disaster ensued immediately after.

"CO, can I get paper?" asked the commode's user. The cop nodded and passed him a bundle through the cage. He received a roll with the cardboard interior removed but soon found there was no way he could reach his own ass; the chain and black box kept him from wiping.

"CO, can you uncuff me so I can wipe my ass?"

The cop didn't bother answering. It was obvious to him that the question was moot, as there could be no unshackled prisoners on the bus. The large man with an unclean rear begged for just one hand, for just one minute. The cop grew irritated with the increasingly desperate pleas until he finally told the convict, "You are not getting unshackled. Leave me out of this. Ask your partner to help you."

The other man, who had been grimly tolerating this spectacle, was not prepared to wipe some stranger's fat ass and preemptively announced as much while the cop with the gun was still talking. He repeated his reluctance to help with the problem, and everyone except for the man on the throne agreed that it was time for this horror to end. The other fifty-eight of us started to grumble.

"Everyone, back in your seats. Any ticket in transit is a tier three," the officer reminded us. That was true; even the slightest infraction on a bus meant you were going to the box upon reaching your destination. The hefty fellow moped back to his seat, carrying a foul miasma with him up the aisle, and spent the rest of his trip riding on an unwiped ass. He had previously been reminiscing with his shackled partner about the fine criminal opportunities available in Brooklyn, but conversation between them ceased.

MOVING FROM JAIL TO jail can involve brief stays in transit hubs—prisons with wards for short-term occupancy that are most primitively and simply furnished. They provide a sheet, a disposable toothbrush, and a meal, but luxuries like your medication and eyeglasses, and even a blanket and pillow, are considered unnecessary. For entertainment you can either masturbate or shout. After men began amusing themselves by flooding the transit hub cells, the toilets were mechanically set to allow only one flush every half hour. Occasionally the cells have a window, but I've been in some of them with nothing but the stench of urine. It was in such a room that I once experienced divine intervention.

As a cost-saving measure, no transport buses move on Wednesdays or the weekends. That consigns hundreds of people on multiple-day trips to long spans with nothing to do but look at the ceiling, flush a toilet every thirty minutes, and jerk off. I had the bad luck to arrive in a hub on a Friday one time, which meant I would be stuck in a torture cell for a miserable Saturday and Sunday. Having the time to do so, I explored it thoroughly. The standard steel combination toilet-sink units have an indentation shaped like a roll of toilet paper. It's a strange touch, shaping it like a standard roll and not the bundle that toilet paper becomes when the inner cardboard tube is removed. There are two reasons that prisons confiscate the cylinder: it can be used as a (very) makeshift pipe, and contraband can be rolled from one cell to another in it.

I reached into the toilet paper indentation of my cell out of boredom and came out with the most surprising artifact. Concealed in the hole was a moist issue of *Granta* dating from 1989. To this day I cannot imagine the process by which that literary journal made it into that cell, but I can recall its contents with ease, having had nothing else to do for two days but memorize it. It featured an interview with Susan Sontag, reproductions of some of William Burroughs's paintings (done by shooting cans of paint with a shotgun), and the whiny tale of a Yugoslav academic who was disappointed in the West. That *Granta* was a true friend to me and certainly kept me from both madness and the growth of hair on my palms during that awful long-ago weekend. Well, almost; I did manage to rub one out to the portrait of Sontag. We had grown so close that I felt as if I should have taken it with me on Monday morning, but nothing was allowed to travel on your person in transit, as it is assumed to be potential escape equipment. I always had to travel with my yearslong growth of hair flowing behind me, rather than in the neat ponytail I usually kept it controlled in. Even the hair tie I used to keep my hair back was an issue for the nervous Nellies. I left the magazine for the next miserable occupant, though I couldn't imagine who might appreciate it.

The pockets that come on state-issued pants, shirts, and coats are deceptive. They are not like the faux pockets that decorate women's clothing that lead nowhere. They have depth and are made of such fire-resistant material that convicts commonly put out coffin nails directly in them in order to finish smoking them later. The uniforms are made in the tailor shop staffed by the inmates of Clinton CF, like the two guys who escaped from that facility in 2015. Tailored specialties also come out of that shop. I had a coat with a thermal lining sewn into it and a pair of "stealing pants," which had enormous front pockets. I wore those until they grew shiny, then developed holes, and finally turned into the deconstructed fabric they started their life as.

However copious one's pockets, transporting contraband in them is generally a bad idea. I used to keep things in my pockets for the cops to find during a pat frisk while the real cargo was "cheeked" in my mouth or rear. Socks also worked for the simplest items, ones you were only concealing pro forma. Sleeves were good to conceal a knife only if you were willing to use it during a pat frisk. Pills were reliably kept in belly buttons, nostrils, and between toes. Rastas have dreadlocks with compartments.

Because of the authorities' abject terror of our escaping, I had to enter every new facility looking like Captain Caveman, as the rubber band for keeping my ponytail together was confiscated on every trip.

Transit put men with beefs, like an unresolved conflict or even a hit on their heads, in a vulnerable position. I've seen fights accomplished by a man kicking or left-handed punching someone, while his shackled partner remained in tow. Even with the strict bus prohibitions, for men who were expecting to die inside, one way or another, carrying a knife was a way of life, or rather of ensuring the continuance of one's life. Being caught without a weapon when facing a determined opponent could mean death. Boofing a weapon is a half-assed solution, as using the "prisoner's wallet" (the colon) for a scalpel defeats the purpose; it's hard to pull a blade out of your butt in time to use it for self-defense.

THERE ARE TWO WAYS to bring a knife on a bus, both requiring a sheath made of black electrical tape for the little piece of something sharp you're counting on to keep your face looking the way it does. You still have to defeat the metal detector, and the tape blurs the ping that a tiny scalpel elicits. But where to keep your weapon, if you're not just trying to smuggle it but possibly wield it?

A piece of dental floss, tied around your molar, will keep a small blade suspended down your trachea. Keeping it hanging there involves a constant fight with your gag reflex. Yard shanks, too big for electrical tape to work, are typically made of a material that will pass the inspection of a metal detector; brass shivs are prized for this reason, a charming atavism. But a transit razor is a medical scalpel, liberated from a clinic. They are tiny, weightless, and hard to use without cutting yourself, but sharp as hell. Eating while "throat-strapped" requires the temporary removal of the blade. Pulling up the thing can be difficult, and getting the knot around a tooth is delicate work.

There is a second option for holstering a razor for transit, but it is hardly any safer. It helps to have a big schnoz, and you have to be able to rigorously control your breathing. Mugsy, a man I knew who carried a scalpel in his nostril, may not be around anymore because of it. He had beef with a gang that had a presence in every joint, so he always traveled strapped. Unfortunately he eventually inhaled the blade he kept up his nose. It was covered in tape, so Mugsy thought it might be harmlessly lodged in his sinuses, but with time blood leaked from somewhere deep inside his head. I begged him to go to the clinic, but he knew that he would be charged with the weapon that would be dug out of him. Possession of a scalpel is worth at least a year in the box. He was coughing and sneezing blood every day when they put him on the draft again. The last I heard from him was a request for dental floss. I sent Mugsy what I had.

The most common thing boofed for transit is simply tobacco, with rolling paper, matches, and a striker. Being able to smoke after twelve hours shackled on a bus is a luxury, but the smoke itself is an acquired taste. No matter how many times it is wrapped, it always has a telltale aroma. When one reaches a transit hub and is locked in with no chance of asking someone for a rollie, even nonsmokers will indulge in a moist cigarette, rectal tang and all.

For years I feared boofing anything, daunted by the very small entrance of the prisoner's wallet. However, tiny pinners of cheap tobacco cost two dollars each in the box. The rectum is copious; you can bring a fortune with you if you have the foreknowledge and time to prepare. Lotioning the balloon makes it easy for the contraband one wishes to stuff to slip past the sphincter. Pros can manage with margarine, shampoo, or even spit. In *Papillon*, the fierce memoir of imprisonment and escape by Henri Charrière, I read about the *plan*, also called a *charger*, which is a smooth metal container that unscrews to hold a prisoner's money, drugs, diamonds, razor, and whatever else can fit into a hermetically sealed anal wallet. While this contraption predates metal detectors, it seemed to be a very common piece of a criminal's kit. Once I learned that the challenge is merely getting your balloon past the pucker, I lost my terror of being reamed by cheap tobacco and brought a plastic glove full of Top to the box with me. I boofed my contraband, and it turned out that you can't even sense it once it's inserted. In fact, the challenge is often getting it out. Some people have so much trouble extracting a balloon that they drink shampoo in warm water to lubricate their entire alimentary passage. The people waiting for the delivery of the package, often the ones who funded the operation, sometimes feed their mules a special meal made with canned corn. It's an old trick to track digestion. If the kernels pass on the other end with no balloon at the head, some kind of bamboozlement has occurred. Violence ensues.

HOWEVER, THERE ARE EVEN worse things that can happen to those riding infernal Greyhounds. A trip can go bad. I'll never forget the frozen morning one day after New Year's when I left the dedicated box facility on the Canadian border. After six months in solitary, listening to the radio out of Montreal, my time was up. Everyone boarding the bus had been in the same confinement, but not everybody shared the joy of being released.

For a variety of reasons, there are men who prefer the box to regular prison.

Most of the time the cause is an enemy. Being the target of an organization, or having a gang hit hanging over one's head, is a terrifying position to be in. One afternoon I saw an old acquaintance arrive at a prison. We talked, and I said I would see him later in the yard, but he warned me off, urging me to stay away until he settled things. Sure enough, that evening he was sliced a few minutes after entering the yard. He had a hit on him, care of a gang to whom he owed a drug debt from another joint. For others, prison itself is unsettling by its very nature, so much so that they fear the stress and commotion of its general population. Some prisoners just prefer the simpler life of the box and will go to extreme measures to remain there.

The incident in question involved the most mundane item possible to thwart a transfer: an asthma pump. The contrast between the chaos stirred up inside the bus and the glacial chill outside, frozen into silence by Canadian cold at five in the morning, added to its impact. But the guy who caused all the fuss couldn't even see past the windows.

We could all tell he was trouble, and that prison had left its mark on him. Only a few teeth were left, his hair was in patches, and he had a wild gaze. He was shackled to a dreadlocked prisoner deep in the grasp of soporific psych meds. The man's manic energy, which I later realized was fear, was no match for the Thorazine or Haldol keeping his partner asleep. Getting no reaction with his stream of consciousness from his medicated neighbor, the crazed man looked for attention elsewhere. The guy next to me had been talking sports and when he mentioned the Pittsburgh Steelers, the lunatic misheard it as what he had his mind on: "That's right, fuck the police! Who is with us?"

Definitely not the sports fan. None of us wanted to engage with him, fearing the outcome. As the bus moved through ice-age Malone County, the troublemaker tried a different approach, calling out the sergeant who rode behind the barricade up front, next to the driver.

"Look here, cracker, I need my asthma pump!"

The sergeant did not have an asthma pump, and he explained as much many times. He began by being polite, taking the request seriously, and then became annoyed, hoping the situation would fizzle out, and finally grew angry, when he realized this was turning into a legitimate problem.

"I want my asthma pump!" the man yelled again, following that up with a cavalcade of racial invectives. The back-and-forth soon caught the attention of the shackled men; all the hushed private conversations had been stopped by the show being put on, but the race riot the man had hoped to spark did not occur as no one wanted to get involved. We had all just finished long SHU terms. Mr. Asthma Pump had but one card left to play. Dragging the shackled and sleeping dread with him, he reached the barrier and viciously banged on the plastic behind the driver's head. That was when everything changed. The bus swerved off the highway.

Suddenly we were all taking evasive action.

The driver knew the protocol in cases of mutiny in transit. The gunman in the back pulled out his Glock. As the bus halted on the side of the road, the crazed prisoner thought victory was finally within reach. The sergeant fished out a bulky telephone from a briefcase; from espionage films I recognized it as a satellite phone. He disembarked and made a call. We couldn't hear what he said, but we knew to be afraid.

Perhaps the the guy who caused all this really believed the sergeant was summoning medical assistance, but his bravado was failing as the gravity of what he had done sunk in. The bus moved on but had left the highway. We were now taking side roads to a new destination. The experienced convicts knew our destination. The huge walls of Clinton-Dannemora loomed ahead.

Whoever manned those walls was clearly expecting us. The doors to a truck trap opened smoothly to allow the bus to glide in. Hell was waiting for our doomed bus in that icy passageway in the form of a kitted-out riot squad, as guards in riot gear, helmets, pads, shields, and sticks were ready, waiting to storm the bus. The operation was carried out efficiently; we never stopped, only slowed down until we were through the truck trap as they tapped the sides of the bus with their batons to scare us.

They let us stew for a moment before boarding. The biggest guard, a giant in a helmet, stepped onto the bus to exfiltrate the problem passenger. The white shirt pointed him out.

"Sarge, I'm OK," said the now-calm perpetrator, "I don't need no asthma pump."

It was only for convenience that he was then unshackled from the shuffling Rasta, who had continued to sleep throughout the mayhem but finally woke up when he felt the cuffs and leg shackles being taken off his scared companion. After the troubled prisoner was removed from the bus the other guys told the Jamaican what his partner had done. He visibly paled when he realized what fate he had narrowly avoided: the riot cops were perfectly willing to take both men, assuming they were both in on it. Our white shirt left with the helmeted giant and his prey and disappeared for an hour, during which we were forbidden to talk and dutifully followed orders. Everyone knew something terrible was happening nearby. The sergeant returned to the bus, visibly worn out from whatever had transpired out of sight. We never saw Asthma Pump again, though the draft bag of his property was obviously trashed when we reached our destination.

I HAD READ ABOUT the cattle cars that brought Jews to Dachau, and the trains crossing Siberia full of death. Solzhenitsyn devoted hundreds of pages of *The Gulag Archipelago* to the murderous ways innocent prisoners were destroyed in being moved from camp, whether by being deprived of water or given only enough dry fish to feed some of the men, ensuring violence. In Holocaust memoirs like Elie Wiesel's

Night I learned about German vans fitted with exhaust pipes leading back into the prisoner compartment, making each ride an execution. The prisoners of war in Bataan were simply marched to death. Reading these accounts put my own situation into perspective and always made my fate more bearable. The waist chains used by the DOC made it hard to breathe, but not impossible. I survived all eleven trips between twelve prisons.

But transit was always a terrifying experience, a loose point in the system of American incarceration that was tightened up with severity and mindless violence. The Greyhounds of the DOC, with their strange rules regarding hair ties and ass wiping, were squarely in that tradition of vileness that dehumanized us. The proximity of normal life, only an inch of glass away, also provoked cognitive dissonance in me. On one trip the bus passed a diner I used to stop in when I drove upstate to go skiing. We turned into its parking lot so the cops could get another hour of overtime. When it came time to eat a cheese sandwich without the use of my hands, which were chained to my midriff, I wondered whether I had actually ever been on the other side of the glass in the past. It seemed unlikely. But as everyone else, I just chewed and hoped the trip would bring me safely to my next destination.

11

LIVE BURIAL

The thirteen months of my life that I spent in the box were not consecutive; the longest stretch of solitary confinement was seven months, and the briefest was fifteen days. I was sent to the "bing" as punishment on four separate occasions, of which I consider only one to have been deserved. The ways of earning a box sentence are numerous and come in a large variety. Some are heinous, others farcical.

My first time was for failing to provide a sufficient amount of urine to test for illicit substance use; that was also the longest sentence I received, an entire year, which was later cut in half. The most ridiculous episode was a three-month box bid resulting from the unauthorized exchange of a human soul for a cup of coffee, followed by two weeks for "harassing" a nurse with an unpleasant facial expression. She had just told me that going out into the yard in a rainstorm was the best treatment for my high fever, and I momentarily lost control of the mask of neutral emotion I wore for a decade as self-preservation.

The sentence in solitary that I did deserve was ninety days for coming up positive for opiates on a random urinalysis. I was indeed guilty; I had swallowed 60 mg of morphine the day before and spent it nodding. Under the influence of drugs one is effectively released from prison. It's a very temporary escape, but one that subverts all the effort and expense invested into making one pay for one's crimes with incarceration. That is why one day of narcotic euphoria costs ninety in an environment designed to hurt in every possible way. Torture is not illegal in the United States; it is used with abandon every time a prisoner is put in solitary. I had the escape route of a literary bent, which allowed me to spend my box bids in the castle turrets of *Gormenghast* and the drawing rooms of *Vanity Fair* and on the tennis courts of *Infinite Jest*. Most of the boxed population, however, was barely literate. To this day I can summon the shrieking and howling, punctuated by teenage madmen banging the walls with their foreheads, that was the accompaniment to my reading.

While there are many ways to fall into the world of the box and more traps meant to keep you in it, there are only four types of destination. The simplest is one intended for temporary use, where you are held while you await your tier 3 hearings. Every prison has such a small, single-bunked box wing dating from back when the use of solitary confinement was rare. If you are already housed there while your misbehavior report (called a ticket) is being decided by a hearing officer, you are already guilty.

Then there are the SHU-200 units, about a dozen of which are attached to older prisons. These identical facilities, purpose-built about thirty years ago, are double-bunked hellholes in which the lights stay on at all times. Identical facilities like this worked so well around the state that the DOC scaled them up.

The destination I was sent to when introduced to this deeper circle of jail was Upstate CF, a third variation of the box. That facility consists of four conjoined SHU-200 units built directly on the Canadian border. One of the prisons I later spent a year in, Five Points CF (apparently not named for the Manhattan neighborhood of yore mostly known as the setting for Herbert Asbury's and Martin Scorsese's *Gangs of New York*), was meant to duplicate the "success" of Upstate and is a carbon copy of it. However, the drop in crime made a second huge box obsolete, so today Five Points is filled with unhappily double-bunked prisoners. During my stay there we were allowed out of our cells, quite the opposite routine from that of the regimen at Upstate. To compensate for the discomfort built into the place, television was provided. We spent our time watching thirteen channels, four of which were PBS affiliates. The abundance of public broadcasting and dearth of cable left many dissatisfied, though I was overjoyed.

FINALLY THERE IS A fourth type, another dedicated box facility for those prisoners considered too crazy or violent to be double-bunked. Southport dates from before the advent of SHU-200 units and the Upstate box. Most prisoners feared this place above all others, but I probably would have preferred to remain in Southport, as every cell is truly solitary confinement. Its benefits were solitude and the opportunity to buy Snickers bars after a thirty-day period of proving yourself with good behavior. Having known hunger in the Upstate box, I regarded the possibility of obtaining candy bars as a luxury. Having a solitary cell to read and write and exercise and jack off in also seemed a hell of a lot better than being locked in a room for months on end with a stranger. Or with a madman, as happened to me after I committed the crime of buying a few second-rate prisoner souls.

To my knowledge Southport was where man sunk the lowest. The "Port" is where dudes "bust their cup"—dousing a neighbor or passerby or random victim with a sludge of shit and piss.

"Shitting niggas down" is the devolved pastime of this miserable place, where men serve their box time in increments of years and every new ticket is a tier 3, meaning that any infraction incurs a further ninety days in the box. Men who wind up there and act out in response to the culture shock of it easily earn themselves additional sentences above and beyond the initial months they had to serve.

They go nuts, and it's a mean sort of nuts. In the SHU-200 units there isn't much trouble they can cause, but that's not the case in Southport. There is a famous story of a handicapped woman who somehow earned the enmity of her wards. She was some kind of civilian employee, a counselor or social worker, who had a grudge against prisoners and was rude toward and dismissive of them. She achieved mobility with a motorized wheelchair, and the day that her vehicle stalled was not a good one.

The men had been waiting for their chance at payback and had ammunition ready. Or perhaps they always kept some handy, in case someone needed to be taught a lesson. As the woman rolled to a halt and started to complain, she was bombarded with shit and piss from multiple angles. The normally grim building erupted in howls of delight and laughter. She cowered on the floor, seeking cover behind her toppled chair. Cops in raincoats had to come to the rescue, and apparently they didn't care much for the woman, either. They took their time and let the guys run out of ammunition, which made it safe for them to collect the befouled woman. She never returned, having apparently been discreetly allowed to retire early.

As hideous as this episode was, there was always a deeper circle of inferno. Neighbors in Southport who hated each other shat their foes down at mealtimes, satisfied with defiling the food if they couldn't "bust their cup" in someone's face. If one's target resided in a cell farther down the gallery, there was still a way to assault him. Even in Southport, the cops had to eventually take you out of your cell, if only for a shower. This was improved upon in the SHU-200 units by building a stainless steel shower stall into each cell, so that prisoners would only have to leave when their time was up or when they needed to see a doctor. Or a coroner. In Southport, however, you were taken down the tier twice a week for a shower. That meant two COs escorted you with your hands cuffed behind your back, but unless you had been ordered by a court to be masked, you could still spit. Clear plastic masks are actually more common than one would think, though they are usually the result of misbehavior in court. The masks are court-ordered to prevent further incidents. Quite a few sentencing judges in criminal court have had to wipe angry spittle off their faces.

But in Southport, where things got serious, a gob in the eye was amateur hour. Merely hocking a loogie at your enemy would barely be noticed. In the Port they spit shit. The shower visits were effectively trips through the firing range, as you were led right past your target or assailant. Filling one's mouth with feces is arguably worse than being struck by it, but it is your own waste. And your only chance at vengeance. Men went back and forth in shit-spitting feuds that lasted a decade, targeting each other twice a week on shower days. The whole building always smells of shit, the residue of conflicts both long-forgotten and ensuing.

THE CONDITIONS IN THE SHU-200 facilities and Upstate were identically rough precisely because they were self-contained. Two men in each unit shared a single shower. However, simply providing taps that could be turned on and off would have been too easy. In the box shower water was offered only for twenty-minute periods for three days out of seven. After a month of good behavior, a fourth shower day was added, making it possible to bathe on both days of the weekend. Hygiene is often the first standard to crumble as madness ensues, so plenty of box residents ignored the water when it suddenly appeared. I remember one exception to the shower schedule being made during a heat wave. My bunky Lacy and I were lying on the cement floor, splashing ourselves with tepid toilet water and gasping for air. The temperature was above a hundred degrees. The SHU-200s have elaborate ventilation systems that would have efficiently air-conditioned the place, but that would have contravened the purpose of the facility. It was hot enough, though, to endanger the old and sickly, so someone must have given the order to turn the showers on.

The water flowed. But someone else in the prison hierarchy did not like this order, didn't like the spirit of compassion in which it had been given. Allowing us to control the temperature of the water would have been way too much; who knows what we could have done with that power? In any case, there were no taps to turn; the temperature was set centrally. Usually the water was lukewarm. That day it was steaming, almost boiling hot. As our room filled with steam, Lacy and I wished merely for the power to turn the water off. But we could only wait for the automatic cutoff that stopped the shower unless you hit the steel button again for another two minutes of water. This system prevented the wasting of water. After a few minutes the steam ceased; we were saved by environmentalism.

THERE ARE SOME CONVICTS who are housed in SHU by dint of administrative segregation rather than by conviction. They are the leaders of men, those who have established their ability to influence other prisoners to riot or rebel. The duration of administrative segregation is open-ended, with only the occasional review by the same people who decided you had to be kept away from the rest of the prison population to look forward to. The ad-seg'd are objects of wonder for the rest of the prisoners, who imagine them to be very powerful and dangerous.

The urine test that resulted in my first trip to the box was triggered by another inmate who had snitched on me, telling the Department of Security that I was involved in a concocted narcotic conspiracy with the facility doctor. As a result, I was tested frequently, but pissing on command was a problem for me. The time it became a huge problem, I just couldn't get more than a few drops into the cup. The atmosphere was tense, and the cops were all over me. My latent condition of paruresis had locked me up; a shy bladder had betrayed me. After I provided my meager sample, the cops took it and let me out into the yard. I had a bad feeling about the episode and barely slept that night, as if it were my last in general population.

They locked me in my cell the next morning. I was moved to the small facility box the following day and fought the "case" as best I could, preserving my strongest arguments for the upcoming appeal. The hearing officer had told me, while the tape was not running, that he'd be finding me guilty, and I appealed by submitting my recording and my defense. Even though I pled that I couldn't possibly have known what the "right" amount of urine was, a real judge, in a real district courtroom, determined that I had interfered with the purpose of urinalysis and my conviction shouldn't be overturned. I couldn't believe it; the legal brief had cost two grand.

During that first trip to the box, I had a bunky who had gotten in trouble for buying someone's Flexeril, a muscle relaxant with a soporific effect considered desirable—though it has the side effect of promoting estrogen production in men. He had been caught with a handful of the pills right after buying them in the yard. I happened to be prescribed that very drug, and three times a day a nurse came to bring me a pill. As my new friend was willing to take my medication and sleep an exorbitant amount, I didn't mind abstaining.

And that is how I managed to complete my first novel, writing in the morning twilight while the snow blew in from the St. Lawrence River. I was wrapped in towels and blankets; in the scratched steel mirror I saw a Napoleonic soldier retreating from a frozen foreign land, denied *lebensraum* by the Russian winter. My bunky snoozed while I wrote with an implement that resembled nothing less than a quill. In the box pens are made safe by being housed in a rubber body.

The vile flexi-pen can be stiffened, however, with a wrapping of envelopes. I used a quill loaded with one flexi-pen after another, until I had an alternate history novel called *Narcotica*. I dreamed about a world preserved in a Victorian state by an opiate amber. I dreamed about what it would be like if narcotics were society's inebriant of choice rather than alcohol.

For my own reading in the box I chose a book in Russian at least once a month and challenged myself with something simple in French every now and then. For the most part I turned to memoirs from distant centuries of travels to faraway places. I read long nineteenth-century ethnographic travelogues. Since I was physically locked away in a dim room at the edge of the world, following Stanley's ("Dr. Livingstone, I presume?") race to the source of the Nile, reading his dispatches telegraphed from coastal coaling stations on the edge of the Dark Continent was nothing if not a luxury. Who else, in our modern and digital world, had the time to go so deep down such rabbit holes? Prison granted me ten extra years to read when I should have been working, and I did not waste the gift. I read everything by Sir Richard Francis Burton in print, including both volumes of his report of sneaking into Mecca, and followed them up with all three tomes describing his penetration of the forbidden Abyssinian state of Harar and city of Gondor, where the polyglot author and swordsman barely escaped with his life.

For fun I consumed the entire Flashman series, which traveled the British Empire in tally-ho style, to keep my reveries Victorian. One detail that kept turning up, both in the period accounts and the brilliant three-volume *Pax Britannica*, a history of the era by Jan Morris, is live burial. Ever since I had crawled into a sleeping bag the wrong way as a child, I was morbidly fascinated by the horror of being buried alive.

The equally morbid Victorians were evidently a bit obsessed with

premature burial, and I sympathized, as it was a condition with which
I was familiar. Victorian cemeteries had arrangements allowing those
buried alive to ring a bell from their coffins. Burials predating modern autopsy techniques were occasionally unearthed showing corpses
in disarray. The most terrifying discovery was nail marks, scratches on
the insides of the coffins. This was a great inducement for the sales of
bells and whistles to attach to corpses, which would presumably
scare the hell out of graveyard workers if they ever rang. Bram Stok-
er's *Dracula* ushered in the vampire on this current fear of post-death
awakenings, and Edgar Allan Poe tapped the fear of immurement in
his "The Cask of Amontillado." But there were places where and
times when this was practiced intentionally. While the British managed to stop *suttee*, the Hindu practice of burning a widow on her
husband's funeral pyre, burying the living remained a common punishment elsewhere. The emirates of Bukhara and Khiva in Central
Asia each had silent fields where the living were entombed.

Locked in my dim room on the Canadian border, the cell door
further buttressed by ice and snow, I had only a sleeping man and my
growling stomach for company. But every morning, the coldest time
of the day when the sun shone, a door to an outdoor cage was opened
to me for an hour. The facility was built with federal regulations in
mind; there was a recreation pen in the back. In this way we were afforded "time outdoors."

The rec pen was reached through a vault-strong door that was
electronically opened from a central control tower. It was as wide as
the cell, which was the width of my spread arms, fingertip to fingertip. It was four feet deep, with concrete sides and a steel grating separating the enclosure's occupant from freedom. In other words, it was
larger than a grave but not by much and somehow passed for "outdoors." One could do pull-ups by attaching some fabric to the fencing
for grip. Exercising with push-ups and sit-ups was a popular pastime,

as calisthenic methods for isolating muscles to train are well-known by box habitués. However, for the most part the limited time outside was used for commerce.

OBSERVED FROM WITHOUT AT the right hour, a box block looks like a bustling spider's web. Lines of thread stretch from pen to pen, connecting the inhabitants even when the rec pen doors are shut. Capitalism flourishes across this network, with men using stamps as currency to buy sealed food items like kosher cold cuts or cheese from one another. The goods travel in pillowcases or other fabric containers. A photograph of the back of the box would reveal the transfers of food and other valuables like books or decks of cards suspended in their travel upward or downward along the walls. A secondary network runs from cell to cell inside. These exchanges are limited to flat items that can fit under a door, so entire books of stamps, pornographic magazines, and slices of bread in manila envelopes make their way across the floor. Connecting one line to another is difficult.

Both parties shoot out their "cars," typically a toothpaste tube with a line attached, and attempt to link them in the broad wasteland of the ever-lit hallways. The idea is to entangle the tips so that the line of your partner can be pulled in. Lots of fabric is required for both methods of intercell commerce, and the cops know to what ends the bedsheets get ripped. To tamp down this destruction of state property, the sheet you're issued is never replaced, though you can have it washed. The need for line material left one bunky of mine with only an eight-inch-wide strip of sheet covering his mattress.

Lines from those two-man oubliettes don't just transverse cells and flights of stairs. Men under these extreme conditions somehow also manage to thread sheet lines across one hundred feet of empty air, in between buildings separated by barbed wire. How? Spear and ball.

Magazine pages are rolled up and combined into two-meter-long javelins reinforced with envelope glue. A thread line is attached; with the lengths required, anything else would be too heavy. The spear is darted through the grid of the cage to the maximum extension of its dynamic potential. A partner in the other building throws a ball made of wadded bread and wet paper with its own thread line. The goal is to tangle with the paper javelin and draw in the line. Chucking the ball through the bars is pure luck, since most of the time it just bounces back. Barbed wire fencing and seagulls attracted to the bread are additional obstacles. And yet man prevails over the elements every time. Upstate all the buildings are threaded together by what Adam Smith invoked in *The Wealth of Nations*: the invisible hand of the market. It is to make a profit that men work together in such superhuman enterprises.

OF COURSE, CONTRABAND IS TRADED. The prices are much higher than in general population, but everything is available in the box. Visitors bring in tobacco, pot, other drugs, and "fire" to their box-bound loved ones. A cage separates the box prisoner from his visitor, but it contains a slot to pass in the food that is available in the vending machines of all visiting rooms. Balloons travel through with the chicken wings. The valuables make their way back to the cells in human rectums. Just about any liquid will serve as lubricant for boofing.

All the matches used in the box are split in half and carefully deployed, but they eventually run out, so fire must be started by alternative means. The power outlets in box cells are turned off because of "third railing." I learned this technique as early as my stay on Rikers. Two pieces of pencil lead are inserted into a socket, effectively extending it out into the open. This enables one to complete the circuit by connecting the two graphite prongs with a third conductor, typically a staple torn out of a magazine. Sparks fly, and the area surrounding the potential arcing is filled with toilet paper as tinder to catch the excited electrons. The inevitable short circuit will blow a fuse, requiring the cops to turn it back on, but the effort is worth it. The resulting "wick"—a dozen feet of tightly coiled toilet paper— can remain lit all day, giving you the feeling of living in a chimney. The smell causes immediate headaches in me now.

To have the electricity turned on in the box, you must prove that you are doing legal work connected to your case. A tape player is provided for the review of your recorded hearing minutes, and the power is turned on. Anyone with something to smoke tries the outlet as soon as the attendant cop walks away. However, the real aficionados make sure that the balloons their visitors provide (a condom wrapped around its contents a dozen times works best, though condoms are contraband inside) come with "red hats" and a "skateboard," which are matches and a striker, respectively.

The cell has a single steel toilet/sink console with a light over it. The fluorescent light is operated by a switch; inserting a piece of foil from the lid of a juice cup or tuna fish container into the crack between the housing and wall can also generate a spark, but it's very difficult to catch with toilet paper. The main light in the cell is operated by the cops. At a certain hour the fluorescent tubes shut off and are replaced by a night-light, which is just as bright as the daytime illumination. After a box bid you will appreciate sleeping in darkness for the rest of your life.

The cell also contains a counter with rounded edges and two stools that swing out from beneath it. The cots are stacked, and the window, which only leads to the rec pen, is triple secured with grating.

Nevertheless, with determination a corner can be pried up. That cell then serves as the "elevator," connecting the first floor of the box to the second. From these pried-up corners the lines are run from the interior of one cell to that of another on a separate floor, passing through two rec pens and a bit of the outside. The information that travels along these lines is enough for people to run entire stamp-driven gambling tickets. Gangs are able to function, and hierarchies are preserved. Orders are given to the bunkies regarding those in need of "washing up"; a note can inform a bunky that he must beat his only source of human companionship. Along the lines both gossip and wickedness are spread.

I lived next door to a pair of dirty white boys who were so poorly behaved that they were due to max out their terms from the box. They had received more time in the box than they had on their prison sentence. With nothing to lose anymore, they did whatever drugs they could get. To pay for them they converted to Judaism and requested the kosher meal alternative. They had a standing agreement to sell the kosher items to a guy upstairs, with whom they also had a dispute over a pot deal; some small sum was in question. So when tuna day arrived, the two rapscallions were a little slow sending the mush up the elevator. The guy upstairs thought they were "deading" him, denying him the kosher tuna for which he had already paid. But the truth was so much worse. The boys had actually spent the afternoon altering the recipe. They washed out the mayo and replaced it with semen—eight loads' worth, though apparently the younger guy had provided five of them. They waited an hour after sending it up before asking a dreadful question.

"Hey, bro, tuna was OK?"

"Yeah, good-looking."

"Feeling pregnant yet?"

The guy just howled in response. He immediately understood and also realized that many others had heard their conversation. It was clear that he had already eaten the fish. The man's outrage and frustration were dreadful. He promised a horrible death to the boys in any prison yard in the state. But they were not scheduled to go to any more prisons, only to be released when their day came. And he didn't have any idea what they looked like. Apart from our bunkies, all of us only knew one another by voice. Many of my neighbors were convinced I was an elderly man.

Troublemakers like these dirty white boys posed a problem to the law. They were already maxed out in every regard, so there wasn't any further punishment with which to threaten them. Shit throwers in Southport posed a similar problem. However, there was still the Loaf.

Food can become a flashpoint with box prisoners because it is the rare area of contact between them and the cops. Men sometimes keep the plastic trays in which it's served, refusing to return them until an extraction becomes necessary. I remember one tray lid that someone had scratched "FEED ME" into. Men also threw food and smeared their observation window with it, or did the same with the waste that is the end-product of the food. Continuing to feed those who "bust their cup" is like providing ammunition to one's enemy, and yet it is against the law to use starvation punitively. Enter the Loaf.

Made of dough studded with cabbage, beans, and other tasteless ingredients, the Loaf is fed to those inmates who cannot be trusted with food, trays, or solid feces. Because it is served in a small portion of dense muck, prisoners on a Loaf diet poop in tiny amounts and not every day. They lose weight very quickly, because it's hard to stomach as well. The Loaf is made with just enough oomph to make three daily, identical portions of six hundred calories each. Technically it provides enough nutrition and is even healthy, lacking salt and fat—and taste, beyond what the cabbage supplies. But the protein (from the beans) and other nutrient counts are kept to a minimum. This is a carefully designed foodstuff, one that will keep you alive, but only barely, and unhappily.

A while ago some guys on the Loaf got around it by demanding kosher food. For this reason the rabbi with whom I worked at the time had to oversee the baking of kosher Loaves. I always thought he should have refused to do so, as it was a way to use the few powers he had within the spiritual realm to improve the corporeal lives of some very miserable people, but a job is a job. In any case, there was always left-over Loaf, and toasted and slathered with butter, it wasn't half bad.

Holidays in the box are celebrated by making "cakes." For these special days bunkies simply save all their meager desserts for a week and then encase them in buttered bread. I spent a Christmas and a New Year's with such box cakes, except that the second one was taken away from us. You are not allowed to save any food while serving box time, so about once a week we were commanded to go out into our recreation pen while the cops searched the box cell. There was never anything too interesting to find, as the men with contraband kept it in the cheeks of their asses at all times to foil these attempts, so the cops focused on the food. On New Year's Eve my bunky and I took all the tiny desserts out from hiding and built a pie out of them with our saved bread and margarine. We had hungered for a week for this treat and eagerly awaited midnight. No one expected a search at 10:00 p.m. on the last day of the year. But one came.

"Yes, we kept some food," I reasoned with the cops through a closed door as they "searched."

"Yes," I told them, "it's all right there on the counter. And it will be gone and out of sight and memory when the bell tolls."

I didn't think they would do it, but they did. I suppose they could have written us tickets for hoarding food, but instead they enjoyed stamping on our cake with their boots and kicking the pieces out the door. They actually did us a favor by booting the remains; I doubt we would have had the strength to resist the oatmeal and canned peaches on the floor. They took away our New Year's Eve that day, but unwittingly let us keep our dignity.

The box is an anvil where man is hardened or broken. Damaged men smear shit on the walls and try to kill themselves by drowning in the toilet, an attempt I witnessed by someone who wasn't in the box.

Some of the ways that man demonstrates that he still lives, despite the live burial to which he has been subjected, are inspiring. Others, like "hunting," are less so. The line transactions are inherently wasteful, leaving all kinds of trash to accumulate in front of the cells. This becomes bait for the hunters' prey. Clean-up crews composed of cadre workers, the same prisoners who cook the box meals and take care of the facility, are occasionally sent out to clear out these spaces. They work fast and take precautions; experienced cadre workers know to wear hoodies and keep their distance lest they become a hunter's trophy. Rolling up a dart gun out of magazine pages is simple, as is shooting pellets of bread or wet paper with surprising accuracy. The men practice on seagulls until the wonderful day when human targets with brooms are paraded in front of their blowguns. The cruelest hunters aim for the eyes and barb their darts with staples. The cadre workers are paid accordingly at the highest rate, twenty-five cents an hour.

THERE HAS RECENTLY BEEN a discussion of the ills of solitary confinement in the courts and press. The issue is a complicated one, as the features of the box that actually breed mental illness (and I heard my share of howling, head pounding, and bunky beating) are not the ones that are commonly identified as problems. In my experience, there were altogether too many people in the box; I would have volunteered for time if I could have done it truly alone. Illiteracy and the lack of interests make the experience much worse for most of the prisoners. Today the box is overused; because the prison population and its percentage of inmates worthy of box-time has shrunk from when the facilities were built, most of the men are serving sentences in solitary for dirty urines. The rapid expansion of SHUs across the state occurred at the same time as the explosion of violent crime that came with the crack epidemic. No one then thought that crime would drop any more than there would be a resurgence of widow burning.

The tale of buying human souls and being sent to the box for this infraction was my first publication, as well as its own chapter here. It didn't pay much, but it confirmed my suspicion that solitary was bizarre, cruel, and not the best example of American justice. Nevertheless, seeing life rise and prosper in men in the box despite the obstacles placed before them was the strongest evidence for the power of human spirit. The men gambled, got high, ate, drank, and made merry despite it all. To wax maudlin (and *Jurassic*), life found a way. I made it through live burial with a newfound confidence. Being merely human led me to that grave *à deux*. And like other men, I survived it without losing a damn thing. All four times. My life found a way.

12

BOLDFACE NAMES

Celebrities seem to emerge in every society the moment a certain density of population is reached; every village has its fool and its strongman. Prison serves as a laboratory to study how men self-organize into societies, and watching that development is effectively a look into our Stone Age past. The number of people required to make up a community of which there is a member or two whom everybody knows is absurdly small. A standard forty-cell tier of a maximum-security prison will have a guy known to be the hardest, a guy who can sell you anything, someone who stinks, a nut, and an authority figure with the most time in. The pattern repeats on the next tier. All the prisoners will know the names of the leading characters, as will the steady cops who have bidded the post and spent almost as much time in jail as the sentenced men they are paid to watch.

But that's just being locally famous. There are also men whose names are known widely among the fifty-eight thousand (2014 census, when I left) denizens of the New York State branch of the Incarcerated Nation. Since everyone who finds himself an inmate has earned his place with a misdeed, the notorious ones are familiar names outside the walls as well as in. In theory, these are the criminals who are the worst of all. Because of cruelty, perversion, or the sheer élan of their crimes, newspapers print their names using the boldface font reserved for the notable.

We all have some memory triggered by at least one or two of these figures, to which I was eventually able to append faces and voices, mannerisms and quirks, as well as laughs shared and favors owed. The Son of Sam. The Preppy Killer. Colin Ferguson, the Long Island Railroad shooter. Mark David Chapman. Mad Dog Sullivan. Joel Rifkin, Shyne . . . At one point or another, I shared air with each of these celebrity prisoners, all murderers except for the rapper Shyne, who most people believe took the rap for Puff Daddy. I was close enough to two men to write journalistic pieces about them; I spent four years in Green Haven with Ronnie DeFeo, the Amityville Horror. I was in two prisons with Party Monster Michael Alig, and reviewed his debut as a painter at a gallery opening. His work wasn't bad.

Both of these men have died since I wrote this book. Michael Alig was tragically found dead, thanks to a drug overdose on Christmas day of 2020, in a cheap Washington Heights apartment. We all knew he had drug problems, and no one was surprised, but somehow I couldn't even get an obituary published about him. Alig seems to have gotten the attention of the police blotter instead. He died on his mother's birthday and there was no one to bury him without a Go-FundMe account started for the purpose. Ronald DeFeo died at sixty-nine in a cell in the spring of 2021. He was still going to parole boards every two years. The system cremated him, as he killed all of the family members who could have possibly claimed his body. True crime doesn't usually end the way it does in the movies.

Having worked at four different prison libraries, I can report that true crime is the genre most favored by the incarcerated reading public. Reading true crime accounts to get a better sense of celebrity criminals, or to understand the mind of a killer, or the workings of a prison, is a piss-poor method of research. The books are typically sensationalized and deal with mythology rather than fact or even analysis. Perhaps the truest description of what it is like, psychologically and every other way, to be in prison, is in a work of fiction. Tom Wolfe sets a hundred pages of *A Man in Full* in prison, and everything just clicks. It's amazing writing for a man who I do not believe has had any personal experience with incarceration. How did he capture the condition so perfectly? Pure talent, I suppose.

A plethora of material has been written about men like David Berkowitz, so he could read entire books about himself if he didn't stick to the Good Book. The Son of Sam found Jesus inside. A lot of the guys claimed that they could identify themselves as background characters in Mafia biographies and narcotic conspiracy accounts. Pretty much all the Italians I met inside were a friend of a friend away from John Gotti. I myself worked out with "John's weights." In order to have a better feel for who was what in the underworld, I read a good deal of true crime myself. I took any ragged paperback that anyone would try to lend me so that I could read what had been written about Gotti, though my own tastes pushed me to the more literary end of the spectrum, the sort of true crime that's read in college classes on genre fiction. I thought Truman Capote's *In Cold Blood* to be a marvelously insightful look inside how exactly people become capable of killing fellow humans. Vincent Bugliosi's *Helter Skelter* also caught my attention by being very well written.

But these books did not offer any deeper insight into the nature of whom I was living with than did *The Napoleon of Crime: The Life and Times of Adam Worth, Master Thief*, by Ben Macintyre, an absurdly fascinating account of a nineteenth-century gentleman art thief who stole the *Mona Lisa*. Similarly, Herbert Asbury's *Gangs of New York* was compelling enough to read twice, but learning the lore of the Dead Rabbits and the Plug Uglies was of little help in figuring out the Bloods. After listening to their coded communication for years, I made do, but without the aid of any book in the library.

One book I did find more useful was *Murder Machine*, by Gene

Mustain and Jerry Capeci, an account of the New York Mafia killers
headed by Roy DeMeo. DeMeo famously worked first for John Gotti
and the Westies, and then against them. The crew was known for
disposing of their victims by chopping them up in a bathtub and then
using corrosive chemicals to further dispose of evidence. The reason
this work was helpful was that I learned particular names in it, like
that of the fearsome Gaspipe (mobster Anthony Casso), which produced interesting results when I dropped them in conversation with
my incarcerated peers. Every New York criminal with a vowel at the
end of his name claimed some connection with Gaspipe. When I later
looked in the back of *Murder Machine*, I discovered that all the same
guys had taken the book out of the library. True crime was not just
a genre that chronicled the underworld but kept its legends alive, and
gave men with wasted lives a bit of meaning to account for all their
lost years.

Much of it wasn't true, and it wasn't even crime, since a lot of the
material actually concerned atrocities committed by the mentally ill.
Working behind the library counters of the Incarcerated Nation, I
learned that books on serial killers were popular, particularly with
sex offenders, for the rape and other sexually dysfunctional behavior
they described. What for regular people would be the stuff of night-
mares were works of fantasy for this set of readers.

The Son of Sam is still New York's best-known celebrity prisoner.
David Berkowitz is the star inmate of Shawangunk Correctional Facility, where he'd converted and become very born again, and works
as the chaplain's clerk. A broad, tall Jew, he has a beard that flows
over his scarred throat, concealing the evidence of an earnest attempt
by someone to cut it inside. I had heard in the yard that a visitor with
a familial connection to one of his female victims had tried to do him
in with a flattened Coke can on the visiting room floor. I only saw
Berkowitz once, through the window of our transit bus when it pulled

in to Shawangunk. It might have been someone else, but the other guys on the bus sensed that they were suddenly in the presence of a psychopathic killer. The vibe in the air was just too weird for it to have been a look-alike.

Meanwhile I was told disconcertingly often that I very much resembled Robert Chambers, the Preppy Killer, just shorter. He left Green Haven Correctional Facility the month I got there. Because of a taste for heroin that he had acquired in prison, Chambers kept getting dirty urines and did every day of his five to fifteen years. He was well-known for being a likable addict; unfortunately he got into some heavy narcotics after his eventual release and is back again, which can easily happen to a person with unchecked drug abuse and parole supervision. His current sentence of nineteen years for the criminal sale of a controlled substance is more than what he was given for the manslaughter of a girl during some rough sex in Central Park in the 1980s.

I spent the years from 2004 to 2007 in the same prison as the Amityville Horror, with whom I spent an hour on line every morning at the prison clinic's medication window. Ronnie DeFeo killed the six family members with whom he lived in a grand house on Ocean Avenue in suburban Amityville, Long Island, in 1974. My retired grandparents lived on Bayview Avenue, three blocks and three canals over in the same town for twenty years. When as a child I started spending my summers with them on the beach there, DeFeo had been in jail for ten years. When I was sentenced, thirty years had passed since his crime, and he had been bouncing around the various prisons of the state. Ronnie had been in Green Haven for a decade by the time I landed there. Sentencing was not as harsh back when he was convicted, so his six twenty-five-to-life sentences were not consecutive but concurrent. He lived in comfort on honor block and still attended parole board hearings every two years. But it didn't much matter how many times he went to the board. *The Amityville Horror* remake, yet another movie cashing in on the murders, was released the year I got to know Ronnie, and when the board denied him yet again, he lodged an appeal claiming that he couldn't get a fair parole hearing with that kind of media attention. It was denied, too.

I used to see Ronnie chewing OxyContin every morning. He had some mysterious ailment that caused enough pain for him to receive a hefty dose of the stuff. The clinic gave him a little plastic cup of the potent pills, which he enjoyed more by crushing through their time-release structure. He used to share them with Rubin, a murderer friend of mine, and because I was curious about the horror, I had the perfect way to start a friendship.

"Hey, Ronnie, I've been in your house," I told him. "There is no red room under the stairs." A year after Ronnie's murders, the Lutz family moved into the house. It was sold at a much lower price than it was worth, even though the bloodstains were washed away. However, the enterprising Lutzes did pay an extra $400 to keep the DeFeo furniture.

They moved out soon after, with a story of spectral swine and ghost armies and a small room painted red under the stairs, where the devil slept over. It was sold as a "true story" in a book by Jay Anson and then found great success as a campy horror film. The sequels, which were published as "fiction," depicted the characters fleeing the house with the evil entities coming along for the airplane ride to California. Then followed movies based on haunted objects sourced from the horror house . . . Amityville became its own industry, one that the town did not welcome.

I had read the original *Amityville Horror* book by Anson and both sequels by John Jones (they are easily available at garage sales in Amityville) and knew the background to DeFao's case. My interest in it predated my incarceration, and I admitted to DeFeo that I had investigated the house as a boy. That claim was basically true. One Halloween afternoon, perhaps in 1990, my local friends and I swam the canal between Grand and Ocean Avenues and breached the satanic property through its adjoining boathouse. As the house was not actually possessed by the spectral hell-pig Jodie but was inhabited by regular people who could call the cops, we did not take our exploration further. The current owners had paid a lot for the house, were sensitive about its history, and had taken steps to reduce attention to it. The number of the original address on Ocean Avenue had been changed, and the famous evil eye windows were altered to prevent exactly this kind of notice. However, everyone in the town knew where the horror house was. Having talked to the locals, I was also aware of which bar young DeFeo went to in order to report that "someone killed his family." We all knew where everything had happened in Amityville, we just didn't believe in the nonsense about supernatural elements. Even if the original book by Anson was published as nonfiction.

I used the interlibrary loan system to get a copy of the original *Amityville Horror* so that I could read it while waiting on line at the clinic, and DeFeo himself began looking over my shoulder and pointing out the bullshit. He was a slight, short, graying man who would get bags of mail from people obsessed with Satanism. He was then on his third wife since entering prison. The women all fit the same profile: lower-middle-class buxom blondes of a certain age and BMI, likely with little self-esteem and a fascination with celebrity killers. The marriages existed on the phone, in letters, and four times a year for conjugal visits—forty-four hours spent together in private every three months, the rest being conversation. And DeFeo was hardly the best conversationalist. Whenever one of the wives threw in the towel, he would divorce and remarry.

He was fairly self-sufficient, however, having inherited the estate of his victims, passed on thanks to a crime he had always denied in court and therefore could have access to. He also sold the rights to his story for a good sum. When I knew him, he was fighting the Department of Corrections, which had found him guilty of "unauthorized exchange" and taken him out of honor block. Over the years, he had taken up painting and dutifully sent the canvases home to whoever was the current wife. Eventually he got a ticket for running a commercial enterprise as a prisoner. What happened next is debatable, as the paintings were bought by morbid collectors for a goodly sum. DeFeo argued that his wife had sold them without his permission and that he had not received any gains from the operation. As the state could not disprove this, and DeFeo's attorney had sworn affidavits from everyone involved saying that the painter himself was kept out of the loop, the decision was overturned, and one morning I watched the Amityville Horror move back into honor block with his thirty years of accumulated property.

Every time he had anyone visit, he would have to get a new ID card made afterward. The prison rules were that the cards were to be handed to the guards while you sat with your visitor, and his would always get "lost," although the cards would later turn up on eBay at prices the collectors would eagerly pay. The COs who ran the visiting room thought it was only fair that they, too, profit off their pet killer, and made sure DeFeo wasn't charged the usual two-dollar fee for a lost ID. Apparently this was all small potatoes; DeFeo told me that in the seventies, when the case obsessed the country and the prison regime was lax, he made a fortune mailing out portions of his own blood and semen in plastic bags. Practicing Satanists kept him in dope money, as long as his body produced the fluids needed for rituals and potions.

Ronnie didn't mind profiting from the common perception that he was demonic. He played up his spookiness if it got his crappy paintings sold or got him married yet again. However, he laughed at the idea that his crimes were caused by Jodie the pig, or the Indian spirits angered by the house's construction on a Shinnecock burial ground, or a demonic red room. Ronnie blamed the Mob.

When we first met, Ronnie told me the same story he had claimed at the very beginning of the affair, in which he ran into Henry's Bar next to the excellent Blue T Pizza to report the murders. His father really was a little mobbed up, but there was never any evidence found for a carload of Mafia killers coming out to Amityville for a family whacking. The Gambino hit man Ronnie tried fingering for the job could credibly demonstrate that he wasn't even in the state, and there was simply no reason for the Syndicate to sponsor such a grotesquely violent display.

Once I got to know Ronnie a little better, he told me another version—what he claimed *really* happened that November night.

It was his sister Dawn who had killed everyone. She shot their parents and siblings and would have put a shell in Ronnie, too, if he hadn't wrestled the gun away from her and defended himself with lethal force. It was quite a tale, and DeFeo has gone to court with it in one of his appeals. An author took interest in the case and came to accept and champion this version of the crime, so there is yet another book about the murders espousing this malarkey. For my part, I still wasn't quite clear on why the sister had gone berserk or why it had taken deadly force to stop a teenage girl. Unlike Ronnie, she hadn't been on acid, speed, or heroin. There had been allegations of violent abuse on his father's part. Ronnie hadn't become a troubled, addicted, and violent kid by chance, and Occam's razor would point to the truth being exactly what he was convicted of. It wasn't like he showed any remorse, after all.

Jailhouse fame is a double-edged sword. On the one hand, it insulates one from some of the struggles of normal prisoners' lives, like

the financial burden. Other prisoners offer a touch of unearned respect to those who make the papers. Ladies come calling. The kind of
women who marry prisoners are drawn to notorious ones more than
the average tarnished bears. However, the parole board is a greater
challenge for celebrity criminals, and true fame often means getting
housed in involuntary protective custody. Tupac, Mike Tyson, Mark
David Chapman, and Shyne all spent years in OPPU, the special unit
for special villains in Clinton Correctional Facility. The rapper from
Belize, Shyne, served nine years in the state before his deportation.

He clerked for the same rabbi I had worked for in a nearby
medium while I was still in the max system. The rabbi served both
prisons, and the rapper was my opposite number. We never met but
handled each other's paperwork. While calling himself a Blood gang
member, Shyne lived with (and off) Punch, a Serbian heist man.
Today Pavle Stanimirovic, his real name, appears on television when
a talking head is required to say something about the Balkan rob-
bers, the Pink Panthers. In prison Shyne became Jewish—very Jewish. This had no impact on his legal status. When he took a nine-year
rap for the gun shot off by someone in the company of Puff Daddy
(P. Diddy afterward), Jennifer Lopez, and the recently signed Shyne,
he also accepted a loss of potential citizenship.

That is the way it goes with green card holders who commit aggravated felonies, even if they are recording artists. Shyne never com-
plained about his plight while serving time, but the subsequent
deportation effectively ended his musical career, as he is not allowed
back in the United States for a decade. His ardent and sincere conversion to Judaism doesn't matter, although he has visited Israel since his
release.

There are many prisoner-celebrities unknown to the wider world.
For years I heard about how Jerry the Jew tried to get out of his life

sentence by dying for a few minutes and being brought back to life to litigate again. He got many people out on reversals but never left prison himself. Some criminals are renowned just for being really hard men.

Blueboy the Crip had a fearsome reputation, and Larry Davis was a criminal legend. Legendary killers like Paddy Irish, who had terrifying eyes, became part of my life, jarring manifestations that appeared in the yard after a transfer. I played spades with him, hoping to lose after hearing the stories. However, the prisoners whose names "rang bells" were stars on the smaller stage of being famous inside the prison system.

Michael Alig, on the other hand, was played by Macaulay Culkin in the cult hit movie *Party Monster*. The murder he committed was described by James St. James in the book *Disco Bloodbath*. I tried ordering it in prison but wasn't allowed to, because its protagonist also had a library card in the joint in which we were both held. In prison Alig was called "Party Monster," or just "Party," which might have been his lovers' preferred term. Or his dealers'. I spent time with him in two jails. He tried to bury me in one.

The same year that Alig made the cover of *New York* magazine, I recognized him floating down the yard at my second maximum, Eastern Correctional Facility. It was an honor max, as good as it gets if you're doing hard time. Mike was haughty, smart, funny, and ruthless. He was very gay, but equally quite familiar to me, as he came from the real world that I recognized. We had eaten at the same places, had friends in common, and thought the same stuff was cool (although I drew the line at dismemberment, while he just drew). I had even worked at the Tunnel, one of his "godfather's" three notorious nightclubs. Peter Gatien, now deported back to Canada, owned the super club on the very west Twenty-Seventh Street where I had a guest list for reduced admission (the Dean's List, I named it) that never made a penny. In Mike's statement to the Eastern deputy of security, he said that I had been his employee. Why did he make such a statement?

I blame myself. Some demon possessed me to say an idiotic thing to Alig early in our relationship. He had a problem; his continuing drug use in prison had become well-known to the security authorities, who had him pulled in for urine testing frequently. By the time we met, he'd already been caught with a half-dozen dirty urines. The consequences for each infraction had increased to their maximum: Alig would get a year in the box for each one. It was lucky that a judge had recently capped the punishment for drug relapse at that; a few years earlier he could have gotten five years in solitary for failing a urine test after so many priors. Alig was a quick study and realized that the doctor at Eastern CF was Russian. He had also observed me speaking my native Russian to the portly physician. There was a way around his problem that could be achieved with a doctor's pen. Alig assumed a connection beyond the ordinary between us Russians and asked me what it would take for him to be prescribed an opiate. That would allow his urine to be legitimately permanently dirty. Even a prescription for a single Percocet a day would have given Alig a license to do heroin.

Why didn't I just laugh his request off? Well, I had seen other prisoners pull this off. One older man I knew would spend his trailer visits shooting heroin with his wife because he had been prescribed morphine and therefore got away with a perennial positive for opiates on all three of the urine tests required to go on a conjugal visit. But the Russian doctor was not corrupt and certainly not about to prescribe anyone painkillers. The prison authorities highly discouraged the practice, and all kinds of red flags would have gone up had Party Monster, of all people, been given an opiate scrip.

Instead I foolishly suggested that I could funnel the required thousand-dollar bribe to the doctor's church through my account. Jodie the pig must have been operating my tongue at that moment. My con artistry was especially ill-considered because the doctor and I were both obviously Russian Jews and did not belong to any church. Alig caught on to the scam quickly and never transferred any money. I thought the episode was fast forgotten. However, tragedy soon befell Michael, and he figured that I might have slipped him an ace for his sleeve.

I soon learned why I was doomed. A law library worker whom I knew from the yard as a fellow stand-up guy had tossed me a cassette tape, telling me that I had to listen to it. It was the tape that had recorded Alig's tier 3 misbehavior hearing. Mike had sent it out to the law library from his cell in the box for help with his appeal. Alig had a more serious problem than his usual dirty urines. Someone had mailed him some crystal meth, and it had been intercepted.

Apparently whatever trick they had used to send it had worked previously, but this mailroom was more vigilant and caught it. Lying on my cot, listening on headphones, I followed the whole exchange. Alig was charged with conspiring to smuggle a criminally controlled substance into a prison. He tried to argue that he had no control over what strangers sent him, but he was still found guilty and initially sentenced to years in the box, though he later got a time cut. Alig pleaded, begged, and wept without any success, and then switched to a different tack.

"You are worried about crap drugs in the mail? What about Danny and the Russian doctor? Selling morphine scrips for a thousand bucks? Danny with the long hair"—I had six years of ponytail by then—"you just have to send the money through his church . . ."

Michael Alig disappeared into the box, and I soon realized I was in the sights of our own security enforcer, our jailhouse Himmler. Stalin's version was Beria; we had deputy of security Thomas Griffin.

He came from one of those upstate families that made incarcerating New York City's worst the family business. Today he is a superintendent of a prison, the most advanced member of a crime-fighting clan of jail authorities. Griffin had by then heard enough about me to make up his mind: I was no good and had to go.

The doctor wasn't questioned by anyone; after passing through the first round of investigation myself, I asked him, and he hadn't heard anything about the matter. It was clear that the entire focus rested on me, and I was the subject of a few extra urine tests, cell searches, and frisks. I imagine my financial account was scrutinized, and perhaps my phone calls got some special attention. Mail watch, too, possibly; I couldn't tell. As I was not in conspiracy with the doctor, the investigation did not come up with anything incriminating. However, Griffin did get me booted from the jail for insufficient urine.

The funny thing was, I was clean and would have come in on my own to give a sample in two days in any case, as I had a trailer visit scheduled for that week. I did not have another trailer in the four years of incarceration left to me.

I came face-to-face with Alig within a year. We both landed in the hilariously named Coxsackie Correctional Facility. He had arrived there before me and was working as the reception porter. I didn't keep him in suspense but immediately told him that I knew what he had done, and had even heard the tape of him doing it. He didn't deny it but tried to buy my justified rage off. "Sorry. I'll make it up to you. You want a little something something?" I was not enticed.

"No condom?"

He was joking, probably. I took fifty stamps instead.

The real reason I forgave Alig was his talent. His paintings aren't bad, although I thought he borrowed a bit too much from Warhol, but back in prison he gave me many pages of a manuscript to read. He had written dozens of chapters of a memoir, which was brilliantly titled *Aligula*. At first I accepted his work with trepidation; having once read an eight-hundred-page novel written by an amateur-writer-cum-violent-criminal, as well as another guy's manic stories complete with rape fantasies, I learned to avoid prisoner prose, which was inevitably a dull pastiche of the mass-market fiction popular inside. Much of the writing was done with money in mind, as the guys imagined fortunes within their reach if only they could out-Patterson James Patterson. And accepting criticism was not a trait generally common in the prisoner population. However, *Aligula* proved to be absolutely fascinating, and the nod to Roman debauchery was quite appropriate. It seems that Alig had actually bought an East German boy once, and the unflinching description of the murder he committed was compelling. Maybe now that he's dead it can get published one day.

And what of my own celebrity, limited as it was? The Apologetic Bandit was only in the news for a single day. Michael Jackson was arrested at the same moment I was, displacing my sorry robberies from the public interest. However, prisoners read. My online material is out of their reach, and I am no Son of Party Monster, rapper, rapist, or *genocidaire* . . . but prisoners do consume media, and write letters, too. I know that old friends of mine still inside have read my articles, and others have listened to my appearances on NPR and other radio shows. They have seen me on the National Geographic channel and in *Newsweek*. I myself have become a bit of a jailhouse celebrity after the fact. Whenever someone else is paroled, I get messages from those I left behind to inform me. Most of them are nice.

13

TAN ARMOR

I spent six years lifting pig iron, pressing rusty weights in ways designed to isolate a muscle and attack it. The repetitive process that enables one to build a body is creative destruction. Stressing the musculature is the catalyst for its growth; you tear gaps in the muscle fiber and nourish yourself appropriately so that the rents are healed with new tissue filling the gap you created by bench pressing. "No pain, no gain" is the rare motto that is perfectly accurate. Bodybuilding hurts, though sore muscles are the only good part. The required diet is obscene, and the inevitable injuries are painful and long-term. It took three herniated discs, a hospital stay, and four years on painkillers for me to finally end my career under the weights. But I don't regret a thing; after years of false starts in college sport centers, YMCAs, rooftop weight benches, and an Arab boxing gym in Copenhagen, the six years I spent bodybuilding in prison yards and correctional facility gyms left me in the best shape of my life. The muscle suit I wore, the tan armor covering my soft bookish self, could not have been achieved anywhere but inside.

There were many reasons for me to exercise while incarcerated. I've always had a tendency toward plumpness. I was never the lithe English aristocratic wastrel or addicted skin-and-bones-and-tattoos punk rocker I wished myself to be. Even with access to the gyms of NYU and the University of Copenhagen, I always ran to fat. One half of my genetics is for the Russian winter, and the other (Jewish) part seems geared toward getting the most out of Chinese restaurants. My metabolism jealously hordes every calorie, so I have to really go above and beyond a bit of diet and exercise to make a dent. Whatever my internal character was, it felt as if my corporal self did not match it. I was facing an extreme situation: Body and soul were not just misaligned—they were at war.

Eating is one of the few pleasures remaining to a prisoner, and at my lowest I took advantage of every opportunity to do so, even if it was outrageously unhealthy. I ballooned up over nine months while fighting my case from Rikers Island, eating pork rinds all day and cupcakes all night. I reached my maximum weight of 250 pounds in under a year. Stress and inactivity assisted my ruinous diet in enlarging me. It's no surprise that I wasn't picked out once in the thirteen further lineups the cops put me through two months after my initial arrest. However alarming the rate at which I could gain weight, I had a plan, and I stuck to it for about six years after reaching Upstate prison. At my peak state, I weighed 185 pounds of muscle and could bench three plates. Achieving that only required working out seven days a week in routines that took multiple hours, starving myself on a muscle-building but calorie-restricted diet, and stealing all the protein I could. Lifting weights in prison is the basis for an entire subculture. With time I became a member of the lifting community and could witness it from inside. *Body Armor*, by Matt "Wiggy" Wiggins, told some of the story. The literature of incarceration contains little about exercise. Prisoners of yore were set to hard labor and would have balked at voluntarily lifting heavy things repetitively after grueling work shifts breaking rocks, cutting timber, or digging holes. The specialized nutrition necessary for modern bodybuilding would have been inconceivable when merely getting fed was a challenge for most prisoners until very recent times. The concept of prisoners strengthening themselves to better handle the violent challenges of the incarcerated world would also have been unrealistic when disputes were so readily handled with weapons.

The musculature of the Russian zek who hammers a nail into your ear with the heel of his shoe is inconsequential. It was only the advent of films and television shows about prison life that foisted the image of the jacked-up convict on society. The reality is that prisoners have been lifting weights for two generations at most, and shows like *Oz* and the numerous B movies like *The Animal,* which depict prison fighting, hired bodybuilders to play roles that require little dialogue. The result is a feedback loop; modern prisoners are aware of their screen image and lift weights to fit it. I once had the idea of providing a weight-training service entirely staffed by ex-con bodybuilders who could replicate the tough workouts and amazing results that lifting in prison yards supposedly entails. By the time I got out, someone had already done it.

The impression the weight-lifting group initially gave could be misleading, since heavily muscled men with convictions for violent crimes in prison uniforms do not generally inspire trust or admiration. Although these men looked as if they could easily wreak havoc, they were rarely violent. Bodybuilding is actually a very good activity to promote the rehabilitation of the incarcerated. It generally results in men with better attitudes and confidence, because thanks to the hard work that building their body required, they have little to prove. Many have never succeeded at anything previously and experience pride for the first time thanks to the weights; that is exactly what you want in the battle against recidivism. Low self-esteem and a reliance on weapons to even perceived odds are a recipe for violent crime. The debate over jacked-up convicts, which has led to prisons around the country removing their weights, posits that the greater violence that buff cons can potentially cause means that they will do so. Banning

weight lifting is simply another way for electable figures to demonstrate that they are tough on crime. The damage that results is paid
for by everyone.

It's not as if we had Nautilus machines or anything more complicated than pulleys. The weights themselves were jerry-rigged monsters. All of the plates were welded together with extra iron in the
rivets and brackets, making any weight assessment an educated guess,
so we had to invent ways to alter them. Leather holsters allowed one
to hang dumbbells off barbells. The swinging of these pendulums
made some lifts downright dangerous. None of our stuff was stainless; rust was the uniform color of the lot. The lowest hand weight
was 35 pounds, and bars started at 135, though we had a 300-pound
monster, too. These are unthinkably high numbers and meant that no
one could start small. You were either naturally strong or preternatu-
rally brave. It was a manly enterprise, with spit replacing powder for
grip and ripped calluses at the base of each finger. Men howled at
each other to "get their money," and we did exercises with grotesque
names like "chest busters," "heil Hitlers," and the "suicide press."

The nutrition required to grow armor was a constant challenge.
We all chased protein, buying stolen eggs and chicken, scarfing down
endless cans of tuna and jack mac from commissary and trading
pizza (Thursdays) for whiting (Sundays). My discipline was iron-
bound; for years I logged every morsel of food that I ate, tallying up
my daily caloric intake and the amount of protein I consumed. I still
have the notebooks full of cryptic lists and tallies. Months went by
without a simple carb passing my lips. I distinctly remember thought-
lessly accepting someone's offered candy in the yard late at night. I
had tossed a few M&M's in my mouth, only to spit them out before
swallowing rather than endure the shame I'd face later when I'd have
to record the transgression. I eventually turned to peeling M&M's for
the protein-rich peanuts. Madness. At the time, I craved a ragged slice

of faux Wonder Bread more than any chateaubriand, lobster thermidor, or tournedos Rossini.

Supplementation was achieved with innovation. Commissary had Tums; the bodybuilding set would chew them for magnesium. Creatine was treated like gold dust; the rare jails that had the supplement also had the biggest guys, even if theirs was mostly water weight. Men smuggled creatine in coffee creamer and Kool-Aid powder jugs. A touch of glue resealed the plastic containers until all glue-seal containers were banned in package rooms. No one went as far, though, as the jailhouse bodybuilder who everyone knew was extorting a kid prisoner. Twice a day the young man was to provide the mountain of muscle with a tissue containing the results of his masturbation, which the bodybuilder balled up and swallowed. It was for the protein and testosterone in the semen. Everyone knew what he was doing, but no one said anything; this was a big guy who was clearly a bit of a bug. When news of his regimen reached the authorities, they put him away for an "unhygienic act" and considered putting the kid in the box as well, until he convinced them that the transaction was not consensual.

Actual steroids came in the regular, rear-passage path. They had to be smuggled the hard way. Rocky, a "roided" character with whom I worked in a routine that sent me to the hospital, had his grandfather come in with two syringes loaded with anabolics and shot a month's worth of grow juice into his legs on the visiting floor. The steroid went into his thighs and then took hold of him. He spent a few days in bed before heading back to the weight pile and outlifting everyone. Rocky weighed an extra fifteen pounds within two weeks of shooting all those anabolic chemicals into himself. He survived, not just the steroids but the 550-pound barbell shrugs that I was not quite able to overcome.

There were also specialized accoutrements: gloves and wrist bands and silly outfits that men would assemble out of ripped clothes. I had a leather weight belt made. This is a four-inch-wide strap that supports the lower back, in theory. In reality it was the ultimate flag, like a boxer's trunks. My insignia-engraved belt was never all that comfortable; the one that I actually preferred to squat and deadlift in was not a fancy leather model but a handmade article sewn out of a cut-up punching bag. Instead of a symbol or nickname, it was simply marked "Spalding," and it was a dream. But I wanted a personalized belt, since I was now, after all, a bona fide weight lifter. Mine cost fifty dollars. The payment was sent to someone in the Bronx by my wife. The belt is black and oxblood, with a gold trim. It has the imperial Russian double-headed eagle at its center, and looks awesome. I wore it even to do curls, and today it hangs on my wall.

The belt was made by "Mafia," a Colombian biker on our court who had a ponytail of black hair that he had been growing for more than twenty-two years. He had a hobby permit for the leatherworking tools and raw materials that he used to make belts, purses, wallets, bookbindings, and weight-lifting straps. He belonged to Pagan's Motorcycle Club (MC), but that did not prevent him from hanging out with enemy MC members. Bikers suspend all standing beefs once inside; there is even a PBB, the Prison Biker Brotherhood. PFFP, "Pagan Forever, Forever Pagan," was Mafia's motto, but he hung out with a Hells Angel he was said to have attacked in the real world. Mafia didn't work out that much, as sizing people for belts and straps instead was a booming business. And his seven feet of braided hair looked great.

My experiment in building armor involved changes in many other elements of my life. I started to tan, switched to tighter shirts, and began collecting tank tops. I never thought that I would care as much about the difference between Hanes and Fruit of the Loom. I worked out hard and ate right, but even before the accident I reached a plateau. I simply didn't have the genetics for Mr. Nap. That was a title I would never hold. Eastern Correctional Facility at Napanoch had a real gym as well as supplements sold in commissary, so it hosted a bodybuilding contest for the inmates. In Napanoch we had an official competition to see who would be Mr. Nap. One year it was even covered by *Flex* magazine and included the use of posing trunks and baby oil for the pictures.

There was always a little more touching on the weight pile than was strictly necessary. Having a man spot you on the flat bench meant having a crotch in your face, and the spooning maneuver used to spot someone doing a squat was nothing if not clothed buggery. Muscles were examined for tautness, and injuries rubbed. After poring over magazine pictures of basically nude muscular men who were depicted sweating and grimacing in pairs, the touchy-feely stuff was the next logical step. Of course, none of this was acknowledged. Lifting weights to become strong and tough was a macho and respected pastime, no matter how gay it looked. I found myself looking over every male body I saw and evaluating it, curious about the vascularity and muscle density beneath clothes.

Guys like me usually gave up on bodybuilding after hitting the wall of the endomorphic body. For those who cannot get abs, there is powerlifting. I was tempted to switch to it myself after spending six months just on abdominals, only to develop a rock-solid core that was invisible, thanks to the coat of lipids I could never shed. I did every version of crunches and sit-ups for 180 days and kept to the strictest diet of my life. I would have gone bulimic if it wasn't so embarrassing. Prison is like an aquarium, with glass walls and nowhere to go; I would have been caught puking. I listened to Dr. Atkins and kept my carbs nonexistent, while tuna was driving me mad, and I dreamed of noodles and rice and bread. And still my DNA denied me abs.

Powerlifting was an alternative. The idea here is to eat as much as possible and work out hard. If you're willing to have muscle that isn't lean, simply doubling your calorie intake and doing extremely heavy, low-rep lifts will make a strongman out of you fairly quickly. However, you won't look like skinned prime grade. Perhaps this explains why the powerlifters were mostly single, angry guys who imagined their great strength would someday be needed.

I don't regret any of the countless hours I spent pumping iron inside. I met men who breathed pure respect among the fraternity of weight lifters. I liked my body more than ever before, but counterintuitively, I became even more critical of my love handles and other assorted flab than ever before. Every defect seemed a terrible one, and there were a thousand chinks in my armor. Tanning helped; most prisons that aren't complete war zones have a "cracker beach" expressly for sunbathing. Tanning one's muscles in sunglasses on a grassy expanse of the yard is an unexpected pleasure and almost feels like freedom. The wafts of cheap Top tobacco smoke are the only clue as to where one is, unless a shot is fired from the tower. First one's always a warning, but if it's your day to stop a bullet, no armor will help.

My wife wasn't all that impressed with my pointless efforts, and my parents congratulated me on acquiring the appearance of a manual laborer. Why, then, did I go through with it? For one thing, I needed the armor. I was not just physically vulnerable due to my weak and chubby body, I was also prey to every xenophobic impulse my fellow prisoners had. I looked, sounded, and probably smelled out of place. But there was a solution at hand. When I got to my first prison, I looked out a window and saw a scene of medieval torment. The yard was crowded and bustling. Muscular men grunted over their instruments of agony, and the rusty weights screeched as they were manipulated. The smell of sweat, rust, and soap from the outdoor shower wafted over all the clinking, moaning, and hissing. The men themselves were the most exotic feature. One of the ways I knew I was out of place was the tattoo explosion. I was one of the rare men without one. The white population was about a fourth; the percentage of the "inkless" was maybe 1 percent.

However beneficial it was to take up as much of the horizon as possible, I had a marriage to keep afloat and couldn't just eat myself into a behemoth, which some men did. I had come into the joint with the intention of losing weight, which is the opposite of what normally happens. I remember how they gave me pants that were three times my size, to which I objected. The clothes-distributing inmate at Downstate was used to ignoring people's requests, but with time my sizes did shrink. Eventually I needed a pair of pants in medium, while enjoying how the cuff of my XL uniform shirts struggled with my biceps. I may not have had tattoos, but with the muscles, long hair I had grown, and yard tan, I looked enough like a real convict to pass for one. It may have been mere image, but it helped.

Of course, the muscles really had made me strong, and I told myself that if I had to fight I'd at least be protected against body blows and could hit someone really hard. Too bad I didn't know how to fight, and the books I read on self-defense felt like fantasy novels. In an actual contest I'd bleed easy because I was so vascular, and because I tried to keep "dry," meaning to be underhydrated so the epidermis would sit tightly on my musculature, my skin was like paint on my muscle. Being "dry" is unnatural and hard to keep up. Professionals cheat by swallowing dry instant oatmeal. It sucks moisture from the rest of the body to make digestion possible. Inside, I relied on cardiovascular exercise instead; I would spend hours running in circles around the yard. Twenty-five laps was five miles; for my heavy frame and sore quads it was misery, but the cardio was my day of rest after six days of lifting.

Not long after reaching the acme of my physical conditioning, I wrecked three discs in my back and was hospitalized for ten days. The end was quite sudden.

I was working out with Rocky, the steroided freak. He had washed out of a semi-pro football league and became the guy in the back of the gym who can get you Winstrol, Dianabol, and a gun. This landed him in prison, where he continued to lift, burning through partner after partner. Rocky pushed it hard. The incident that put me in the hospital is embarrassing to recount. We were using wrist straps to work out with weights too heavy to grip. I wound up shrugging 550 pounds of pig iron with my deltoids—the muscles that turn your neck into a pyramid—by tying the barbell to my hands. I got my comeuppance within seventy-two hours.

The herniated disc must have hit the sciatic nerve in a unique way. A day or two later I was walking away from the lunch line with my tray when I felt a horrible pain in my quads, in the front of my legs rather than the usual rear. I couldn't budge and thought I'd been poisoned. A cop was yelling at me to move it along. The best I could do was drop my tray on the floor. At the clinic they suggested I go to the yard, until I lay on the floor and waited for a white shirt. The sergeant came and told me they would admit me to the hospital if I didn't get up and move myself to the yard. I agreed and continued to lie on the floor. They finally started to believe me after a few hours of this.

Finally I was admitted to the hospital unit, where I was put on Percocet after giving them some brown-colored pain-urine and extraordinarily high blood pressure readings. Agony can only be self-reported, and prisoners always lie, so they had to have some kind of proof before helping me.

THE HOSPITAL WAS A NEW experience for me. Conditions are luxurious there in comparison to a cell, so earning a bed in the jailhouse infirmary requires some proximity to death. I shared my room with a kid who had a lethal brain tumor and months to live. The nurses were extra kind to him because of this and tolerated his illicit smoking in the shower.

The kid with the fatal tumor lived. I saw him alive and well four years later. During our time together he thought I was the one in greater danger after watching me make twenty-five lines out of my Percocet and methodically snort them one after the other. He almost called the nurse, thinking it was an attempt at suicide by nose candy.

Unable to walk, I spent the time there reading the complete collection of Evelyn Waugh's travel writing, five books in one huge tome. Traveling the world of the 1930s and snorting the Percocet prescribed to me helped pass the time. I also read books like *When Bad Things Happen to Good People*, by Rabbi Harold Kushner, and even Alcoholics Anonymous's *Big Book*, but found more to elucidate at least part of the cause of my pain in *The Brothers Karamazov*. Families are complicated meshes, and when any one node becomes outsized, it warps the structure of everything woven around it. In my own case

my father was the family star, the talent, the genius; and the shadow
he cast over the rest of us closed many avenues of possibility for me.
I wasn't supposed to compete or submit. I wasn't encouraged to join
his field of expertise and was simultaneously mocked for considering
any other field, which was considered spectacularly deficient. My life
was, at various times, lonely, complicated, challenging, painful, mean-
ingless, and ecstatic. The one variable that remained constant was
that I felt better with some opiate in me.

But the pain in my legs was barely addressed by the pills. I had
compressed my spine, disforming the discs so severely that a cortical
steroid was required to reduce the inflammation. I was discharged after ten days in the hospital with a prescription for the painkiller tramadol. Ultram is meant to be used only for ninety-day periods; I stayed
on it for six years. Unlike traditional opiate pain pills, "trams" don't
show up in urine. Unlike a prescription for Percocet, they aren't a "license" for doing heroin. For that reason, just about every prisoner who
needed pain medication was on the stuff, despite the side effects that
set in after exceeding the recommended prescription time. One guy on
tramadol had seizures. After he bounced through the inside of a steel
bleacher, he was found unconscious with such a variety of injuries that
he was suspected of being the victim of a gang assault. While tramadol was an excellent painkiller that carried me through till the end of
my bid, I found I could no longer stand its side effects after my release
from prison. Erectile dysfunction was too high a cost; as a prisoner I
could ignore this problem, but not as a married man.

During my six years in prison dependent on Ultram, times were
sometimes rough. Being on a habit-forming medicine as a prisoner is
giving up even more liberty than was already surrendered by conviction. My physical state was entirely dependent on what the nurses
gave me at the medication window, and I could not count the number
of times I waited in line only to be told that my order had expired and

I would need to see the doctor for a renewal. This condemned me to several days of withdrawal, which in turn left me buying pills from other convicts in order to not collapse into the diarrhea, nausea, cramps, and insomnia of opiate withdrawal. The nurses knew the medication was physically habit-forming but did not care. So many convicts had been caught cheeking their meds to sell them that they assumed everyone was crooked. One facility enforced a general crush order, and all the pills were powdered.

Arriving at another facility with this crush order in my chart, a new nurse assumed I was a known pill-cheeker. This prison did not enforce a general crush order but used it when necessary. The woman took it upon herself to punish me. She gave me cups of plain water, leaving me in withdrawal until the next shift. I can only guess at what happened to the pills I had been prescribed. Once I realized what was happening, I put in a grievance, which is a formal complaint. She retaliated by recommending that I be evaluated for paranoia but stopped giving me the cups of H_2O. The worst part of that episode was when my parents reacted by taking her side. They surmised that I really *was* paranoid, and a good state employee would not do such a thing to a bad junkie like me. That hurt.

When I was released from the hospital, the doctor also told me that I couldn't lift for a year. But his timing was abysmal. For years I had timed my nutritional schedule according to when I had trailer visits with my wife. Basically, she saw me naked every hundred days. That meant that for fifty days after each trailer visit I ate carbs and lifted weights for mass, and then spent seven weeks dieting on a brutally strict Atkins regimen of pure protein and lifted only for cuts and definition. I learned how to cycle my bodybuilding this way by adapting the methods I had read about in *Flex* magazine, among others. These homoerotic publications were endless pictures of the same fifty men straining under weights in little shorts and lots of oil. From a distance the muscle mags and my porn stash were hard to tell apart. There actually were pictures of bodybuilding women as well, but to me they were uniformly hideous. Prettified heads in makeup on top of slabs of male body with the tits tacked on.

What these magazines blatantly lied about was the use of steroids. Every single one of the men displayed in their pages was a product of a team of biologists. The human body cannot look like Ronnie Coleman without extreme chemical manipulation, but the magazines pretended that their models just worked out extra hard and ate right. I thought it a cruel trick to play on the ignorant masses who didn't know about all the Deca and Dianabol and Winstrol. They tried so hard, trying to achieve results like their heroes, unaware that it was impossible without illegal drug use. The magazines were popular inside, and while I did learn a few things from them, there are only so many ways to exercise a muscle, and there's nothing new to say about the bodybuilding diet. In a sense, you really only needed one issue of *Flex*.

So I was discharged from the hospital with a trailer coming a month away. Having wasted so much time lying around in agony, I ignored the doctor's advice about the gym. I worked out for the weeks I had left before my wife came and wound up bringing on another attack at the very moment she arrived when I took the heavy grocery bags from her hands. I spent the next forty-four hours allotted to us on the couch, and for once she cooked. Working through the *Kama Sutra* was not expected of me, and I was massaged. It was actually one of the best trailer visits as far as I remember it.

14.

GULAG ALL-STARS

The contemporary Russian identity, marred as it was by seventy years of Socialist occupation, has confirmed prison's place in the list of elements that now define Russianness. Some of the other ingredients are the Orthodox Church, birch trees, the Volga, Tatars, eunuchs, Byzantium, the jewels of Saint Petersburg, the Stalinist skyscrapers of Moscow, and the curbside vomit of alcoholism from the Pacific to the Baltic. However, one of the most persistent of the Soviet regime's contributions is the reek of prison cells. Every twentieth-century Russian knew a zek, had a friend of a friend or a relation, distant or close, who had been inside. A зек was short for заключеный, someone held "by key," or a prisoner. In my world, I turned out to be the zek whom the people of my circle knew.

Before realizing that, I had to come to terms with my Russian identity. After an American childhood perpetrated in Russian, an urban public school but borscht for dinner, I was a bit confused and needed to work out which nationality was really mine. Doing so in prison turned out to be quite natural.

With everything else stripped away, identity became the contested bulwark that prisoners took their last stand on. The answer to the question of who you are is much more complicated inside than it is in civilian life. Perhaps teenagers looking for a mantle of identity to don can better relate to the dilemma faced by the incarcerated than adults for whom the quest has mostly passed. Upon reaching the cusp of adulthood, the young are overcome with the angst of not having a clear sense of who they are yet. In reaction, they try on ready-made personas, often ones created by the mercantile world. They are temporary, stopgap measures that stand in place until a mature sense of self emerges to express one's individuality. Fledglings sold or sold on music, clothes, ideologies, and manners of speaking can become Goths, or thugs, or punks, et al. For each identity, there is a regalia, soundtrack, and code of conduct. All of these costumes are prêt-à-porter and make for very good business for their suppliers, as the need will always be there.

Prisoners, however, are in their own category. They are grown men who have had all the trappings of their identity taken away by the law. In Descartes's *Leviathan*, the social contract is described as a compromise we as civilized humans make. By relinquishing some of our freedom of choice, we are able to live in the safety and comfort of society. Paradoxically, one of the features of a free society is the ability to be an individual. Once you break your end of the deal, which is what committing a crime is, part of the disenfranchisement that is the punishment is a limitation on the expression of your individuality.

For prisoners, preserving an identity becomes an exercise in willpower. The system begins the battle against you almost immediately. Your very name is replaced by a Department Identification Number (DIN); 04A3328 was mine, or rather it *was* me. That sequence of digits and letters—which indicated that I was the 3,328th prisoner to be processed through Downstate in the year 2004—is indelibly engraved on my soul. I will be cognizant of it to my dying day.

Reading Victor Hugo's *Les Misérables* did not give me much insight into Jean Valjean's struggle to be a man rather than 24601, but only revealed that I was hardly the first to recognize the process.

Hugo used that specific number for his hero because the author believed he had been conceived on the twenty-fourth of June 1801.

Some men simply succumbed to being state-assigned numbers, to the point of tattooing them on their bodies. I met one fellow who had accumulated three DINs before the age of thirty, all inked on him as if the state ever forgot. But others insist on being more.

Because part of identity is coded in language, qualifiers involving pronouns took on great importance inside, adding nuance to the hierarchy we all studied to find our place in.

This exercise in anthropological taxonomy began with sex. I often heard the platitude expressed by the prisoners that we were all men, first and foremost. This bit of obviousness acquired importance and levels of meaning, even though if we weren't men, we obviously wouldn't be in a men's prison. Another common refrain was that one shouldn't abuse the "fags" because they were men, too. This gender labeling defined men as more than merely "not women"; we were dangerous, capable of violence, and therefore demanding of respect. Sexual orientation added an asterisk to the definition, but in the hierarchy of identity, gender came first.

After cocks came pelts. Race mattered; this being American prison, an entire bloody history came encoded with the melanin that determined skin tone. Nobody had the luxury of not picking a team, and the mixed among us had it a little tougher. Race mattered to an extent I had never witnessed previously. It was both a reason to oppress and to redress perceived wrongs. It was overwhelmingly believed that race was associated with collective common traits, ones usually not acceptable to the subjects themselves but perceived truth to everyone else. Thus Hispanics were considered by the other prisoners to have a proclivity to crimes and misdemeanors of the libido. (Remember how many times you said "Latin lover" before virtue signaling your offense.) Blacks were thought to be immoral, violent, and untrustworthy by those who weren't black.

Whites were viewed as inherently weak, addicted to drugs, and soft, while sneaky. Asians were believed to be mysterious, and Jews cheap and dirty. Stereotypes of race were factored into evaluations of individuals without any debate. Political correctness was useless in prison, as any available organizing method was vital to our tribal lifestyle. A man without a name or a shirt still has his skin, and thereby a racial identity.

I noticed that those reliant on a race to define their identity had the least going for them of anyone. Claiming superiority or even self-worth simply because you were black or white was a stretch. Racial collectivism was accepted with fervor by some and scoffed at by others; not too many were neutral on how much race mattered. The authorities certainly thought it did. After decades of bitter experience, the policy on double-bunking was one of racial segregation. I spent a week alone in my first cell until another white prisoner came along to fill the bunk above mine; the administration wouldn't move a black or Latin prisoner into a tiny cell with me. There was no acknowledged ideology behind this policy, just bitter precedent.

Race was not the terminus of identity by any means; there were white Muslims and Hispanic Nazis inside. However, the next layer of identity was sophisticated, expressive, and often included an element of individuality disguised as taxonomy. Using makeshift congregations, tattoos, accents, and nicknames ("handles" inside), incarcerated men found ways to express their nationalities. We had a villains' UN upstate, described at length in another chapter, and, crucially for me, plenty of Russians.

The tremendous variety of nationalities could be sampled by their handles alone. Among the black prisoners were men from Africa and the Caribbean, Panama and Belize. Every day I addressed men as "Sudan," "Pana," "Nigeria," and "Trinny," as well as a half dozen simply named "Africa." The Asians were likewise known as "Thailand," "Nam," "Chinatown," and "Tibet." I was acquainted with a few guys named "Argentina" and "Brazil," as well as a "Uruguay," while the numbers of Mexicans made it impossible to use the nation alone as a handle. Those descended from European countries had the same problem. We had a whole court of Italians, with a Sicilian faction among them. Poles, Czechs, Ukrainians, and Yugoslavs of every stripe were also too plentiful for eponymous handles, though they were all called "Russia" in a pinch. Despite everything, I never was.

Russian was my first language, though for most of my life it has been my second tongue. I was born in New York, but I think I was conceived in Rome, during my parents' exodus from the Soviet Union. I was ignorant of English until I became old enough for school.

Sent to kindergarten in a Dominican neighborhood, I picked up Spanglish with the storied speed at which children learn languages. Culturally I'm nevertheless a product of the USSR. My father's traditional Russian cooking, frequently centered on a cauldron of soup disbursed over three apartments in one Washington Heights building, gave me a taste for Slavic food that stubbornly persists. The thought of borscht makes my mouth water. It gave me something to talk about with the other Russians, but that's not to say my inclusion was smooth.

My father began my Russian education early on. Other kids were paid an allowance for chores like doing the dishes, but only my family included reading the classics in our native tongue as one of them. When I got older, I translated English books into Russian and kept a journal on it, pecking away on a Macintosh and printing out my efforts for my father to correct. I still make mistakes in written Russian but can read it with ease. I've always been grateful for the gift of bilingualism. I never guessed that mine wasn't quite the correct Russian to speak as a zek in the zone.

I speak fluent, unaccented English in complete sentences, so the other Russians weren't quite sure what to make of me. Having learned our language entirely from my intellectual family and from nineteenth-century literature, I'd never acquired an ability to curse. My on-the-fly learning curve in that area was steep and peppered with idiocies like "Fuck your mother's balls." I also spoke formally, addressing my peers with the formal Вы to their general confusion. I used Soviet vocabulary unknown to nineties kids. And I knew not one word of Fenya, the criminal argot. I think some of the Russians who interacted with me before I learned how to swear and spit felt as if they were serving time with their mothers.

Russian prison culture evolved in the pressure cooker of the Gulag, which is an acronym for "Government Directory of 'Lagers.'" That term was first used in the Boer War of 1899 but is perhaps more familiar from the German Konzentrationslager. Or concentration camp. The Germans certainly scored high in brutality, but it was the Soviets who made an entire world out of *Lagers*, a world with its own history, culture, and language. While I read about this hell on earth in Solzhenitsyn, Shalamov, and other Gulag scribes, I also experienced its living remnants. The books helped; I'd pick up a phrase in *Fenya* that would have been an abstraction to most people and try it out that very afternoon in the yard.

In the 1930s Stalin delighted in building a system of labor camps that ground twenty-five million Russians to death with work. The population of a midsized country was turned into zeks and sent to an archipelago of zones in the frozen north and endless Siberia. These areas were cut off from the rest of the country but not from one another, as the zeks were moved by sealed trains from camp to camp. Scattered among the hordes of innocent political prisoners were the *vors*, the thieves, a population of tattooed criminals. They had a hierarchy, and there was (is?) a special rank in hell for "thieves in the law," *vor v zakone*. The culture that emerged from this grim world was founded on an opposition to mainstream life. It was so antisocial that it required its own language, Fenya. It was not spoken in my home, but today's Russian criminals indulge in the zek affectation of speaking this uber-slang, which has an alternative vocabulary for even the simplest of terms. During my first year inside, I spent a lot of time listening to Russian conversation that I nodded along to, pretending to understand. Eventually I borrowed books that my father would have balked at, cheap Moscow editions of crime tales, with guns in tattooed hands on the covers. I learned the violent, vulgar, and sometimes inventively funny Fenya from them no less than from my compatriots.

Vors-in-the-law also make themselves "blue" with tattooing, each of the marks meaningful and earned, like merit badges. *Vors* have rules; for example, they don't eat pussy. If you're a regular guy, a "friar" like I was, these rules don't apply, but you must disclose your caste when meeting another zek and especially when it comes to sharing something. *Vors* in the law are supposed to kill you if you split a mug of *chifir* with them without revealing this defilement, as they have now been disgraced by your romantic mouth, and only blood can wash away the stain of cunnilingus. The drink that thieves and the juvenile *urki* get high on, *chifir,* is a cup of cheap tea (bricks of it are sold in the zones), brewed from enough tea leaves to make twenty cups. *Chifir* is thick and vile and makes your heart patter and your skin sweat, a high that was and is chased throughout the zone. It is slowly sipped and allowed to bathe the gums (leaving green or missing teeth), because a gulp of such strong stuff will make you vomit before absorbing enough caffeine to catch a buzz. After reading about it in every Gulag book, I had to try it. I drank it with a

Russian who was tattooed with a simple version of the Russian *vors* in the law stars. The eight-pointed nautical stars are applied to one's shoulders; stars on your frontal delts signify you are a *vor* of rank. Having another two on your knees are an additional honor, indicating that you refused to work in the Soviet zone, since you will never kneel and stain your stars with the floor. The Russian who brewed me a ten-Lipton cup of tea had probably merely applied the stars to himself. He claimed that he had gotten them in a Russian prison, and after his eventual deportation he would claim to have earned his stars in the American zone. Other Russians I knew had no stars, but my friend and teacher, Dmitry, had a Jewish one covering his forearm, with an eagle atop it. It was his second bid and second stint in the kosher kitchen of Green Haven. He knew there were times when it paid to advertise one's allegiance to the kosher cause.

A friend I had made early on, Dmitry taught me that one could become accomplished even as a prisoner. He had about twenty years in, and he used the time to get good at everything. Since he smoked cigars, he spent many of those years out in the yard. So as not to waste time, he mastered all the games that were played there. Not only could Dmitry beat anyone at chess, checkers, spades, and tossing horseshoes, but he also mastered the eldritch arts of pinochle, cribbage, and even Scrabble. The latter he won at even when playing native speakers (and men of words like myself). I realized Dmitry had simply memorized the right parts of the Scrabble dictionary (fourth edition), when he showed no knowledge of what the two-letter words actually meant. It was for me to marvel at a "jo" (Australian slang for "girlfriend") and "li" (oriental unit of measurement). When the fifth edition was released claiming that "za" is a short way of saying "pizza," I saw his point. These words were just a means to an end.

The man also taught me that you could be good or bad at being a prisoner. He was definitely a maestro of incarceration; Dmitry had figured out how to make money in jail. The huge Star of David on his arm was a memento of a kosher kitchen job years earlier. He stole in such volume that Russians were unofficially banned from working there for a generation afterward. But Dima could also make things. In the real world his mother ran an escort service, but the family had once worked in the garment trade. The man was brilliant with thread. I still have a pair of green mittens made of repurposed blanket and lined with the fur of a lost pet, which he sewed together with dental floss. The price was a pack of Newports. His raincoats were legendary. Prison rules said you had to have clear ones, so they were a desirable commodity. They came with Velcro closures, pockets, and vents, and didn't rip the way the crap from catalogs did. He made them out of transparent shower curtains, but they also came with an expiration date. Every now and then the cops would confiscate every rain coat and poncho in sight made of "altered materials." It was darkly rumored that Dmitry lined the cops' pockets for those rainy-day searches; he always had a fresh batch for sale immediately after his last line was destroyed. To make it less painful of an expense, the most recent line always had a new feature.

Dima was clever enough to marry three times while incarcerated. He put ads in Russian papers, pleas from a lonely man looking for love, slyly noting his American citizenship. The ladies were eventually disappointed when they found out that a prisoner cannot attend an immigration interview, making it impossible for them to become US citizens by marrying him, but he gave them some good exercise during conjugal visits. Dmitry used to entertain me with lurid descriptions of these pairings involving bathtubs and slippery hair conditioner, but after I met one of the women, who was rather large, I asked him to cease and desist.

I learned from Dmitry that life goes on, as he insisted on living as much as he could as if he wasn't inside the wall. He was very Russian, when it benefited him, and not at all the rest of the time. Dima even thought he'd lost his accent—that was for scrubs like Gelman. I liked Dmitry, though I never understood why he was on a Dominican court rather than ours. He played chess at his table next to our Irish court and knew all the guys, but wasn't a member. When I looked him up eight years after last seeing him, I learned why. During all the hours we spent together, my "mentor" had avoided mentioning the rape he was in for. And that explained why he was on the Dominican court rather than mine.

Gelman, on the other hand, was a known arsonist and brilliant violinist. He was a perfect example of how one could fail at being a prisoner, in Dmitry's way of thinking. Not only was he physically and mentally broken by incarceration, Gelman also did not get respect from anyone. The preponderance of prisoners wrote him off as a bug; the guards agreed, and the Russians considered him an embarrassment. I had to visit with him secretly, but I respected his talent immensely. Gelman had a fiddle that looked older than the seventeen years he'd been down. It was very obviously taped together, but he could draw amazing sounds from it. Gelman played at all our Jewish events and once serenaded my mother. The other Russians pretended they couldn't hear the divine music that came from a destroyed violin played by a broken man.

The story was that he had been on the cusp of an amazing career. Gelman had emigrated at the same time my family had and graduated from the renowned Juilliard music academy. He played at the Carnegie Recital Hall in 1982; I read the *New York Times* review. Alas, per the *Times*, "It was not a happy occasion." However, he'd also invested unwisely. The downtown building he bought had tenants from whom it was impossible to collect rent. He made the paper again in 1986. Burning it down for the insurance was worth more than the initial investment. It also cost him fifteen to life.

Gelman had lost it some by the time we met. He looked absolutely bloodless, pale from a yardless decade inside, enforced by agoraphobia. He emerged only for fire drills, and every year or so when his cell was forcibly cleared out. Gelman was a hoarder. He obsessively collected newspapers, paperbacks, and stranger things. I frequently saw him filling his shirt with lettuce. The other Russians, looking for someone to bully, made Gelman a target. They mocked and abused him and once threatened that they would tie him up and keep him tucked under a table during a family event. Instead he played his violin expertly for the appreciative families visiting, but he escaped back to his cell as soon as possible. The state was no kinder to him. They deported him after seventeen years; the parole board demanded two more years after he served his minimum fifteen. Gelman was sent back to a Ukraine he hadn't seen since his long-ago youth. He took his instrument but left the newspapers. Few noticed his departure.

Years later, when I read Thomas Mann's *Doctor Faustus*, I couldn't help comparing the case of the composer Adrian Leverkühn with Gelman's. Mann's protagonist sold his soul for brilliance. Had Gelman made some kind of shoddier bargain? Why does a brilliant musician commit arson? Dmitry said it was because Gelman was an idiot, but he considered many to be idiots.

The final Russian to make an impact on my bid was called "V-cubed," as all three of his names began with the letter. "Volodya Vladimirovich Verov" is close enough to his actual name to explain the moniker. The prison staff issued him to me, unable to communicate with him, and the only other Russophone in the medium-security jail we were in was a half-Algerian troublemaker. The state insisted on sending V^3 to antidrug and -violence classes. To demonstrate what they thought of their own therapeutic programs, my ward was considered to have completed both of them, merely by sitting next to me in my translator role. We both agreed I wouldn't really bother translating the platitudes being supplied, but I had to say something to prove we were paying attention. I used to declaim poetry, explain recipes, and recite the list of Communist Party general secretaries to him when pretending to share the wisdom of the adult substance abuse treatment program.

V³ looked deceptively terrifying. He had childishly scrawled tattoos all over him, which I mistook for prison work. His face was alcoholic-colored, and his teeth were made of several types of rotting Soviet metals. I suspected that V³ was probably trouble when he was assigned to me, though it turned out I was the problem.

In fact, he was a decent family man who couldn't help the crimes of Soviet dentists, general secretaries, or tattoo artists. The pictures on his skin were the result of long and dull Siberian winters. He didn't know any English, but his Russian wasn't needlessly overdeveloped, either. V³ definitely didn't know a thing about crime; the world of *vors* in the law and the zones was as foreign to him as it had once been to me. What he did know was how to hunt.

V³ had killed more deer than any of the NRA member cops. He lived off venison for years when surviving in Siberia as a bootlegger. He had once been a grain alcohol dealer in some backwater, although his participation in the operation ended when he overindulged and ran out before winter ended. At least the deer were plentiful there. Back in eastern Ukraine, he had to switch to canine meat. When communism fell, family dogs were abandoned by the pack. Initially the dog hunters were welcome for addressing this nuisance, but eventually pets began to disappear, too. First the meaty ones went, but progressively smaller breeds soon followed. By then V³ had three sons. His wife knew how to cook dog expertly, although the whole family learned to hate poodle.

They soon wound up in America, thanks to the efforts of Pentecostal missionaries. In the nineties American Christian fundamentalists,

Jehovah's Witnesses, and Mormons swamped provincial Russia, accumulating converts. Once they had established a stable community, they would import it. The churches petitioned Congress for refugee status for their wards, claiming they were oppressed because of religious intolerance in Ukraine. V^3 was relocated to Utica, in central New York State. He was the unlikeliest immigrant and brought many of the typical Russian ills with him.

The man worked hard but drank hard, too. He was used to meat and potatoes for his supper; one night after a long day, the sight of "yellow worms," or macaroni and cheese, did not please him. He banged a knife on the table; his Russian wife knew her cue and ran outside crying. But an American neighbor interfered, seeing tragedy where there was merely habit, and dialed 911 for her. The felony charge for "menacing" was satisfied with a sentence of probation, but V^3 didn't understand that he wasn't supposed to drink during it. Violated for reporting under the influence, he was doing one to three years when the deportation papers came.

Because he only had a green card, he was eligible for that. Menacing is an "aggravated felony." The wife was on mental health meds; the children were going to foster care. I saw this all unfurl before me, and even though I wrote letter after letter to agencies and activists, I knew the family was going to be destroyed. In the meantime, the wife visited her husband in prison and brought fatback, which is hog jowl fat cured like ham. We ate the pure salty fat either sliced and crunched with garlic or cooked into noodles. It was the unhealthiest food in the world, and delicious. The woman had no idea where all this was heading. V^3 was being sent back to Ukraine, forbidden from even visiting the United States for ten years, and her children were going to be taken away. I continued doing what I could. Mostly I listened to his exotic tales of hunting German shepherds and being baptized by Americans in a hole in river ice.

My family helped by sending up a crate of Soviet adventure stories for V^3 to read. It's never wise to take things for granted when it seems cozy inside. They locked me up and sent me out of the jail for buying human souls, an episode that will be recounted in another chapter. This put V^3 into a tragic state of hampered communication. I heard that another prisoner, a former Franciscan monk who is himself mentioned in yet another chapter, put himself on a crash course of Russian to be able to speak with him, but I never heard whether he defeated the department of Homeland Security. In the course of a moment I was dragged to the box, and my life with V^3 was ended. The parallels to his condition are clear.

Echoes of old Russian prisons followed me for years because of my reading as well as my relationships and friends. The literature of the Gulag was crucial in teaching me how to deal with a world I had one foot in, while the other often seemed stuck in my mouth. I studied much of the prison writing in Russian, reading labor camp classics like the *Kolyma Tales* of Varlam Shalamov in expatriate editions because the USSR wouldn't print them. I read Solzhenitsyn in English because there was so damn much of it, but I don't know anyone else who read all three volumes of *The Gulag Archipelago*. The underrated *Heart of a Dog*, by Mikhail Bulgakov, was magnificent, giving me some context to what socialism did for the underclasses. *Faithful Ruslan*, by Georgi Vladimov, also about a dog but one that remains a camp guard animal rather than being turned into a proletariat human as in the former text, was absolutely moving. That was the rare work that gave me some insight into our overseers, the cops.

Faithful Ruslan is the tale of a prison camp told from the perspective of a castaway guard dog, knowing that he is supposed to bite but not why. Many of our guards were similarly conflicted, knowing they were supposed to hate or at least mistrust all of us, but not sure if they really should. That Soviet novella was considered very subversive in its day. I believe I am the last person to have read the work in *samizdat*.

The word means "self-publish," though that term has taken on a connotation far from its literal Russian meaning. The Soviet Union banned many books, but copies were still moved around the nation. Works like *Gulag Archipelago* came in Russian editions, printed in the West, but were widely promulgated thanks to the work of fevered nighttime typists. Anti-Soviet Russians would retype works like *Faithful Ruslan* to spread the good word. A friend of my father's got caught and served three years for making *samizdat* copies of Barry Goldwater's anti-Red menace *The Conscience of a Conservative*. He was never warm enough again after his time in Mordvinia, in the north.

I read *Ruslan* in a photocopied version, snuck through a draconian confiscation routine. I expected I would have a quarantined week after being sent to Downstate from Rikers Island, when I'd have nothing to read while locked in a cell. I knew and feared this alliterate state, so I took advantage of a loophole. There is only one thing that can travel with you: legal work regarding an open case. My father made me a copy of the entire novella and removed its title page and table of contents. Since my photocopied pages were in Russian, I was able to pretend they were one big legal writ or transcript, translated for my benefit. The cops didn't like it, but they respected their own rules. Once the paper clip was confiscated, I was permitted my countercultural, anti-Soviet *samizdat* novel. I read it a handful of times over the week. Of course, by 2004 most dissidents had retired. But not all.

Being Russian in prison meant being a hyphenated American. It was the first time for me; even as a student in Denmark I presented myself as simply Russian to avoid discussion of American foreign policy. I met many other Russians inside and out, of varying degrees of "otherness," but we all had one thing in common. History had left its mark; we were influenced by the Gulag. Many of us had never

visited Russia or had been born after Gorbachev tore down the wall.
A very small minority had actually known the pain of Soviet prison.
Furthermore, none of us had been a political prisoner. So why did we
all know the special vocabulary? Who was taking Fenya classes? Like
any zek in a zone, we all know a tattoo of a pretty girl on a man's
back meant that he was used for rape. The image was to give the sod-
omist something to look at. We all knew that a "cock with ears" was
a modified penis, one that had glass beads inserted under the skin,
adding ribbing for pleasure. Of all the nationalities one could be, it
was being Russian that made the incarcerated world a little closer
to home.

Russia had put away so many millions that its Gulag world bled
over into the ordinary realm. This kind of culture is like cockroaches,
hard to kill and ubiquitous. The Gulag survived to reappear in my life
over a barrier of decades and continents. As America puts away an
even greater percentage of its population, signs of a growing awareness of prison culture are everywhere. I wish being Russian didn't
include an awareness of the stench of prison, and I fear that being
American doesn't evolve into such a state. However, more than 2 million of our 330 million fellow Americans are behind bars, with many
more having some form of experience with Team Prison. Prison culture has already entered the mainstream in the form of sagged jeans
and "drop the soap" jokes. In certain underprivileged communities,
everyone knows someone who has been on a prison softball team.
In a better world, prison would be an experience that is rare and a
last resort, but the American incarcerated league just keeps growing
without a Stalin heading it. Two million American prisoners is an
unfortunately large roster for an all-star team that would be better
off benched, say in treatment or through sentencing reform. But the
game plays on.

15

COOKING WITH ELECTRICITY

The food in prison was bad, though better than the diet of gruel and rot one finds in descriptions of the gastronomic challenges that prisoners in literature faced. As I was locked away in an American big house of the twenty-first century, there was always more than enough of it, and the United States actually has a costly problem in the obesity rate of its incarcerated millions. Rikers Island was recently sued by an ex-convict who developed all the health problems that come with morbid obesity. He won a settlement, having argued that choices of nutrition had been taken out of his hands and handled irresponsibly. The jail reacted by swapping out all the junk food items in its commissary for diet versions. This is a blatant miscarriage of justice, as it is part of prison culture to eat as well and as much as possible and not the fault of what is sold in commissary.

Prisoners put enormous amounts of effort and ingenuity into feeding themselves amazing meals. The state has little to do with it. The output of the mess halls could be bad, and when it was, it was the worst food imaginable. The meals we cooked for ourselves could be good, and when it was, it was the best of food. In our preparation, a plate of choucroute, or paella, or lo mein, or any of the simulacra we contrived with ingredients stolen, grown, bought, and improvised, tasted amazing to a degree beyond what even the best chefs can create. Nothing tastes as good as when you are starving for it. If hunger is the finest spice, then years of it compounded into a deliberate famine (prevented from turning into actual starvation with servings of soy protein and limp noodles) made a flavorful burst of eggplant Parm, strawberry cheesecake, or fried mackerel into a verdant oasis in a food desert.

Aleksandr Solzhenitsyn opened his three volumes devoted to the Gulag with a citation from a geographic survey that noted that prehistoric salamanders found frozen in glacial ice were discovered to be still edible. The author concluded that the expedition that found them employed zek labor. Starving prisoners carrying the scientists' geological equipment were clearly the ones who came upon the creatures, as they fell upon them and ate the lizards immediately. Reading this account in the comfort of American prison, where three hot meals were provided every day, made for a stark contrast. Even on the limited rations of the box, no American prisoner would eat bread that had fallen on the floor.

Unlike the hapless animals that wandered into Soviet camps and were devoured, our local fauna were safe, apart from the predations of one nutcase who caught seagulls and prepared them in his cell. He even planned to make a business venture out of this, but no one would pay to eat the stinking gray meat. I was morbid enough to try the seagull stew he whipped up, and found it dreadful. I told him that he was not going to make any money with his plan, and since he kept clogging the toilets by flushing feathers, he was going to get caught and punished for animal cruelty. There would never be enough demand for calories, or even for meat, that could support a seagull kitchen.

However, certain items were simply unavailable. There were foods that I could eat only four times a year on conjugal visits, assuming the joint I was in even had trailers for such visits. In preparation for the two breakfasts, two lunches, and two dinners that we would eat, I sent home menus with lists of ingredients. My wife would subsequently marvel at how I could devour a dozen eggs sunny-side up at a single sitting. The yolks were the rarity; the mess hall only served scrambled or hard-boiled eggs, which tasted as if they'd been stored in buckets of formaldehyde. The scrambled eggs came precooked in five-pound bags and were doled out with three-ounce ladles in the mess hall.

Commissary had had pints of liquid Egg Beaters available. While better than frozen lizards, none of the options provided the rich pleasure of chicken embryos. Details like this could lead to cultural misunderstandings. I had a neighbor named Light, who was a decent guy who had experienced some bad luck; his wife had left him when a clerical mistake identified him as being HIV positive. Everyone is tested before going on a trailer visit, and when she received a letter saying that her husband was now afflicted with the disease, she concluded that Light had been misbehaving in any manner of ways. He eventually got the matter straightened out, but by then his wife was gone, and he didn't have anyone to bring stuff for him to eat on trailer visits. Light said that he missed eggs more than anything, so when I had a chance to bring a few back from my own trailer visit, I did. I fried him two jumbos as best as I could, but he was turned off by liquid yolk as he never ate eggs sunny-side up. He asked me to cook them hard, and I refried them, wasting the precious egg yolks and learning a lesson. A youth spent in institutional settings like group homes and juvenile detention left one unprepared for certain tastes.

You learned to notice the signs of such a childhood. The guys raised rough were accustomed to mashed potatoes made from powder, thought lemon juice came from a plastic squirt jar, and never ate vegetables. They always ate their dessert first so that no one could take it away from them. Plastic cutlery was another part of their lives. Only I ate with a fork in my left hand when handling a knife with my right, or rather, the spoon that I had to cut with. Many men were quite fine with a spork for everything and I often saw spaghetti cut into mush with an upside-down cup so that it could be spooned up with the hybrid implement.

The prison doesn't need its inhabitants for much, but we did supply the labor and skill necessary to feed its population. Three hot meals a day for 2,500 hot-tempered men every day of the year is beyond the capability of the generally good-natured nurses, secretaries, and chaplains whose temperaments always won them the worst jobs. You need inmates to run chow.

Mess halls operate according to a uniform statewide menu that repeats in two-month cycles. Chow is served at seven, eleven, and five, though the meaner prisons push dinner ever earlier into senior-citizen territory to be done with the day faster. Coxsackie CF ran last chow at 3:30 p.m., leaving half a day to live off your dinner until breakfast.

The mess halls also marked most holidays with celebratory dishes. However, because of "budgetary concerns," the meals often felt like a way of informing us that we really didn't deserve holidays. The paucity of the annual Thanksgiving dinner only reminded us that we had blown our chance at enjoying a nice one. For eleven Thanksgivings in a row, I ate the official holiday luncheon of three slices of "turkey roll"; a ladle each of stuffing, instant mash, and peas; cranberry sauce from a giant can; and a piece of shitty cake. This holiday meal was hard to tell apart from the standard turkey dinner that we got one Sunday out of eight, except that the latter featured only two slices of turkey roll.

Five holidays, four of them federal and one a law enforcement favorite, had special meals. Christmas was roast beef, slices of rough brown substance that would terrify a civilian. New Year's meant chicken breast; Easter was turkey-ham and pineapple.

Surprisingly Martin Luther King Jr. Day was not marked with any special meal at all, while St. Patrick's Day, which is not a federal holiday, was celebrated with corned beef, cabbage, and potatoes.

Actually, no one was surprised. Minor holidays like Independence, Memorial, Labor, and Columbus Days all called for the same festive dinner of two hot dogs and two burgers, both made of chicken and soy protein molded into different shapes. Compared to the care that convicts put into their own baked mac and cheese, salmon croquettes, linguine alle vongole and other holiday food supplementing the turkey roll, etc., the prison kitchens' output was a cold comfort.

The mess halls themselves were large, impersonal spaces where the atmosphere was always tense, because like the yard, it was a place where a substantial portion of prisoners could congregate. And riot. The yards were overseen by men with guns in towers while the chow halls were guarded with technology. At decent intervals there are special three-hole blocks in the ceiling with a cop always on duty. Too much rebellion and he can make the holes launch gas canisters. A room to the side holds gas masks for the cops to don in case of a gassing. Prisoners know to tie wet T-shirts around their faces during these incidents; having had a few whiffs of tear gas, I can report that it makes armed insurrection a challenge.

Silence was once a tool used by jailers to "correct" their charges. Jeremy Bentham's panopticon required it, and Alexis de Tocqueville describes Quaker-run institutions of penitence kept so quiet that everyone wore slippers to mask even the racket of footfalls. While it is now generally understood that forcing quiet upon man, a social animal, is much likelier to foster insanity than contrition, certain rituals survive from the days when mess halls were places where prisoners ate without speaking. Before a prisoner leaves the table, he knocks on it. That is how "May I be excused?" is conveyed. Another prisoner will knock back, meaning, "No problem." I was taught how to politely knock before I ate my first morsel of incarcerated food.

Because this is America, hunger could not be used as a tool or weapon. Even during punitive lockdowns three meals were served a day. When a lockdown is announced, the prisoners are all confined to their cells, as one is usually enforced because of an unsolved violent crime or the disappearance of something dangerous. The entire prison staff is drafted to make sandwiches and hand them out. Twice I was fed bologna on white with mustard by the pretty secretaries. We'd never seen them before, as they worked in the front offices of the big house.

One time a lockdown was called because a cop had boiling oil splashed in his face, and the second time a weeklong one was conducted, and the prison searched from top to bottom, cell by cell, when a case of medical scalpels went missing. These were particularly dangerous things to get loose because they do not set off metal detectors.

Everybody with any experience knows that it is rare for such items to be stolen but common enough for the second-rate staff to lose them. All of the prison employees had reasons why they compromised on their jobs, as positions there were nobody's first choice. One doctor we had was court-ordered to practice medicine on us plebs after causing the death of one of the patricians he was used to healing. His bedside manner was noticeably absent, but there was also an Indian pathologist who just couldn't find work in his field and treated all of us like dead bodies.

A prison was expected to run a lockdown every year or so, just to confiscate all the contraband that inevitably accrued inside. On each block a cop would walk around at the beginning of the process and take all the lamps and Dutch ovens and electric woks and hand-sewn long-sleeve shirts and carved wooden spoons and cobbled-together stools and carved soap crucifixes and stash the stuff in his own locker. There it sat while the cells were searched, to be returned afterward. Because lockdowns were expensive they typically didn't last long; the lengthiest one I ever heard of was two weeks, in response to the unsettling discovery of a bag of bullets hidden in the prison. You wouldn't actually have needed a pistol to shoot them; a zip gun made out of a radio antenna could do the job.

Stripped of every other avenue of consumption, we prisoners used our alimentary system above and beyond its capacity, a logical extension of the role consumption has in ordinary society. Given the limitations on drinking, dancing, and fucking, we ate to mark occasions, an entire category of cultural enterprise that was officially denied to prisoners. The celebration of holidays, for example, could only be accomplished with feeding, as the requirements for every other ritual way of marking a day were unavailable to us. The mess halls may have made holiday meals that were underwhelming at best, but the prisoners cooked feasts that would blow your mind even outside the hungry context of prison. These traditional food-oriented events became warped. Thanksgiving turned into a competition of edible excess, with more food prepared by groups of prisoners than could be eaten. Much like in Native American potlatch custom, the power and wealth of communities was expressed in their ability to waste it. Every year I saw a friendly three-way competition between the three majority racial groups to host the most elaborate holiday meal. It was actually a rather good-natured struggle, as the resultant abundance made everyone share, and even the brokest inmates got a plate, although in exchange they were typically expected to clean up.

The reliance on food for celebration and to contrast the bleak and gray lives of repetitive misery that prisoners led did have unusual consequences. While Christmas and New Year's Eve remained traditional times for feasting, prisoner culture missed no occasion to celebrate something with good eating. Every year I saw elaborate nacho trays and heroes made for the Super Bowl. The Italians sometimes did Columbus Day meals, and St. Patrick's Day was marked by the Irish. It seemed that any occasion served a pretext to celebrate with gastronomic endeavors, since raising a glass was impossible.

Ramadan deserves its own discussion. Islam is the most successful of religions vying for prisoners' souls. According to the 2013 figures, 11 percent of convicts in American prison are Muslim, with a further 4 percent registered as Nation of Islam. In the general population, only 1 percent of Americans are Muslim. These prisoners are almost all black; the converts who are white and Muslim are typically also sex offenders or graduates of Protective Custody. Being Muslim in prison means much more than being a member of any other religion, because the community functions as a tribe or gang as well as a faith. Having unified under the banner of Islam, this block of black prisoners has won certain privileges and concessions from the administration, often in courtrooms. Jailhouse Muslims have "beard permits," allowing them facial hair beyond the permitted inch. They also cannot be transferred on Fridays and are allowed prayer rugs in their cells. Following the precedent set by the Nation of Islam, the Nation of Gods and Earths has graduated from being the proscribed gang known as the "Five Percenters" to recognition as a legitimate religion. It's no accident that the guards use the term "Prislam" to describe the phenomenon.

Islam has had a great effect on the mess halls. Pork was banished a generation ago. While a kosher diet is offered to adhere stricter rules of kashruth, there is no need for a halal alternative, since today *all* the meals are halal. However, every year there is a big affair around Ramadan. In theory the large Muslim population has been fasting all day. During the weeks of Ramadan, groups of men attend huge meals after the sun sets every night. Since hardly anyone is really fasting, much of the extra food from these feasts is sold off. Sometimes it is interesting: I was able to eat goat once a year inside. The spices ordered for the Muslim prisoners to cook their break-of-fast meals were another valuable commodity, though the staff was savvy enough to know that a tablespoon of nutmeg will make you trip and forbade it. Bodybuilders playing with their insulin levels used the

Ramadan cinnamon to alter their body chemistry. Outside Muslim organizations typically didn't offer too much help for the imprisoned converts, but a few of the men were actually Shia Muslims who did get attention from sponsors. As a result, I occasionally ate dates marked "Made in Iran," the only foodstuff I ever had from there. My parents fed me exclusively Russian caviar, never Persian.

For the neophyte Muslims of the incarcerated world, there wasn't much guidance on how to be a practitioner of *al-Islam*. The rare Middle Eastern prisoners were turned off by the frankly racialist nature of the Islamic congregations inside and kept their distance. As a result, the challenge to abstain from pork, so common an ingredient in soul food, played an outsized role. The suspicion that swine was being added to the meals as a way of defiling Muslims was a common one, and echoed the accusation that provoked the Great Mutiny against British Rule in India. I read in Jan Morris's brilliant *Pax Britannica* trilogy on the British Empire that in 1857, the revolt against the British East India Company was driven by a belief that rifle cartridges (which needed to be bitten open) were greased with pork fat to dishonor the Muslim soldiers of the Raj and alternatively with beef tallow, to break the caste of the Hindu soldiers. None of it was true, as the cartridges were lubricated with inorganic petroleum, but by then a lot of innocent people perished horribly in the Black Hole of Calcutta and by other innovative ways to kill sahibs and memsahibs.

While reading Morris's account, I heard my Muslim neighbors complaining about the latest place where they thought they had discovered pork. It was supposedly in the thin strip of glue on the rolling papers that came with Top tobacco, the cheapest smokable in the commissary. I didn't engage with this paranoia; by then I'd already heard enough about swine having been snuck into the unlikeliest meals of the mess hall. I asked true believers why they thought the state would go through so much trouble, risking lawsuits and revolt, just to get a lick of pork into them, and received the same type of responses that accounted for the supposed actions of the British Raj long ago.

Prisoners cooked in their cells for a variety of reasons, beyond avoiding the dangers of the mess hall. Some do so for money; I've spent many a pack of Newports on labor-intensive fried jack mac and yellow rice. Canned mackerel is the cheapest source of protein going; for a dollar you get a slab of South American fish in deadly brine, covered with slime but no scales, and almost completely gutted. It is technically already cooked, but is further prepared by being battered in corn flakes and fried in oil derived by freezing a jar of mayonnaise and siphoning it off. With a cold soda and rice, it made a nice dinner. I preferred the work of a Chinese entrepreneur who would fill a plastic glove with steamed dumplings for a "brick" of Newports and include a separate finger of dipping sauce.

More common was the chef who worked on demand. Such a jack-of-all-cuisines had spices, supplies, skill, and equipment, which he would deploy for ingredients you provided in exchange for a portion of his own. That was how I ruined a clothes iron making steak for fourteen Asian criminals.

A certain Tommy lived across the hall from me. He was reclusive, but everyone knew that he had a sentence longer than his life expectancy and that he hadn't just killed, but tortured. Chinese triads kidnap businessmen with cash or gold reserves, then torment them until they divulge the stash. If they're not wearing masks you know you're dead, but the job of a guy like Tommy is to make death preferable to life. Apparently match heads under the fingernails is a currently favored technique.

One day Tommy came to me with a request. When he asked if I could cook the bloody swaddled thing he was cradling, I momentarily backed away, preparing to make apologies for my lack of experience cooking babies, until I realized what I was looking at. It was a beef shoulder, fresh and bloody in butcher's paper. His crew inside of fourteen had scored it somewhere and decided they wanted American steak and potatoes. Even though they cooked elaborate meals for the gang every night, this was beyond their expertise. I took them at their word and nabbed the cellblock's clothes iron, used for pressing "visit shirts." Butchering the cow's deltoids into fifteen slabs of meat with two can tops was a difficult task that left me bloody to my elbows. Tommy looked into my cell and grimly nodded in approval at the by now terrifying sight of me.

The browned potatoes and mushrooms (both from a can) were easy enough to sauté in my wok, but getting the meat medium-rare using an iron was no simple matter. I had to press the hissing appliance into each side of the meat, and after a few slabs I could tell no clothing would safely pass under it ever again. Nonetheless I did manage to cook all the meat and sent the plates out, keeping an extra-rare one for myself.

They were all returned within fifteen minutes. For one thing, the diners thought I'd neglected to cook the meat all the way through. They all pointed at the blood pooling on their plates with distaste. There's apparently little appreciation for rare meat in the Chinese palate. I'd also not factored in their utensil of choice. These were mainland guys; each had his own set of hand-carved chopsticks. They were a mark of status, as the sticks were technically contraband. The intricate meals they ate nightly were always served in bite-sized morsels. Tommy decided I was just an idiot who didn't know to cut the meat small enough and, taking pity on me, brought over his own serrated can lid and chopped my carefully butchered steaks into hash. As the meat went back on the iron, he doused it with soy sauce, sugar, garlic, and MSG (which we had in the form of a seasoning called Sazón). As he flipped around the sizzling stir-fry, a Korean gangster came over carrying a garbage bag full of rice he had steamed.

My potatoes and mushrooms went into the rice. The meal was re-made into beef chop suey and placed on the rice. The men ate their food with gusto, claiming they knew they liked steak after all and I was just a typically stupid round-eye who needed their help.

The iron was a measure of last resort. The official methods of "chefing up" were the immersion heater and hot pot. The former was a three-buck coil with a fuse that would blow if you plugged it in without immersing it in liquid. For years I wondered how the little devices knew whether they were immersed or not until I learned that they contained pressure-sensitive sand. These cheap "stingers" could be retooled by soldering the fuse back to run off the current directly. That required patiently sawing open steel piping. The most radical method for boiling water was a wired nail clipper. Breaking the im-plement into two pieces—it didn't have to be a clipper; any steel would work . . . but don't try this at home—and attaching them to the positive and negative wires of a power cord with something non-conductive separating the poles is all you had to do. The rig would boil the water into which you dropped this terrifying device. Of course, you got what you paid for. The water would shock you if you touched it while it was plugged in, and the metal would visibly oxi-dize into rust while the reaction occurred. Everything you cooked by this method would have a reddish hue, which was probably harmless. Adding a pinch of salt made the water boil twice as fast, though you also get double the rust. Having once tried making this work in a steel sink, I can assure you that the consequences of letting the cur-rent complete the circuit with any medium but water are explosive. In older prisons, more than one cell is dependent on a single fuse, so I can also suggest being prepared to deny it if you should blow the power out for an entire tier. I sure did.

The clear plastic hot pots were eighteen dollars and couldn't boil. They had a thermostat that would stop the heating coil from getting the water any hotter than that required for instant coffee. It was not hard to get them to boil by rewiring them, but that was against the rules.

The cops knew what to look for and could simply put a bit of water into them to see if it boiled while they were digging around elsewhere during a standard monthly cell search. Different jails had different standards of vigilance. My first maximum security, where my decade sentence was considered short, had so many real problems that the cops would move my pot aside to search for serious contraband behind it. But at another jail, I had to electroplate a nub on the inside of a stainless steel shower to hang my cooking rig. Otherwise it would not have survived the searches.

I lost a dozen hot pots over the years by rigging them to boil, but the device really was useless as sold. The plastic cylinder and glue it's attached with could not handle the temperature needed to boil water. My first meal ever made in a retooled pot was a box of mac and cheese. I ended up eating raw pasta congealed into a plastic-laced ball.

The jailhouse aficionados' tactic was to disassemble the thing and discard all the plastic, as well as the aluminum base plate and internal electronics until the naked coil was all that was left. When its poles were hooked up to a current, it turned red-hot, just like the coils of an electric range. Once your coil was wired directly to a power cord and mounted on a tin can, you had an eye. Next you had to source a large can to use as a pot to cook in, and then collect whatever fat was needed to deep-fry chicken. You could be shocked by the open current, burnt by the blazing coil, or sloshed with boiling oil from a can balanced on the eye, which was without a lid or even a handle. But you could now cook delicious food in the privacy of your cell. No one would call this arrangement safe, but it functioned with brutal efficiency; cooking with pure electricity.

To cook with the stinger, either the homemade nail-clipper kind or the three-dollar version from commissary, you also needed plastic bags. Inside, clear plastic garbage bags are the most common option. When I was released in 2014, there was a fad for sous vide cooking—food sealed in plastic and immersed in a hot bath. It was familiar stuff; I'd been boiling bags of every type of food for years. There was some talk of dangerous chemicals off-gassing from the plastic being heated, but the worst incident I suffered was the loss of three heads of broccoli that my parents had kindly brought me. While draining a bag full of spaghetti and broccoli by jabbing holes in it with a fork over the toilet, I became impatient and was being scalded by the steam, so I tried to poke an extra hole in the dribbling container. Suddenly the whole thing released my lovely vegetables into the toilet bowl. Aghast, I started picking out the stalks but was caught in the act by Chino, my cooking partner. He simply asked me when I'd last cleaned the throne. We flushed the hot greens away.

Years of cooking with the limited ingredients I had at hand left me with a peculiar stove-side manner. I don't waste a damn thing, adding even the residue stuck to the inside of a can to pasta water. I never underestimate the value of a fresh piece of produce, compared to the second-rate products from cans, bags, and pouches. I ate one head of cabbage a month for years, so I know to peel it rather than cut it, if not using the entire thing. The same goes for an onion, no refrigeration required as long as you consume it layer by layer. I know that you can fry with mayo or extract the oil from it. In the summer you boil the (vented) jar, and in the winter you freeze it. Most important, I learned how much I appreciated good food, its comfort and its sustenance. It always gave me a reason to get through a day, to make it to next breakfast (egg pizza was the best, which they've since removed from the menu). Whether by limiting it or giving out extra, the authorities also recognized that food is undeniably the stuff of life.

16.

WHITE-POWER
SHOWER HOUR

In New York State there simply were not many Aryan Brothers or members of the Aryan Nation. We had a small population of incarcerated white men who claimed to be white-power driven, but they played a leadership role. Most of them were lifers, after all, with nothing to lose and no hope for parole. The ideology gave them something to live for. Being the minority of a minority, they didn't have much occasion to advertise, so as a show of force, they instituted a mass descent on the outdoor showers at the close of each yard period.

There were two looks available to the white-power guys: hairy and bald. They either sported Viking manes with braided beards, or boneheaded baldness and Fu Manchu mustaches. Both tribes used their white skin, so conducive to scrolling explosions of tattooing, as canvases. They relied on carefully composed images in ink to a far greater extent than the gangstas, Chicanos, or good ol' boys. The bodies of the white-power men could be read. Whether abstaining from shampoo altogether or employing quite a bit of it, the Viking types and skinheads both used communal bathing to compare the work they did on one another.

The abundance of ink was deployed for predictable and repetitive imagery, some of it primitive and hastily done, while other examples were meticulously detailed works of beauty and craft. There were traditional pieces that I would see over and over during my travels through the Incarcerated Nation. Swastikas often went over the heart. Some were crude, with lines not quite straight, angles short of ninety degrees and even tattooed backward at times. These were likely self-applied in county jails, often by the single white resident of a pod, pricked on in a rage perhaps after a beating or even rape at the hands of men of other races. Whites may be the majority of the American population, but, at least in New York State, they only accounted for 23 percent of the prison population. The chest swastikas sometimes came with adornments, or were composed of ax heads. Those that included splashes of red, black, and even the rare white ink were planned works, put on carefully and slowly as the centerpiece of the expression of a worldview. The neck was traditionally for SS lightning bolts, sometimes accompanied by a Wehrmacht helmet.

Tattooing the numbers 1488 was a Californian affectation, and denoted the fourteen words combined with a repetition of the eighth letter of the alphabet to indicate "Heil Hitler"; it could be inked anywhere. The back of each arm was a canvas for the words "White" and "Pride," respectively. The more daring replaced the latter with "Power." The former was more common; not all showers could be taken solely with white fellow bathers.

IT IS IMPOSSIBLE TO SERVE time as a white man and not have some relationship with the concept of white power. One cannot be neutral on the subject; the other prisoners do not allow it. Being white means being a minority, and a hated one at that. Not only are white inmates of the same race as the ultimate enemy, the prison staff that keeps the men imprisoned, but they are also of the race of the oppressors who make up the majority of the American population. And have the majority of American assets. Prison is where the tables are finally turned; whites without protective affiliations are hunted. Right and wrong left this room long ago. The categories that matter to white prisoners are "raped" or otherwise. Being a member of a white supremacist organization preserves one from such fates.

There are those who have tried to take the high road, preserving the moral ideology that is a luxury of those outside. Things don't end well for them. But you don't have to become a Nazi or a racist to survive the joint. I spent ten years as a Jew. However, you do have to pick a side, and if you make your choice based on the morals of the wrong society, the society you used to be a part of rather than according to the realities you now live under, you will pay dearly.

The presence of white supremacy in prison is almost universally misunderstood. The only writer I've encountered who perceived where it comes from is Andrew Vachss, who writes vigilante crime tales cast with romanticized ex-con characters. Vachss corresponded with New York convicts for material, so I actually read some of his letters. In books like *Flood* and *Strega*, he explores the dynamic that I witnessed every day.

Whites in prison suddenly find themselves to be a minority with the majority comprised of a population that is in the minority in the outside world. With the roles reversed, scores get settled. Until recently this meant rape; even during my term the one case in which "blood on a knife" prevented "shit on a dick" was interracial. The hardened kernel of tough white men use swastikas, learning the fourteen words ("we must defend white children . . .") and greeting each other with the number 88, to make themselves sound even harder. Vachss understood it correctly: an enormous amount of jailhouse white supremacy is simply born out of a desire to not be fucked in the ass.

THANKS TO AMERICAN TELEVISION, I expected the Aryan Brotherhood to be running the joints upstate. While I did meet plenty of pretenders, I did not, in fact, encounter any formal, active white-power organizations. A gang called the Dirty Dogs, which offered me a spot as a prospect that I turned down, used a barbed wire swastika as its patch, but it had Hispanic members and was not ideological or political in essence. White gang members are rare, and the ones I met were Bloods and Crips and not Nazi Lowriders, Hammerskins, or the Texas Syndicate. The latter three are white prison gangs from other parts of the country. This is not to say that the Brand, as the Aryan Brotherhood is known in the federal system, is not a force to be reckoned with.

Germ, a friend of mine doing time in Colorado, was told to cut the shamrock tattoo off his leg since he carried a "rock" without being "in the car." In that state having a shamrock tattoo indicated that you were an AB member. They offered Germ the chance to prospect, since he already had the ink, but he wasn't up to killing someone with his little four-year sentence halfway up. He had to take a few beatings before finally being left alone.

The media actually provides quite the feedback loop for prison gangsters. They learn how to be what they are from the screen, while the screen delves into jailhouse memoirs and hires ex-cons like me as consultants in its ever-deepening quest for authenticity and outrage. I experienced a remarkable interplay between televised fiction and reality myself in regards to this subject. The movie *American History X* was playing on the dormitory TV on Rikers Island on the very first night of my incarceration. I walked in at the moment when Edward

Norton says, "Put your mouth on the curb," and proceeds to kick a black man's skull in. At that moment everyone turned to look at me, the new guy who'd just walked in, and the only white in the room.

There were skinheads and self-styled "Aryans" even in New York City county jail and on Rikers Island, as well as in the state facilities. On my first day in, I was concerned enough about these groups that when it came time to declare my religion, I claimed it to be "none." No one told me about the benefits of claiming Judaism, and I did not realize that half of my peers in the same situation insisted they were Jewish just to get kosher trays of food. In later years I witnessed groups of men tattooed in full Third Reich regalia queuing up for kosher meals, joking that getting the Jews' good food through the subterfuge of claiming Judaism as their faith was an act of resistance against the ZOG machine. That would be "Zionist-occupied government," of course.

Plenty of prisoners knew the vocabulary of white supremacy and even had the ink to match while being culturally somewhat less than committed. For example, I knew dozens of guys who claimed white power while listening exclusively to rap music. This kind of prisoner would say the word "n——" to whites with one meaning implied while (carefully) deploying it in conversation with black friends in a very different way. The use of that word was a very easy way to justify a gang beatdown.

Many of the people drawn to white power had deep personal problems and insecurities. They longed for the kind of family that racialism promised, even when it was clear that the established white-power guys would prey on the new and young ones. After all, there were always drug bills, which were typically and hypocritically owed to members of other races. The drug trade certainly did not respect racial boundaries, and the demographic that the committed racists came from was particularly susceptible to substance abuse. The truth was that I never met a soldier of the White Resistance who wasn't a chemical enthusiast.

For some reason fascism and dope usage often run in tandem. I read in Albert Speer's *Spandau: The Secret Diaries*, about Hermann Göring, second in command of Hitler's Reich and a venerable morphine addict. Jailhouse junkie neo-Nazis knew about his history and often cited it. Göring picked up his addiction to morphia while recovering in Sweden from airborne warfare in World War I. When captured by the Allies, he was medically titrated down from a morphine habit greater than the army doctors had ever encountered before. When he managed to commit suicide by convincing his American guard, Tex, to bring him a cyanide capsule, he was still being treated with ever-diminishing doses of the opiate.

Reading Albert Speer's accounts of addicted Nazis made me wonder about the paradox. *Mein Kampf* was all about healthy minds in healthy bodies, and the German enthusiasm for sport and nature and "naturism" did not jibe with dependence on opiates. The answer might be that men are drawn toward both fascism and addiction by personal weaknesses.

The neo-Nazis also embraced tattooing, which was not a cultural artifact of historical fascism. In fact, it was the European royals and royalist aristos who had themselves tattooed, as well as lower-class sailors. Joseph Roth's *Radetzky March* and Frederic Morton's *Nervous Splendor: Vienna 1888–1889* opened up worlds of nineteenth-century life to me. When Archduke Franz Ferdinand was autopsied after being shot by Yugoslav nationalist Gavrilo Princip, thus starting the First World War, he was found to have an inked Japanese snake winding itself around his entire arm. Czar Nicholas was also known to have an elaborate tattoo. The Nazi SS officers above a certain rank did have their blood type tattooed in their armpit for emergency battlefront transfusions, but by their time tattooing was no longer an aristocratic affectation. And even those tiny letters denoting blood types proved to be sufficient to get them killed after the war, when Sturmführers attempted to melt into the population but were betrayed by this bit of Teutonic efficiency.

Nevertheless, tattoos were everything for the Nazis I knew, despite the absence of a line of continuity between their heroes of yore and the scribbled street criminals of today. The tattoos were often fading to blue, poorly drawn, and even misspelled. A friend and I used to compete to find the worst tattoo in the yard that day. I won the game by finding a guy who had "Born to Loose" tattooed on his arm. The loser was actually a rather pleasant fellow, though a murderer, and wasn't aware of the horrendous spelling he carried for the rest of his life on his skin. I once played lookout while a white-power junkie called "Tattoo Bob" inked a letter on the back of a kid's neck. Bob had his eye on the two-Newport-pack payment for the tattoo, as he was dopesick and it would buy him the 60 mg of morphine that would set him straight. Tattooing in the yard was dangerous, being strictly forbidden, and therefore rushed; Bob made a mess of the letter. I was only supposed to be the lookout but got pulled in deeper when the kid asked me how the scribbles looked. What could I do but lie? I said it was great but without the expected enthusiasm. He noticed my hesitation and asked what letter I was reading. Bob barely had enough time to mouth "G," which I promptly parroted, satisfying the poor client. I had been deciding whether to guess "K" or "X."

Many of the swazis and bolts get inked inside, as few tattoo shops are willing to commit the pictorial equivalent of hate speech, or at least they don't advertise that they do that kind of work. The jailhouse tattoos are applied with machines made from Walkman motors driving a guitar string, or even more primitively, poked in with sewing needles and ink made of charred chess pieces. The latter were inevitably bloody affairs that often got infected.

My fascist lifting partner Chris Slavin actually did have his work done in a Long Island shop. It was the most egregiously offensive tattoo I have ever seen, and he had it in full technicolor right on his belly. I first noticed the antisemitic atrocity as he spotted for me on the bench press when we exercised together. His stomach had two figures drawn on it: a skinhead executioner in boots and braces who loomed over his pleading victim, a *landsman* of mine. The boot-boy swung an ax over his head, about to lop off the bearded rabbi's head.

Slavin was a white-power guy, but also one of the few men I ever met who was in for a hate crime. The tattoo helped convict him, as the image was presented as evidence at his trial. By making the assault he was convicted of into a hate crime, his sentence ballooned into what other guys serve for murder. The tattoo was the only evidence of that kind of motive in the assault, although the victims were Mexican. Slavin appealed this abuse of the First Amendment, as he viewed it, though he did not deny that he had assaulted a man. He protested that it had not been for ideological reasons and argued that a tattoo put on his body at another time and place should not affect the evaluation of a later incident.

My job as the facility rabbi's clerk did not change the fact that it was me who Chris looked for to have conversations with in the yard. He knew I was a Jew, and I knew he was a neo-Nazi. He sought me out because I could keep up my end of a historical-political dialogue and play the straight man, representing mainstream society (a role to which I was unaccustomed), as a foil to his radical ideology. He insisted I read the newsletters he got from Resistance, which provided white convicts in the prisons that did not ban it with news and support for a certain worldview. Under the rules proscribing gang materials, a lot of white-power material was forbidden. The authorities feared it would stir up race riots in the yards, while prisoners believed this censorship was evidence of the great truths concealed from them by the ZOG.

Resistance was the same outfit that sold cassette tapes (exclusively for the antediluvian prisoners who had never graduated to CDs) of bands like Skrewdriver, Johnny Rebel, and the Blue Eyed Devils. The members of the latter skinhead band were very active in the movement and came up to Green Haven Correctional Facility to visit Slavin. Because he had been convicted of a hate crime by a tattoo, a perfectly legal form of expression, according to the First Amendment, Slavin was considered a small-time martyr among some. I even saw an interview with him in a German nationalist publication online. Having his cause embraced by the extreme right wing did not help him win a reversal, dooming his appeal in the court of public opinion as well as in court.

BEYOND CHRIS SLAVIN AND "Skinhead Stevo" and "Nazi Dave Luck" and "SS Will," there was a crowd of white prisoners whom I nodded hello to but didn't really know. In turn, the WP guys didn't quite know what to do with me. I was blond, blue-eyed, and covered in muscles, but insisted on claiming myself as a Jew. They knew they were supposed to hate Jews, but few were clear on exactly who they were. Were Jews still Jews without beards? Did Jews remain the Enemy without yarmulkes? Or without a finger in international finance? To confuse matters, there were actual incarcerated Jews wearing full Hasidic regalia, or just a skull cap, and then there were wannabe Jews who wore a *kipa* after converting themselves, and crazies who wore them to stay warm, as only Jews and Muslims were permitted headwear inside the drafty halls. Defining a Jew was hard, because some Jews dressed like Jews and some didn't. Some had control of the media, and others did not . . . Most of the purported anti-Semites had had very little experience with actual Jews. I will never forget the one neo-Nazi whom I asked why he hated Jews so much.

He kept trying to avoid answering me until he finally said, "Because they're so fucking stupid!"

The forces of Aryan Resistance had a state-sanctioned religion all their own. I intentionally mispronounced "Odinism" as "onanism," but no one ever got my joke, even when I referenced Genesis as the source forbidding the sin of Onan. The materials for the resurrected worship of the Norse pantheon came from cold Midwestern states, and it was clear that the majority of Odinists were incarcerated. All their documents insisted that the dagger required for their ceremonies could be symbolically represented, in hopes of placating the authorities who already didn't trust this newfangled religion. The Odinists had already won the right to wear a symbol of their faith in court. You could order a Thor's Hammer from Resistance, and that was the first thing neophytes did once their change of religion papers came through.

It was hard for me to take the resurgence of Viking faith seriously. There were rituals honoring Thor, and I found it hard not to imagine the American comic book hero. Considering the limited reading most of the men had done, I imagine I wasn't the only one. That didn't prevent one blond-maned killer from Indiana, who earned himself a life sentence with a forgotten murder committed as soon as he crossed the state line into New York, from adopting the name Thor for himself. I met him in my first year, when he was young and hirsute. The last time I saw him was years later, on a bus headed toward my last prison. Thor was being taken to Southport CF, to go serve a year in solitary. He proudly told me it was for "ventilating" someone. Age had apparently put enough gray in his hair to send him to the bald-headed end of the white-power spectrum.

However, he still had a long plaited Viking beard.

The same court decision that upgraded Odinism to a recognized

religion also allowed its practitioners to join Jews, Muslims, and Rastafarians in being exempt from the rule limiting beards to one inch in
length. Correctional officers looking to make their bones carried tape
measures to enforce the rule for those without beard permits.

The majority of Odinists were exactly who one would expect;
skinheads like Chris Slavin or biker types. I never encountered a
black member, but plenty of Latinos were involved. After meeting an
Arab with a back-sized Third Reich tattoo, I knew not to be surprised
by any combinations. However, there was one Odinist named Uzi.
Borrowing the name of an Israeli gun seemed like a poor choice for a
white supremacist who was already Puerto Rican, and sure enough,
he turned up as a practitioner of Santería, the Latino voodoo, a few
jails down my road. He still had a prominent swastika tattooed on
his chest, right where a bow tie would go. But in this milieu, I learned
not to be surprised by anything.

AS A STUDENT AT NYU (class of 2000), I had spent a semester abroad
at Copenhagen University. I had wanted a far-flung locale where English was spoken and I could smoke weed. Somehow I had the sense
to realize that Amsterdam, with its no-nonsense drug culture, might
be the death of me. Denmark was the perfect compromise, though I
still made the worst of it. I studied Norse sagas and found bad influ-
ences. I learned to smoke heroin from Arne, a warlock who made
sacrificial daggers to fund his "hobby." He tempered the hand-
wrought steel blades in blood in the Swedish northlands and arrived
by ferry with a canvas bag of them to sell at outrageous rates to waiting covens in the sophisticated Copenhagen suburbs. Once the daggers were sold, Arne bought a lot of heroin in Vesterbro, the Danish
version of a bad neighborhood. The study of Danish history was my
official reason for spending 1997 in Denmark, but I also learned how

to roll balls of smoking heroin into figure-eights on a foil from this pagan jack-of-all-trades. Arne has since drowned, a sad coda for the first messenger from Valhalla who hinted that the gods I knew from the Icelandic sagas had living devotees.

My professor, Michael Lerche Nielsen, took care of my formal education. Learning the two dozen ancient runes was part of the course. I never imagined how this would come in handy and where, but I wound up teaching a prison class in the runic alphabet. I was already exercising on the same court as the Odinists and was on friendly terms with their only member who had been convicted of an actual hate crime, Chris Slavin. I was willing and able to teach the runic alphabet, but of course, I was also the rabbi's clerk. Nevertheless, I could use a bit of acceptance from these people who didn't understand me, let alone have any fondness for Woody Allen characters like myself. As if by consensual hallucination, my Zionism was elided, and in the end the Odinists mostly shrugged and figured, "Doesn't look Jewish."

I taught the class with both great success and none. Many of the Odinists were struggling with the English language, so Old Norse did not make a big resurgence. I knew more prisoners who had taught themselves Hebrew than Odinists who mastered runes. The Elder Futhark comprises twenty-four runes, and even though I diligently wrote them out on the blackboard for every class, no one ever seemed to gain any familiarity with the alphabet. At the same time, having someone spend time to teach them something arcane and obscure flattered the white supremacists to no end. They never missed a call-out, as somehow my lessons legitimized their crackpot faith; I re-member how bitterly disappointed they were to learn that modern Vikings of the five Nordic states (six, counting the Faroe Islands, seven with Greenland) were Lutherans rather than pagans. They imag-ined modern Swedes sacrificing heifers to one-eyed Odin, god of thunder, patron of raping and plunder. I opted not to tell them about Scandinavian feminism and humanitarian superpowers.

Chris was amazed by my associating with the Odinists but was intelligent enough to understand that I would never tattoo a swastika on myself, and not only because I was Jewish. Having read Spengler and Goebbels (as have I; *The Goebbels' Diaries 1939–1941* are compelling reading), he understood that another determining factor was class. I was too educated, too foreign, too distant in socioeconomic class from his own background. Chris Slavin was the rare prisoner who valued me for these traits rather than despite them.

When I asked him how a smart guy like him had come to such views, he tried to give me *My Awakening*, David Duke's book. I was curious but ultimately declined, worried about the impression it would make on passersby. I didn't want to be mistaken for one of these guys. Even in prison they are some of the most despised. I felt I had disappointed Chris, so I took a volume called *Complete Sagas of the Icelanders* instead. It came from a mutual acquaintance, a skinhead from Queens whom I had known as far back as Rikers Island.

I'm sure only I read the huge thing. It took me a while to finish, and although I was able to add the tome to my booklist, it did not add to my understanding of the Odinists.

I did read two books by a real Nazi. Speer, Hitler's architect, offered more insight than others. The first was called *My War*, and it described how an intellectual of his class could have been seduced by vulgar, lumpen Hitler. Speer weaves endless rationalizations, but in the end his accession to the cause was a form of stockholm Syndrome. That term was popularized during the trial of Patty Hearst. She was an heiress to the Hearst publishing fortune when she was kidnapped by the Symbionese Liberation Army. They kept her in a closet, raped and beat her, and on their next bank robbing outing, she joined them, toting a gun. When she was captured and put on trial, the family deployed its resources to hire a brilliant defense attorney. He got her off by claiming Stockholm syndrome, a psychological condition in which the utterly powerless gravitate to whatever source of power is available, even if it is the oppressive power of an enemy. All of Weimar Germany can be said to have been in the thrall of the syndrome, with Hitler as the power vector. Speer admitted as much in his own case; only Hitler had the power to make his architectural renderings reality. The entire nation of Germany, sick and poor during its Weimar period, was in the syndrome's thrall to Hitler. Likewise, the white minority of prisoners, suddenly finding themselves weak after a lifetime of strength drawn from membership in the majority population, also gravitates to the only source of power available to it, no matter how questionable, hypocritical, and immoral it is.

But Speer wrote a second book, describing the twenty years he spent in Spandau prison with the other Nazi war criminals judged unnecessary to hang. In it he describes his gradual distancing in Spandau from the men who told themselves over and over how they could have won the war, how they should have won it. Speer came to recognize that their convictions were a symptom of their malady, one that he had once also been a victim of, but no longer.

As the years passed I found it much easier to ignore the white-power guys. Whoever found his pride in his skin didn't have much to begin with. When I looked up Chris Slavin on the outside and saw that his appeal had been denied, I wasn't surprised. The argument that a tattoo on a perpetrator cannot turn his actions into hate crimes required those judging him to actually see the tattoo. The First Amendment argument was clear, and yet it was one nasty tattoo. And so, in Chris's case, first impressions remained the final impression. The image defeated everything else. In one sense, the white supremacists, both hairy and hairless, depend on exactly that fact. And in the end, they are also doomed by it.

17

MUERTE

Every breath you take is one subtracted from the total allotted to you. Every step you take is another toward your grave, and every moment lived is but another in the countdown to death that is the very definition of mortal life. One of the blessings of youth is the ability to live in ignorance of that wretched truth, and a great part of the bitterness that is aging consists of a progressive inability to no longer exist without the knowledge of where it all leads to. A stay in prison, at any age, is a poignant reminder of the enormous role of death in life, because death is seemingly far closer to the surface of things in a prisoner's life. Much like in war, the possibility of death is around every corner of the big house. And inside, death is not treated in accord with the modern methods of sanitizing and sweetening it. There are no euphemisms; men can be "taken off the count." No one "passes away," and bodies are treated as the soulless meat that death leaves them.

The death penalty has not been used in New York State for more than a generation. Capital punishment was only taken off the books in 2007, but it hadn't been used since 1984. There is no "death row" of prisoners condemned to death, appealing the decision, and milling with activists determined to save them. Many more prisoners than you would think support capital punishment because they have elaborate justifications for the murders they committed. Also, most death penalty cases are rape-murders, and according to jailhouse morals, rapos deserve death.

Green Haven CF still has a death house, with a scary wooden electric chair shown to visiting dignitaries. It was called "Old Sparky" and had been transferred from Sing Sing in 1971, along with the horror movie leather face mask and straps and copper skull plates. A cop who wanted to repay a favor I had done for him unlocked the door and let me sit in the chair. I did not experience any sensation of haunting or anything else while seated there.

You hardly need to receive the death penalty to die in prison. The sentence of "natural life" is a very rare one, but plenty of men get twenty-five to life at ages when it is tantamount to a life sentence. And death comes to the prisoner at a rate much higher than it does for normal folks. It comes through violent means, through natural causes, and by invitation. The latter, death by one's own hand, was perhaps the most frequent unnatural cause, since murder inside is much less common than it used to be. "Jail bodies"—casualties involving prisoners—were prosecuted more leniently before the nineties. Taking another prisoner off the count would only prolong your sentence by a couple of years back then, and there were men who had killed fellow prisoners several times. I met men who had killed inside. They had "thousand-yard stares" and solid reputations.

After having demonstrated their capacity for murder, they spent the rest of their bids without being tested and driven to commit any further acts of violence. However, I cannot say if it changed them. Some were marked by their crimes, others were like anyone else you would meet.

Perhaps the state considered this situation a means of fighting crime, or cutting costs. However, in the nineties murders in prison began to be counted toward the crime rate of the counties where they're located, and at that point they could no longer simply be swept under the rug. Today killing a bunky will get you twenty-five to life. Nobody with a chance of going home wants to die in prison over some yard beef, so there is a resurgence in the popularity of cutting instead of stabbing. So many men walk around with scarred faces that the term "gangster slash" has become common.

Of course, things still have a way of happening. As soon as I got to my first joint, a likable man named Kojak was killed in a terrible way. He looked like a black version of the character Telly Savalas made famous, and always had a crowd of listeners for the street sagas he told from his wheelchair while out in the yard. Kojak was a paraplegic, and you might wonder why it would be necessary to keep such an invalid in prison. In fact Green Haven had a whole wing for them, and there were even some quadriplegics housed there. I once asked a new superintendent, who went out in the yard to meet the guys and demonstrate how progressive he was, why it was necessary to incarcerate the handicapped. He motioned pulling a trigger, and said that as long as they could do that, they were a danger. And yet that was clearly not a possibility for quadriplegics. Each of these men was assigned an inmate assistant, which was considered a plum posting, because the paralyzed men were prescribed morphine, which they doled out to cajole their nurse-convicts for the help. The state paid nineteen cents an hour for the job, and it was a hard one. As well as feeding and serving another inmate, you had to bathe him and help him defecate.

Prisoners are known neither for their compassion nor their empathy. Kojak's assistant got into a disagreement with his ward, probably over narcotics. He ceased using his finger on Kojak's asshole; the man couldn't feel the difference anyway, so he never knew his bowels were not being induced to work. He couldn't feel the build-up of feces over a few weeks and was told he was defecating by the assistant, and when he died, it was put down as natural causes, even though everyone knew what had happened. I liked Kojak and was shocked by how casually everyone took this death. It being my first year, I hadn't seen as much death as they had. I ended up reading the cartoonist John Callahan's *Don't Worry, He Can't Get Far on Foot* for a better understanding of quadriplegics and the tormented dependence they have on their helpers. Callahan was doused with his own urine and left for it to freeze on his face for three days when his unstable nurse ran out on him. They had argued over drugs. Kojak's sad end, it seemed, wasn't unusual.

The first violent death, caused by a blade rather than neglect, on my watch was actually an accident. A very slight black guy who didn't weigh much over a hundred pounds was paid a bundle of dope, ten bags of heroin worth $300 to $400, to take a Puerto Rican dealer out. He was just supposed to injure him enough to send him out of jail, but he pierced an organ with his homemade aluminum ice pick instead. Everyone knew everything, but no one said a word. The crime went unsolved. From observing my fellows, I learned that taking the news stone-faced was part of being a stand-up guy.

I'd heard of Ñeta gang executions, sit-downs where court was held and judgments passed. If a conviction is voted for, the unlucky victim gets garroted with an electric cord the moment his guilt is ascertained. The Ñetas were notorious in the Puerto Rican prison system for making bodies disappear. The flesh and crushed bones would all be flushed down the toilets, and skulls were famously broken apart inside of pillow cases. It would drive the guards crazy when their counts wouldn't add up after a convict was flushed into oblivion.

The condition of incarceration sometimes preserved men, causing them to appear to be dozens of years younger than their age. The enforced sobriety and regularity of routines helped. But at the same time, the prevailing stress made long lives rare. The end was often brought on by a grinding sense of menace, daily fear, and the demands of maintaining a level of aggression.

Old age was the biggest killer I witnessed. Medical care was provided in prison, and men were treated for conditions ranging from cancer to HIV, but inmates couldn't get organ transplants, though a friend of mine did manage to give his mother a kidney.

Everyone smoked, and the food was unhealthy. The state prison system, enlarged for the crime wave of the crack years and now forced to close prisons as the population dropped year after year, found itself having to deal with the novel problem of the incarcerated elderly. The senile, dying prisoners among us were shuffled into purpose-built hospice units. There they remained inmates but were simultaneously patients. They had no yard, which meant no friends. Men grown old inside rarely had anyone left outside. So no social life, no human contact, except for the nurses, and the nurses who work in prison hospices cannot work anywhere else for whatever reason. Hospice convicts can't make their own food. They can't even smoke cigarettes. All the old guys feared the hospices and avoided them for as long as they could, because once admitted, there was only one way out. The poor bastards in jailhouse hospices can only do what was expected of them and soon drop dead. And they mostly do; it might be the preferable option.

Keeping the elderly incarcerated is obviously costly because of the medical care required and makes for bad politics whenever the huge DOC budget is attacked as wasteful. The state recently opened a second hospice unit to deal with its fast-growing and most expensive demographic. The problem of a growing proportion of senior citizen inmates explains the existence of something that is disguised as a compassionate element of the system. There is a procedure for medical parole, which is theoretically granted to terminal cases, allowing men to die outside the walls. In my ten years I'd never seen it granted.

The requirements to qualify are almost impossible to meet. You have to have a diagnosis of six months or less to live, to start, but there are other limitations intended to prevent a freed convict from using those last months to misbehave, which eliminates anyone who actually needs the medical parole. After all, the behavior of a prematurely released criminal could end a political career. In Massachusetts the crimes committed by a man temporarily released on a similar program called a furlough ended the entire furlough program and played a role in denying Michael Dukakis the presidency. Willie Horton, who raped a woman when the candidate was governor of the state, was brought up to show how soft on crime the Democrat was. New York hasn't had furloughs in decades.

As one might guess, there is a frequently changing Oldest Prisoner in the New York State Department of Corrections. I knew one who had a month or two to live but a decade to serve; Joe was in his eighties but had whacked someone at the age of seventy. He almost got the release, as he actually satisfied the criteria. However, it was discovered that he had committed a felony before his tour in WWII, and this juvenile record disqualified him by being a multiple felon. Someone had searched through the paper files predating the digitized archives and the microfiche material just in case. Joe took it well. He died one morning soon after in utter silence. It was a long time before any of us seeing him go with such dignity broke it.

Death made all kinds of magic usually beyond the pale a reality for prisoners, much as it had required the death of his mentor for Jean Valjean to reach freedom in Victor Hugo's *Les Misérables*. Funeral visits to the outside world were a possibility for some, the "death-bed visit" another opportunity to leave the incarcerated world, however briefly. But not both; you could either say goodbye to a parent or appear at their funeral. Civilian clothes were issued for those attending funerals, but so were two armed guards, and the shackles were never removed. The local police were informed of the presence of a convict in their domain and would also appear at the funeral. Not everyone can get releases in these cases. The man in charge of security in each prison must evaluate the threat posed by each individual funeral trip. Some men are considered too violent to go, while others are too well connected. In my first year upstate I was shown the patch of pavement on which a DOC captain was stabbed after he denied a man the chance to attend his mother's funeral.

When my grandfather died, I had the option but did not choose to go. Guests had come to pay their respects to my father's father from three continents. I loved him dearly but did not want anyone to see a grandson in shackles. It was probably bad for my grieving process, but my parents were relieved. I was sent photographs of the service. I never looked at them much.

The loss was followed by that of my grandmother three years later. It saddened me greatly that my grandparents died with the bitterness of their beloved only grandchild serving a sentence. I never had a chance to show them I could do better. Those are the consequences of my bad decisions. Other men with longer sentences had to suffer through the deaths of their entire families. One man I knew lost his in a car accident while driving upstate to see him. He devoted his life to heroin from then on. I was fortunate to still have my wife and parents living when I was released.

The correlation between incarceration and suicide has been evident since man came up with the concept of jailing man. Primo Levi described Jews choosing death over the camps, and Solzhenitsyn wrote about suicide as the last choice left to a man, usually turned to when all others were extinguished. "Taking yourself off the count" was something that would happen, punctuating the bid, with alarming frequency. All the naive suicide prevention measures in place ignored the fact that this population had the best reason to off itself of any.

Why shouldn't a person ordained to die in prison choose the time to do so? The cops are trained to arrest suicide attempts and notice the signs of planned ones. It's hard to believe the authority's stated motives in preventing suicide, since they spend every single moment not saving lives but poisoning them. And in the end, the guys who want to go cannot be stopped.

The men who intended to kill themselves were not the same as the ones who threatened to do so. I learned this lesson most personally when selling off a few extra bottles of shampoo, a brand I stopped using after this episode. A neighbor serving a long bid for a murder came by and sniffed the azure goo I was hocking with appreciation. He was a man from upstate, a working fellow. I knew he had no money, so I just gave him a bottle of the blue soap. He said thanks, put it in his cell, and went outside to use the phone.

Whatever he heard on that call caused him to hang himself behind his door that afternoon, after waiting for the cops to do their count. A few hours later they found him, hanging quite dead in his cell. We were all kept locked in, while the bureaucratic procedure of reducing the prison population by one grinded through its gears. Someone in a suit came and signed off on the cause of death. While ruling out murder was good for the prison's individual statistics, it was terrible for the cop whose shift it was. In theory the cops were supposed to ascertain every fifteen minutes that each inmate was breathing. Sometimes a newjack would take this seriously and wake up men sleeping at night with blankets or coats over their faces. In reality, nothing could have prevented this man's suicide. He had never even hinted at any self-destructive tendency previously and timed his hanging over a shift change.

They took his body out on a vintage steel mesh stretcher, but got tired halfway down the tier and dropped it right in front of my cell. The angle was perfect for me to take a good look. My neighbor's face was the same shade as the shampoo I had given him just that morning, a cheerful lurid blue. Later that evening I went down to his cell to ascertain whether he had ever washed his hair with the shampoo he so clearly coveted.

The bottle was unopened; I concluded that he had not intended to die that morning. Death really did come for him that afternoon and not a moment earlier. Soon after, I was personally involved in another suicide attempt, being the one to discover it.

A man we called the Crow because of his Gothic look decided to take a big ball of crack off a dealer, with no way to pay the several hundred dollars it cost. He spent the whole night smoking the stuff and tried killing himself in the morning. That must have been the plan all along, because the people he had taken it on credit from were not easy guys to owe. It cannot have been a very pleasurable evening of cocaine, if death was to be the last hit.

I worked as the block porter and had to be the first one up and about in the morning, handing out hot water. The cells had taps, but only for cold water, and federal regulations require prisoners to be given access to hot water for bathing. This was accomplished by my pouring it into prisoners' wash buckets through a long black plastic watering spout, which I replenished from a wheeled garbage can I filled with hot water from the showers. When I got to the Crow's cell, he was waiting for me. He was too weak to speak, so he just showed me the bucket he had filled with his blood. His wrists were slashed, but he could still walk. It turned out he didn't want to die after all. I called the cops and locked myself in my cell, knowing that all hell would break loose while the Crow was being saved.

After his hospitalization, he was given three months in the box. That was for dirty urine; they didn't charge him for self-harm, although they could have. Suicide is against the rules. The authorities did find out why he'd done it, and didn't like it one bit. In a perverse form of outlaw justice, after solitary they did not transfer him to another prison. Instead they moved the Crow back into the same block as the guy he owed. The dealer put him on a payment plan that had him turning over his meager state pay of four dollars every two weeks for more than a year. The COs had no intention of doing crackheads any favors, it would seem.

SUICIDE IN THE BOOKS of Yukio Mishima or James Clavell's *Shōgun* can appear noble, the ultimate way to take one's life into one's own hands. The works of Marcus Aurelius and Epictetus also suggest that the Stoics died when they wished to. Choosing where, when, and how you die appears brave on the printed page, but the reality is rather different. A palliative taking of one's own life in the case of disease is hard to oppose unless relying on the strictures of religious faith, but such conditions didn't describe the cases I saw.

Every one of the suicides that touched my experience was the expression of mental illness. And they hurt everyone they touched. The Crow was actually married, so I imagine a woman somewhere eventually paid for his attempt. My neighbor with the shampoo had children. They were grown-ups and already had to live with a father in prison, and now this. Killing yourself is selfish. It simultaneously and terminally kills a part of everyone who cares about you.

Perhaps the most disheartening jailhouse deaths are the ones that strike after the bid is over. My friend Red, actually named Anthony Jenkins, served out an entire term with humble dignity for killing his wife. He wore a daily smile on his face. But after the fifteen years he completed, he relapsed on drugs and hanged himself from a tree less than a year after his release. I'd been out for two years by then. My friend texted me that night but was already dead as I frantically called him back, over and over. Because his body was not discovered for a few days, we all thought he might still appear, perhaps at my home. I didn't know anyone who handled incarceration better than Red, but it got him in the end. It was hard to process and took me years to erase the texts from my phone. My wife took me to the woods, made me cry about the injustice of it all, and I got rid of those final words he sent me. Always the gentleman, he had simply written, "I'm proud of you." When I had read that, I knew Red was saying goodbye.

Another friend who died was Oscar Ramos, aka Chino, and by now familiar to the reader from these pages. He survived almost twenty years of incarceration as an inveterate clown. His sense of humor was as twisted as my own; we used to greet each other with the ultimate fighting words of prison, "Suck my dick." He made it back to the real world after his long bid for a murder committed in a nightclub over a beef his younger brother had with people whose names he didn't know, but died of water in his lungs a year later. Like Red, Oscar superbly adapted to the rigors of the hard life Inside. Perhaps their adaptation just went too well, and returning to regular life is what did them in.

Since death cheats the state out of its years, no one is riding it out to freedom like Jean Valjean. They autopsy everyone who dies inside in the locked wing of the local hospital, and there is more than one Potter's Field for burying the men who never make it out. In a cost-saving measure, policy is to cremate the bodies. The state won't even let people kill themselves out of jail, as it's a tier 3 offense and you get ninety days for your first attempt, a year for your third. I'm sure the dime I served will cost me as much in the end. While I was sober and healthy for ten years, I lived in a world of daily stress and fear. But having watched death pass ever closer inside, I've lost a little of my fear of the valley of the shadow. I know it leaves you blue. I know that when it comes, there's no avoiding it. You can invite death in at any moment, but you cannot decline such an invitation yourself. Death certainly visits us prisoners more often than it does the residents of think tanks, or submarines, or kindergartens. It's not because death likes the place. Maybe he thinks he's doing us a favor. But he's wrong, just as Red was wrong. Prison may feel like a living death at times, but even that's preferable to the alternative. There's always breakfast in the morning, if you can't think of anything else to live for.

18

SYMPATHY FOR THE DEVIL

My name was called over the yard loudspeaker, never a good thing on a sunny morning, and I had a bad feeling about it. Praying that I was doing this just in case, I bid farewell to guys I'd been talking to—Leo the former monk, and V³, who politely listened to our discussion of George Bernard Shaw without understanding a damned word of English. After our *adieux*, I walked to the gate of the yard to discover my fate. Cops were waiting for me, and I never saw either of my two friends again.

Suddenly I found myself handcuffed and roughly thrown into the back of a prison van. The contents of my pockets were all tossed in front of me, lest I pull some kind of MacGyver with the earplugs and Tootsie Roll I'd had on me. Going to the box at Cayuga Correctional Facility meant a van ride to the attached special housing unit. Even though it was in easy walking distance, it was considered its own facility, so I was subtracted from the Cayuga count and added to the SHU population. Vans were considered a safer form of convict movement than walking us. Perhaps that is why we were referred to as "packages" across the cop radio band. The handcuffing was to prevent a last-ditch escape or revenge attempt. The van was brutally spartan. It had no seats or benches in the section for "packages," and because I was cuffed behind my back, whenever I was inevitably thrown to the floor, I could not get up. When my ride was over, I was dragged out because I couldn't maneuver very well anymore.

After the seven years that I'd already done in the incarcerated world at this point, I had become accustomed to how rapidly one's situation could change. When lying on my side and bouncing around the dirty van, my wrists already chafing, I could only think of one thing: *Why on earth was I here when just a minute ago Leo and I had been talking about* Major Barbara?

During the intake at SHU all of my clothes were taken away, including my watch. I read in Solzhenitsyn that denying prisoners knowledge of the time was a KGB method for destabilizing and weakening the psyche. I managed to preserve only my wedding band and stiff upper lip. I asked the guards repeatedly what this was all about, but to no avail. After I stripped down, my ears, nose, mouth, and other cavities were inspected, my toes spread, and my hair combed through. Cleared, I was given an ill-fitting uniform and led in handcuffs to an empty cell. Once I was locked in, a guard unlocked my handcuffs through a slot in the door. There was a second slot for attaching or removing leg shackles.

Nobody had yet told me why I was in the box, but I had an intuition that it was because of the souls. In fact, my gut knew that was exactly why I was in there. But my head refused to believe it. This was not medieval times, and I was not Mephistopheles or a character from Nikolai Gogol's *Dead Souls*. I was innocent of buying the souls of dead serfs and had not trafficked in them with the devil. The souls I had purchased were low-grade by some measures; they had second-rate GED scores, felony records, and abysmal credit scores. That's not to imply that my own was better.

But after all was said and done, my terrible crime was going to cost me three months of solitary and nearly prolonged my ten-year prison sentence by ninety days. My rational side could not believe that in 2012, the New York State Department of Corrections would write up a misbehavior report and lock somebody up, all done officially and on record, for the Dark Age crime of buying five human souls. For coffee.

I had spent the first seven years of my sentence in maximum-security prisons. Most prisoners look forward to the day when their security classification drops and they are let into medium security. They view the maxes as effectively being locked in a cage, days mostly spent behind bars. But I saw the gate as locking others out, and had grown accustomed to my cells in the four maximums I "visited." Behind a steel gate meant NPR on the radio, a pot of coffee percolating on my handmade "eye," and my hundreds of books to read in solitude. It was the life of a monk without having to believe in God. But it had to end one day; it's much costlier to keep men in individual cages, so whoever is eligible for dormitory life gets transferred to a medium as soon as possible. Any sentence under six years was served in the lesser-security prison, but I was held back a supplementary year because of my bad behavior: a dirty urine kept my classification a max for an extra twelve months.

Eventually I moved to a medium, and things changed. Entering the larger population of prisoners, I was suddenly surrounded by a chatty and social bunch of villains. Though the internal architecture of the medium-security prison was designed, as Jeremy Bentham would have approved, to muffle sound, imprisoned men communicate without difficulty by screaming to one another. And they really relish one another's company. I preferred my peace and quiet, especially at night. I had to learn how to achieve this in a new setting.

My first night in a sixty-man dormitory, I didn't sleep at all. From my top bunk, I could see all the other prisoners in the hall. It was like slicing open a beehive; I marveled at the action all around me. Gang members used their plentiful time to methodically pluck their beards into perfect shapes; high on opiates, hyperattentive, and unable to feel the pain, they spent hours carving out their facial hair designs with tweezers. Other men waited until the questionable privacy of darkness to whack off under their sheets. From my perch, I could not avoid seeing mass masturbation. That first night I doubted I would ever be able to sleep. As I adjusted, the unpleasant realization dawned on me that just as I could I observe my brothers in arms, they were observing me. And not just me, but my possessions.

For the last seven years I had lived on one hundred dollars a month from home and whatever I earned in the joint. Inside, this made me a member of the economic top 1 percent. State pay, which only narrowly seems to circumvent slavery laws, is on average three dollars, biweekly. My "white-collar" prison jobs, working for libraries and clerking for rabbis, netted me fifteen dollars, also biweekly. This sum was supplemented by my family with a hundred-dollar money order a month. I was privileged; few of the men were on their first bid, or had families that could afford them, or had not long since burnt their bridges.

My peers viewed me as vastly wealthy, and once they realized that they had a fat cat among them, I was set upon almost at once with requests. In the maxes this wasn't an issue, since my possessions were locked in my cage with me. For me to lend someone something, I would have to sneak it out into the yard, which meant saying no was easier. I still felt taxed when I was on the court, but I had gotten better with deft evasions over time. I wished I had had more practice; who expects to start each day with twenty asks for a cigarette? It's hard to say no because the requests are worth pennies, but en masse they add up, and I had a line of supplicants every morning.

Living communally brings Marxist fantasy into existence, as property loses the sharp edge of proprietorship, and everybody has a little bit of a claim on everything. Or at least everything they can see.

This is not always bad. There is a certain lending library aspect to dormitory life. Of course the porn gets passed around, spreading God knows what kinds of germs, but guys also read one another's books. I've been in dorms where all the men read all of Harry Potter, and enjoyed listening to debates over how "the little nigga with the glasses" should have blasted "Rolling Mort." The men with the largest collections of James Patterson and the gruesomely detailed true crime novels get hit up the most, but the sheer amount of reading material I had drew my own visitors. The best way to discourage too many borrowers was simply to let them browse, and after scanning my collection of literature and history they would wander off muttering, "Motherfucker weird." Magazines are also popular; a single issue of *Maxim* or *Stuff* was likely to be read by entire dormitories. The cartoon covers of my *New Yorker* subscription sometimes drew neighbors to ask for a read, but the magazines were quickly returned, since I was such a weird motherfucker.

As I did not want to appear a Scrooge—or, more to the point, as the sole Jew in the place, I did not want to encourage the usual slurs—in my first month there I gave away a lot of stamps, coffee, and cigarettes. Soon I realized that I had many repeat customers. I also figured out that having spent their own resources on gambling or drugs, they were relying on me to feed them and their habits. Something had to be done. Becoming Dr. No was beyond me. I had to live with these people, share a shower with them, and trust them not to slit my throat while I slept.

In fact, in that very dormitory, I had already witnessed a nighttime atrocity when a Dominican, heavy and old, came to a dreadful end. He probably had sleep apnea, and for that was attacked by a crew of gang kids who had decided they'd had enough of his snoring. They loaded up a sock full of AA batteries. One night after the Dominican had begun to snore, they whipped him in the face with this brutal weapon, striking as hard as they could. He sat up with his eyes and mouth wide-open and immediately fell back into unconsciousness. He ceased to snore. In the morning the old fellow was taken away to a clinic, and we never saw him again. No one was implicated. The lesson was clear; I did not need to make myself resented when we were all so accessible.

I had been deploying my own resources carefully, making sure they would carry me through the month. At the beginning of my sentence a hundred dollars a month would last me above and beyond, but as the years passed everything went up in price while my allowance and the state pay remained the same. And I still smoked then. I had to come up with a solution.

Having sold my own soul, in a manner of speaking, for a sentence of twelve flat, I decided to find relief in buying those of others. Thomas Mann was already on my mind, as I had recently read his magnificent four volumes of *Joseph and His Brothers* followed by *The Magic Mountain*, whose mountaintop sanatorium seemed like a serene paradise to me. The *Zauberberg* became my fantasy when I closed my eyes, but the incident with the Dominican had proved how far I was from its Davos setting. Having recently dipped into *Doctor Faustus*, another Mann masterpiece, I had an idea. The composer Adrian Leverkühn got twenty-four years of genius in exchange for the gift of syphilitic creativity, after which he was punished with madness. He sold his soul for brilliance. In a bit of television I could not forget, John Larroquette, playing a scummy lawyer on *Night Court*, got a hundred dollars for his soul. For my soul-sucking criminal compromises with my own morals, I got half the time Leverkühn did, probably none of the genius, and certainly not Larroquette's Emmy. In any case, as the disease that Leverkühn deliberately contracted ate away at his mind, the composer embraced the Mephistophelian figure with whom he began to interact, the metaphorical buyer of his souls.

Mann wrote the character with aplomb. The devilish is always appealing to those of a bohemian bent, and even though I was but a half-assed Rimbaud locked away in a place of simple values and harsh rules, my sense of play never left me.

Humor is often the answer, at least to most of the questions I have faced. For the entire ten years of my incarceration, I laughed as much as possible, feeling that every chuckle was a moment stolen back from the Department of Corrections. I picked up the idea in Solzhenitsyn's *Gulag Archipelago*, where the innocent prisoners laugh at political jokes that are treacherous because of the informants all around, but laugh nevertheless to remind themselves that they are more than just zeks. Central European, as well as German, literature is remarkably suited to jailhouse reading. They have a native sense of absurdity, a condition I walked around in for years. Having seen men attempt suicide in toilet bowls and murders committed a dozen feet from me, what could I do but put on the same sardonic smile that I imagine Bruno Schulz wore when his brilliant brains were blown out by a callous SS officer. I loved his *Street of Crocodiles* and *Sanatorium Under the Sign of the Hourglass*. The Polish Jewish writer had been an SS officer's protected servant, but the German lost him at cards to a sadistic SS man who killed the writer. Perhaps it was the blood that soaked the soil of these authors' *heimland*, but I also adored Hermann Hesse, especially *The Glass Bead Game*, better titled in the original as *Das Glasperlenspiel*. German writing on man and his place in this ungainly life of ours appealed to me when I was so lost in this one. Kafka's *Castle*, with its cruel absurdities and nightmare bureaucracies, felt like an apt metaphor for prison life. I went further down this rabbit hole and discovered other Czech literature to revel in. Hašek's *The Good Soldier Švejk* taught me how to laugh off the worst life has to offer. Karel Čapek's *War with the Newts* suggested that any oppressed underclass has a certain power. Since I had the time and inclination, I also read Günter Grass and Joseph Roth. I loved to read history in the form of fiction. Gore Vidal entranced me with some of his work, like *Burr* and *Creation*, in the same way.

But let's return to *Doctor Faustus*. Mann's most consequential work is a retelling of an ancient story that has also been recounted by many others: Christopher Marlowe and Goethe in plays, and Gounod and Busoni in opera and the musical *Damn Yankees*. I had read the other material, but the growing madness and greatness of Leverkühn spoke to me very much of my own efforts to seek creativity, or at least explore my inner realms with drugs. And I had also read, as a younger man, *Dead Souls*. Gogol's beloved Chichikov had engaged in a scam to purchase the names of dead peasants who were still listed as living. It was certainly a smarter scheme than my own robberies. Meanwhile, every time I turned on the radio, it told me to sell my own soul (too late) for rock and roll. There was something in the air, and I was in the right mood to buy some souls. And prisoners were willing to trade theirs for far less than for what Leverkühn had demanded.

For the entire time I was in prison I owned a typewriter, and it was on this typewriter that I created the contracts to purchase the souls of fellow prisoners. My peers had always assumed I'd bought the machine for legal work: most typewriter owners in prison get the expensive devices as investments, because they are, in fact, jailhouse lawyers. With them they can write legal briefs and motions without being subjected to the scrutiny of the cops in the Law Libraries, and without having to deal with the libraries' shoddy typewriters. Doing legal work for other prisoners is technically illegal, but it's hard to get caught and easy to make a fair amount of money. Typewriters are also used for gambling. Little tickets are printed up and sold for packs of cigarettes. The same odds as Las Vegas are offered on football games and such. Usually someone in the joint has a cousin or associate in

Nevada, and the odds are as fresh in the yard as at the Borgata. If someone wins, they can earn dozens of cigarette packs.

I was never involved in any of these activities, though I was frequently asked for use of my machine for both. The clear typewriters—transparency is required by prison guidelines to ensure nothing is hidden within—are made by only one company in the world, Swintec. The swine gouge the price to match the demand of its captive clientele. Typewriters are for the most part unused relics in the real world, but cost over $300 in the catalogs for the incarcerated. Over the course of ten years, I ran through three typewriters, costing me over a thousand bucks.

I usually spent my own time either typing translations from Russian, which was a paid gig my father had found me, or writing. I composed short stories and one and a half novels, as well as essays, reviews, and letters. I knew every function of the 1980s-era machine, even the ones only included in the Ukrainian manual. The company was global and covered prisons there, too. For some reason the manuals were not the same; I learned how to paste blocks of text from the Ukrainian version. Only 7 kb of memory was permitted to us convicts, so I had to work in four-page chunks. After every four pages, I would print out the text and clear the memory for further writing.

My skill on the typewriter was part of my undoing: my contract for souls just looked too real in the eyes of the cops, who were horrified by what they had discovered. The document simply stated that in exchange for a desired item, which was a cup of coffee in three of the five cases, the seller would transfer ownership of his immortal soul to the buyer, me. It took me only ten minutes to type up these one-page contracts. I used the legal jargon that was inescapable in prison and added in little bits of sarcasm to amuse myself. To this day five of these signed documents are in an Albany evidence locker along with the shanks and drugs confiscated in other less metaphysical cases.

Some of the fellows who were pressuring me for one of my possessions were hesitant when I explained the terms of the deal, and I remember one religious jailhouse Muslim who needed more convincing: "Yo, my man, you could spare a shot of mud?"

"No problem, but only for your soul. Sign here."

"You want me to sign my soul away for a cup of coffee?"

"It's Folgers." The cheap stuff was Maxwell House, at half the price. It was hard for anyone to resist those Folgers crystals, and despite this man's reservations, he could not, either. I included a clause stating that the souls would be returned in the event the Rapture occurred; there were many readers of the Left Behind books in prison. My contract was supposedly endorsed by the Better Business Bureau, and in the final version mentioned the UCC, or Universal Commercial Code, a common reference work.

This was bad miscalculation on my part. UCC materials are banned inside; I was eventually found not guilty of possessing them, however. In the incarcerated world the Universal Commercial Code is considered a book of spells by the prisoners and a weapon of sorts by the authorities. In recent years prisoners had attempted to use the procedures in the code to put liens on their enemies' properties, and targets included superintendents and deputies of security. Once there was a lien, no matter how baseless, the property or item in question was frozen financially and could not be bought, mortgaged, or sold.

Liens required a lawyer to untangle and could cause damage and money, even if groundless. They also clogged up the court system, and convicts are a litigious lot. Having a UCC is a tier 3 offense, the highest level, as was my "crime." Had I been found guilty of possessing the UCC, years could have been added to my time. To this day, I have never even seen a copy of the Universal Commercial Code.

However, there was also this madness going around about becoming a sovereign entity rather than an American citizen and not having to do prison time or pay taxes. Although this idea also exists in the wackier reaches of the internet, prisoners have embraced it as the alchemical solution to all of their problems, be they financial or legal. Milton Friedman's "no free lunch" doesn't ring true to people who really have had a couple of free ones from soup kitchens in their time. And the UCC supposedly holds the key to freedom. For some reason, the fact that prisoners' names were written in all capital letters on our ID cards seemed especially compelling evidence of this secret information to the believers, who think you can free yourself from the bond made in your name upon birth, collect your millions, and walk out of American jail, which no longer will have the right to hold you once you are a sovereign entity.

I had five takers on the night I printed up the contracts. I dutifully handed out three cups of coffee, with creamer and sweetener, to the first three. Another signed away his soul for a granola bar, and the fifth did so for a single stamp. With only one soul to sell, these fellows could not come back for more. I found this to be an excellent solution to the constant requests that deluged me ever since I'd received my security clearance.

Everyone in the dorm witnessed this exercise in absurdity and had a good laugh, including the cop on duty. I had always lived my life as if I were the protagonist of a novel, and this just seemed like a humorous chapter. But apparently I was dangerous enough to be locked away in the box. The Department of Corrections does not appreciate jokes.

If I had learned anything over the previous seven years, I should have known to immediately destroy the contracts. Instead I left the papers out in the open on my locker. The cop who worked mornings was a member of a fire-and-brimstone evangelical church just down the road. He came across the contracts and called in a sergeant. I dearly wish I could have been present at that conversation rather than in the yard, but somehow the two decided that I was a menace that had to be stopped.

The first few days in the box, before I received my ticket and the little bit of property that I could have, were so mind-numbing that I thought I would go insane. Some use the time to sleep without interruption, but I stared at the ceiling and looked for something to read. The cops had learned what I was in there for before I did, and many actually had sympathy for me. I was smuggled a local newspaper, which I read twenty times. To this day I remember the spate of cow tipping, or "farm animal attacks" as the paper put it, that was terrorizing Cayuga County. The two and a half days before that newspaper arrived was the longest stretch I've gone in my adult life without reading a single word.

I spent seventeen days in that room. It was a transitory place, as I was still technically "fighting my case," though Josef K. would have had an easier time getting acquitted from that kangaroo court. But at least I had the blessed luxury of solitude. After four days they let me go through my property, in handcuffs, and I saw that while all of the fresh food had been taken, my precious manuscripts and books had survived the cops' packing. That meant that the fellows assigned the detail felt some sympathy for me. For those prisoners at whom the cops are angry, anything of value gets given away during the process and sometimes open jars of grape jelly, followed by pancake mix, are dumped into bags of clothes and papers. The sex offenders get it the worst. I saw one pick up his bags after a stint in the box and discover that they were entirely filled with the contents of a garbage can. In any case, my possessions were relatively sound, including a rare book I had borrowed from another inmate, Steinbeck's propaganda piece *Bombs Away.*

I was allowed to take five books back to my cell, and with those in hand the box became a vacation. I decided to use the time to read the lesser-loved plays of Shakespeare, as well as a thick volume of science fiction for when I had no attention span. I consumed fifteen plays in fifteen days, enjoying *Coriolanus* and *All's Well That Ends Well*, works I probably would never have read without having absolutely nothing else to do. I also did push-ups. Clips of a hundred between every scene at first, then after every act when I found the pace was unsustainable.

Meanwhile I had my "case" to fight. None of the real security staff wanted to touch this one, as the potential later embarrassment was a career danger. Instead the food service manager was deputized to be my hearing officer. As I stood handcuffed before him, he read the charges with a straight face. I already knew about the unauthorized exchange, of which I was guilty in the most technical of terms, and the possession of UCC materials, of which I was not even theoretically guilty. As soon as he took a breath, I asked him whether he was taking this seriously.

"Without a doubt," he answered, a cold, puritan glint in his eye.

SHRINKS, SOCIAL WORKERS, AND PRIESTS roam the SHU halls and talk to the inmates through thick plastic, forcing both parties to yell. Their presence is considered a suicide prevention measure to allow them in, even though the cops don't like it. Because the box is relatively easy to get into and very hard to get out of, many inmates choose the path of self-destruction. I have witnessed both hangings and wrist-slashings there, the latter carried out with stolen and sharpened plastic spoons.

In Cayuga Correctional Facility I was visited by representatives of every religion. The well-educated Algerian imam came to apologize, on behalf of the faithful, for what he viewed as an outrage. But he conveyed this message in French, as he was a state employee and didn't want to be seen sympathizing. The rabbi, a Manischewitz enthusiast, did not bother employing his slurred Yiddish; he had twenty-five years with the state and expressed his disgust with the situation openly and without any fears. The Catholic deaconess was very kind, and went as far as comparing my trial to the Inquisition. The African American Protestant minister mentioned the Salem witch trials. Apparently the clergy of Cayuga Correctional Facility had resented this involvement of security in what they considered their immortal realm, but to no avail.

At my hearings, during which I was always tightly handcuffed and made to face a wall, the incident was treated with the utmost gravity. It was clear from the beginning that the UCC charge wouldn't stick. It was also clear that I would never see the yard of Cayuga again, because they were sending me to spend time in a real SHU, where I would have a bunky, the worst punishment of all. Later I learned that the glorified mess hall clerk-cum-arbiter was a fellow member of the church down the way, so he didn't mind prosecuting a "Satanist," no matter how ridiculous the charges.

My bags were packed even before I was found guilty. I made the obvious argument that I had intended it all as just a joke, and asked if any souls were discovered either on my person or in my property. But the fine print of the rule on unauthorized exchange also includes gifts, and the cups of coffee were being interpreted as such. So whether I was satanically buying souls or merely giving away cups of coffee, with creamer, I was guilty. A witness was called in. It was the owner of *Bombs Away*, of all people. I asked him whether he felt that I had truly bought his soul. He freely admitted that it was of course just a joke.

"Case closed?" I asked hopefully.

"But did you receive a cup of coffee from Inmate Genis?" asked the hearing officer.

The traitor replied that in fact he had, with creamer and sugar.

"Case closed," said my Pontius Pilate, smug and satisfied.

And sure enough, in writing up my disposition, he stated in a document admissible to a court of law that through witness testimony it had been demonstrated that a cup of coffee had been "exchanged" by Daniel Genis to their collaborator, making me guilty. Perhaps because it was a legal document, no souls were mentioned, only an oblique reference to "contracts."

I was given three months in solitary, plus another three months of recommended loss of good time. That was serious. It meant that because of my foolishness, I might have to leave prison later than I thought. Luckily, when the day came for me to explain myself to a Time Allowance Committee in another prison, it happened to be Halloween, and the group's members found the story humorous enough to ignore the penalty. I did not try to blame Thomas Mann or Nikolai Gogol for my misconduct, and went home on time.

After the trial I was shipped to a special unit so far west in New York State that the radio signal came in from Erie, Pennsylvania. I had already put in my appeal, and then a supplementary and rather metaphysical appeal was appended by the Prisoners' Legal Services, who found the whole episode outrageous. A letter of mine was also forwarded to *Esquire* magazine, which printed it under the byline of "Entrepreneur of the Month." A Jewish organization, the prison outreach arm of Chabad, involved itself to make sure this wasn't one of those Christian-blood-in-the-matzah cases.

None of it mattered; I served every one of my ninety days. The first seventeen counted toward the overall ninety, but the next seventy-three days were spent locked in a room with a man named Radar, who showed all the signs of being a schizophrenic. He also had three months to do, although his sentence was for throwing a tray of coffee cake at someone. Radar—who called himself that for his finely honed abilities in handball and had never even seen the show *M.A.S.H.*— would have been a terror to share a nine-by-eight room with for even a single day, let alone seventy-three. He had a bump on the back of his head, a relic of some 1970s New York cop's billy club, and when he lay back on it, his vision developed a hairline crack and he had auditory hallucinations. However, he soon decided that these symptoms were actually caused by my racism. On top of that, the hallucinations told him that I was a police spy, sent to finally "catch" him. The tension grew thick; I tried not to speak to him, though I did leave little treats on his side of the desk. I wasn't such a racist that my cookies were inedible.

At one point Radar noticed that we had extra T-shirts and tore the additional ones into strips with his teeth, causing a bloody mess, since he didn't brush them or see dentists. He flushed these strips down our toilet, and within a day the entire unit's feces all gurgled out of the toilet and onto our floor. I scrambled to save my books, but eventually a team had to be called in to both unplug the toilet and power wash the cell. While this took place, Radar and I were moved to the outside cage, which serves for the court-mandated one hour's "outdoors" recreation.

TO LIVE THROUGH THIS experience, I needed engrossing reading. I had recently started a monstrously large novel of ideas, Robert Musil's *The Man Without Qualities*, so as soon as I had access to my property I retrieved it. (Upon seeing the cover, Radar immediately concluded that I was a homosexual.) The monumental book and protagonist Ulrich's ambivalence toward both morals and life in general were a good reflection of my own troubles. The characters, however, lived in the wonderfully decadent *fin-de-siècle* Vienna, while I had to collect food trays through a slot in a steel door. Musil was a comfort nevertheless, and I lived with him and the Emperor Franz Joseph. Despite the novel's 1,700-page length, it eventually ended, and I still had a month to be locked in that room.

As more books arrived, Radar looked at them with horror. The nineteenth-century portrait on the cover of *Vanity Fair* particularly disgusted him. When my post-Musil stack of books arrived, Radar immediately decided that I was crazy, satanic, and gay.

The exposure of Radar, first to Musil and then to Proust (which he pronounced as "Praust," like "Faust," ironically enough), even if only by cover art, was jarring. His conclusions, from today's distance, are funny enough, but when a man tells you such things with a straight face, you wonder how you're going to sleep at night. Especially after he threatens to "get you" while you dream. When a cop kicked the door to wake Radar up for the count one day, things got worse. He concluded that I was there, in cahoots with the law, to somehow subjugate him. With time, Radar devolved into a howling, weeping lunatic. On shower days, three a week, when the showerhead built into a corner of our cell turned on for twenty minutes, the interaction was torturous since he finally had my attention to deploy his hostility on. In a sense the major modernist works kept me safe from Radar, as well as from the general madness of the box, with its screaming gang members and angry cops. But the absurd reason I had for being there, my identity as Mephistopheles, never left me. Radar might have believed that I was enslaving black souls, and threatened violence, but I knew that one day I would have a good story to tell. And sure enough, this tale was my first publication.

Sartre wrote *No Exit* to make a miserable point that I had rejected years earlier as a younger man. As a student at NYU, I could hardly take seriously his simplistic idea of the French existentialist that "*L'enfer, c'est les autres."* I loved people, and people loved me. But locked in a room with Radar, ironically almost duplicating the conditions of the play, I realized that what I once thought was facile nihilism was in fact a terrible truth.

Hiding from Radar in Musil and Proust, with five extra souls on my account, absurdity had come to visit me just all too literally.

Upon my release from being locked in a closet with a violent lunatic, I felt reborn. I never imagined I could value the "freedom" of a prison yard so much, or the "safety" of general population, where at least one was safe to sleep—though not to snore.

Whether I am still in possession of the souls is another question. They were never returned to their owners, but because the contracts are kept in Albany, perhaps the state of New York holds them, as it does so many others. It is not a legal question but a philosophical or literary one. To answer who owns the souls now, who you gonna call? Kafka, I'd suggest.

19

THE OLD BALL AND CHAIN

A decade of my marriage was spent talking on the phone, writing through the post, fighting at plastic visiting room tables, and fucking in modified trailer homes installed for conjugal visits. I watched men with forty years of incarceration under their belts cuddle their own wives in the visiting rooms in which they had grown old together. I saw other men transition from passionately calling every night to cursing the faithless whore who he discovered was now doing his best friend after less than a year of separation, and he only had a dime to do!

Before I was dragged away to Rikers in 2003 and not released again until 2014, my wife and I had only known each other for about a year and gotten hitched just four months before my arrest. The more standard pattern was to be left by the woman one was married to in the free world and then get married to another one. After all, most women entering into a marriage are not signing up for trailer visits every three months and huge phone bills for the rest of the time, except for those who surf the convict matchmaking sites.

I initially didn't have too many expectations that Petra Szabo would wait my incarceration out. Who was this woman? Petra is a fit brunette who teaches yoga and looks like she does. She's from Budapest, but we speak English mostly, Russian occasionally—Petra had worked as an animation manager in Moscow, so could get by in my

native tongue—and French when we need my parents to not understand. We used our three mutual languages (her Portuguese was as
useful for us as my Danish) to cover the spectrum of human expression. Under the flag of discretion, we deployed the most lethal of our
ultimatums and heavy artillery salvos in French or Russian. Despite
the time available and not for lack of trying, I'd never been able to
learn enough of her native Hungarian to absorb insults beyond "cock-
roach" (*svabbogar*, Swabian bug!).

The intellectual Genises were no novelty to her; in fact, they were
comfortably familiar to Petra and probably won me someone better-
looking than I deserved when she became my girlfriend back in 2002.
She got along with my parents until she didn't and then did again.
Petra had been in a relationship with one of Hungary's premier artists, who is also an obnoxiously sincere saxophonist. He played the
instrument shirtless at the age of sixty, and was also married with
children, then and now. Petra compromised. She had become accustomed to the particularly Eastern European combination of Clever,
Bad, Talented, and Arrogant.

Petra brought lovely food on the trailer visits. And, of course, she
waited. And, of course, we fought; it was, after all, a decade of long-
distance marriage. Mostly we didn't, as I had tried to learn from the
mistakes of others. I saw the pitfalls of appearing needy or attempting
to be controlling. I made sure to be interested in the minutiae of her
life rather than complain about mine, even *when those fucking cops
called me a . . .* Convict grievances are truly the most boring of topics.
I didn't smother her with them, and kept the letters interesting and
funny, and tried to make my life real to her. I thought I'd succeeded,
though years later I was surprised to learn that she actually suspected
me of all sorts of malfeasance. But she kept all that mail.

My wife is a brave and magnificent soul. Or she might be the most
indecisive woman ever. I had relapsed on heroin before our June

wedding in 2003. The marriage was not the most sincere; true, I was her boyfriend, but her visa was up, so it was either get married or break up. She was willing to leave it at "We'll always have New York," but I suggested we wed. Then I became a junkie (again; she had somehow managed to meet me during a period of clean time that I'd managed to put together between habits). On our first visit after the fall, I pointed out that she was young, accomplished, and beautiful and should probably leave me. She said she'd wait and see. Now that seventeen years have passed, I suppose she's no longer deciding. Petra saw some potential in me when no one else did.

Because the marriage was necessarily a conjoining of minds more than bodies, we got to know each other unusually well. Petra is a hard one, but how could it be any other way? Her aggressive intelligence bristles at the possibility that she is being led or, as she would see it, dominated. It was difficult for me to be twenty-five and have a pretty wife free to enjoy New York City every evening while I rotted in prison, so I had to be careful to not press that particular button. But because it is a big red one that depresses very easily, I naturally did so plenty of times. Nevertheless, I was cognizant enough of what questions not to ask after ten years inside to keep my marriage intact. Most of the guys I saw obsessing over whether the wife they effectively abandoned by selfishly committing crimes was fucking the mailman or neighbor eventually did get letters informing them that they would always be the best of friends, but . . . The presence of children in these families made the splits harder; we did not have any. Breakups and divorces were a constant source of trauma for incarcerated men, and even managed to blow my uncle's mind.

My uncle Igor, who played a big part in raising me, since my entire family consisted of only five people, was wary of the whole prison thing. I never even added his phone number to my list of those I might need to call. He did not offer. He wrote an occasional Christmas card and sent a carton of cigarettes once, but never visited Rikers and didn't visit upstate for the first few years, even though I was only a hundred miles away. He was obsessed with other things, and he forgot about my existence. However, eventually his conscience awoke and he made the trip to Green Haven CF.

Igor was sitting in the visiting room next to an immaculately made-up Hispanic woman of a certain age. The prisoner she had come to see was brought from the box, so he was only unshackled once he was seated. He was obviously a gang member, probably a Latin King, and had a fresh scar on his face. My uncle was oblivious to what was about to happen, but I could overhear enough of their conversation to foresee a violent tragedy. She was clearly scared to death of the guy, who had likely terrorized her for years while keeping her hostage with a mutual child. He was handling the long stretch ahead of him badly. The woman had seen a chance at happiness. She had come up to visit that day in order to break up with the prisoner.

My uncle was chatting about the horsepower of his Honda as she did so. I stopped listening to him by then and was on the tips of my toes, though I couldn't figure out how to protect Igor. There was a steel table between the visitors and us, but that didn't stop the newly single convict from leaping over it. In his hand was the jagged pop tab from a can of Coke. While on top of the screaming woman, he tried again and again to slash her face with the little piece of metal. The struggle seemed to go on forever. My uncle had also been knocked down and had a little blood on him. The cops eventually yoked up the prisoner, who must have had many years of box time added to his sentence for this outrage, and took him away. The woman left in a mess of tears and blood. My uncle left soon after. And never visited me again.

Although this is the chapter devoted to the wife who basically served my sentence with me and the perverse form marriage takes on in the lives of the incarcerated and those partnered to them, it is also an opportunity to discuss telephones in prison. We are no longer the epistolary society we were as recently as WWII. Prisoners are afforded the possibility of calling even in the cell behind every courtroom where they put you after a judge or jury convicts you. Rikers Island had its own commodification of the phones, as discussed earlier. Upstate, some prisons had an abundance of phones, mostly in the frozen yards, while others had a shortage. Coxsackie CF had five telephones for a population of almost two thousand inmates. Obviously each phone was claimed by a particular gang or race, which didn't stop Michael Alig, of *Party Monster* fame, from being on one of them every time we were in the yard. He simply paid the Bloods a hundred dollars a month for the access. But the biggest exploiter of this captive market, the biggest bully running the jacks, was the DOC itself. Since my marriage to Petra was conducted fiber-optically to such an extent, we were victims of extortion. But those calls were a lifeline; when we didn't fight, they were worth every penny.

When we started in 2004, the standard thirty-minute phone calls were eight dollars each. As this was already in the age of Skype, Petra's calls home to *Magyarország* cost ridiculously less than speaking to her husband, who would make his calls standing under the frozen sleet or baking sun. The price of phoning had an effect on the discourse; when having a really good talk at the twenty-ninth minute, having wasted the first fifteen or so on some long-forgotten fight, taking the plunge and dialing back for another half-hour meant something. Either we could abstain the next day, to save the money spent, or face the reckoning from my parents, who paid the triple-digit phone bills. At least there was never a line for the jacks, and there was a marked racial skew to the callers, as more of the white prisoners had families willing and able to pay so much to speak to them. Still, charging those families that amount of money to talk to their loved ones was blatantly criminal, and halfway through my bid, a court found that to be the case. The price of chatting with Petra for half an hour dropped to a dollar fifty. At this point the situation regarding access to the jack changed dramatically, as the low price now made it a resource to squabble over, just as it had been on Rikers Island. Nevertheless, I wrote a two-page letter for five days out of seven, putting something in the box every time the mail went out. Petra sent me hipsterish cards and photos. Like her, I kept everything I ever received for a decade.

Of the married prisoners, a larger portion had been married while convicts. This is so common a practice that there is a set procedure for the weddings; I've been a witness at one. Unfortunately the bride in that case was an undocumented immigrant who went back to Mexico after the marriage and was then apprehended crossing back to America and her incarcerated husband. She was banned from entry into the United States for ten years, and they never saw each other again.

But who are the women who marry prisoners? Today there are websites they can browse where inmates have posted advertisements for themselves, usually with a dashing picture but not too much about the crime that put them in their position. Location matters, of course. A friend of mine started an epistolary romance with a woman from Perth, Australia. Each phone call was eighty dollars and had to be carried out in the presence of his counselor, who was also the leader of a rape survivors group and not very encouraging. The clergy who work for the state have a long waiting list of prisoners to marry. These prospective husbands must meet all kinds of requirements, involving waiting periods and disciplinary records. Their intended wives are told of the details of each man's instant offense and his HIV status. These women are not being coerced; they want an incarcerated husband. More than once I've seen a woman leave one prisoner for another. Sometimes they marry sex offenders, who are not allowed conjugal visits at all. Why?

Celebrity prisoners like Ronnie DeFeo get heaps of mail, and much of it is from morbid women who want to share in the life of someone far from ordinary, even if in an unwholesome way. Other women recognize that they will be a goddess to an inmate no matter how many donuts they eat. Then there are the women with trust issues who like the idea of always knowing where their husband is, and that it's far from any other women. My own wife was convinced my blue eyes had the gay prisoners aflame. She was especially jealous after big Pole Majiec gave me a kiss on the cheek in front of her on the visiting floor and lisped that he'd see me later. I thought it was funny, but Petra found it hard to believe that anyone in prison would play such a joke. It took me a while to convince her that this muscular Adonis was just my friend and toying with us.

Of course, prisoners also do extreme things to make themselves more interesting to women. They are sexual creatures, even if the state seeks to deny them this aspect of life. One jail I was in had a crew of Hispanics who installed "pearls" for whoever wanted them and could pay for the service. The "pearl" is a piece of domino, carefully filed into a smooth heart, circle, triangle, etc. It's the size of a nickel, and as thick. Once ready, the experts make a slit in the skin of the penis, slather the pearl with Bacitracin, and insert it under the epidermis. Then a stitch or two is applied, and the person newly endowed must take care not to have too much of a hard-on until it heals. In theory these enhancements were meant to please the women waiting for these men, but considering all the hands-on work involved in installing one, I had my doubts. Some men had many pearls, going up the shaft or armoring around it. I thought of a great design for one, and one is all I can fit: an old-fashioned bomb outline, which could also appear to be a fish. But I lost my nerve when a prospective pearl wearer caught an infection that swelled his penis into the painful size of a Coke can. I left the joint without any extras.

While the women who marry prisoners may seem to have questionable motives, the inmates they target certainly do. These men know that women see them as projects and wounded birds and often consider these marriages as an arrangement to last only for the duration of the bid. The women somehow never see this coming and are always surprised by the betrayals that come after release, if one is even scheduled. Granted, I've known plenty of couples who found happiness despite the limitations of incarceration, and my own marriage survived and then some. But as much as it pains me to write this, to any ladies looking for advice on whether to take the plunge with a jailbird, mine is not to.

Reading the literature of great romances and affairs of the heart did little to help me sustain my marriage. Dante's worship of Beatrice from afar was not what I wanted out of life, and the cruel and crude works of Michel Houellebecq merely unnerved me; I did not want to come to despise what I desired. Learning anything from other inmates who had sustained much longer marriages despite incarceration was also a limited proposition. So much of their interaction was based on what they could get the spouse to do for them, using the negotiating tools of mutual children and guilt. I made sure to not be a burden of any kind on my wife, to make it as easy as possible for her to be married to me. I tried to be as much of a presence in her life as I could, ergo the endless letters. But one thing that both my fellow married inmates and the occasional Jackie Collins book I read agreed on was that women are very seldom satisfied by words alone. They value physical contact in a way different from men. All of us prisoners dreamed of sex night and day, and marital vows would have been conveniently forgotten had a brothel operated in the yard. I read that nineteenth-century men of letters, like Kierkegaard, wrote "hygiene" in their journals to denote a whorehouse visit, as sex without love has never been an obstacle for the male of this species. Women, however, value the expression of love through touch more than a thousand pictures, each of which may be worth a thousand words. For this reason, it was such a blessing that for years of my incarceration my wife and were allowed trailer visits.

Conjugal visits are held in modified trailer homes, which, while not actually tractor trailers, still get called "the trucks." The word that rhymes with this name plays a big part in its popularity. For years visits to the trucks were the basis of the long-term schedule I lived by. It was a good year when I got four trailers in twelve months, but a rare one. Had I been stationed farther upstate and had a wife who was nearby, I could go once a month, but since I was close to a hundred miles from the city, cancellations from other couples, opening an opportunity to go on a truck in a few days, were rare and reasons to deny or prolong the wait common.

A truck stay lasted forty-four hours, spanning two evenings and one full day. They came at mandated intervals of ninety days, spent without the least infraction of discipline. To go out on one, you had to give urine two days before, then again the day you went out, and finally the moment you came back in. The vigilance of this regimen was carefully thought out; the middle sample wasn't tested unless one of the others came up dirty. The middle test could therefore pinpoint your use of drugs directly to the trailer period, and your visitor could be accused of smuggling in the drugs.

You would think that prisoners afforded the luxury of conjugal visits would take care not to lose them, but the guys weren't in prison because they thought this way. The trucks were a hotbed of contraband and smuggling, although the wife-swapping that was rumored to happen in every facility during a Family Reunion Program (FRP) was not something I can confirm. Most people just brought in vodka in water bottles, but this being the joint, sex and crime were inevitably conjoined. But there was a cute domestic aspect to it as well.

Each of the trailers has two bedrooms, and some have three. Because the program is dedicated to "family reunion," many accommodations were made for the presence of children. There was a video game system, a high chair/crib combo, and a playground jungle gym outside. Mostly the children I saw were fascinated by the thirty-foot-high wall keeping us in; the trailers were typically located in a corner of the prison so that a guard tower could watch over us. The wall was perfect for handball, and I once found myself playing the game with an energetic little monster who got his finger under my sneaker. I didn't mean to step on him, and he took the injury with a sense of humor. The next morning a chorus of children stood outside my trailer and called for Bigfoot to come out and play.

Sometimes extended clans, including grandparents and toddlers, visited their scions inside. Of course, the women were all afforded careful appraisal by the guards. The more attractive the visitor, the more attention she got. I remember one poor West Indian kid who had a gorgeous mother; she was always checked with special care. Every visitor's documents had to prove a familial relationship. Over the years Manhattan escort agencies had made a fortune by helping out the Mob guys on ice. But they sent up too many of these "sisters and cousins" to the wise guys, so by my time this was impossible. To introduce any variety into your sex life you really did have to marry and divorce. That is a glacially slow process but still common enough for me to have met more than one spouse for men I knew over the years inside.

Even with so many stringent rules, the trailer program was not squeaky clean. As well as the *aqua vitae*, all manner of contraband entered through this window. Sneakers were exchanged, soaps with alcohol content like Neutrogena came in, and clothes with a swath of thermal lining arrived. Perhaps the most exciting case of my years going on trailers was the "gang of six." There are six trailer units in each jail that sponsors the program, and in one prison I visited there was a conspiracy among the men to flood the joint with weed. One man's wife was to deliver a half-pound of marijuana, and six men were going to smuggle it in at over an ounce each in their rears . . . until someone snitched.

The woman was apprehended by the New York State Police, searched, and found with the weed taped to her stomach. The trailers were terminated for all six until a punitive year had passed and another application submitted, which was often rejected. I only saw the guys again in another jail two years later. One marriage had certainly ended with this episode; the smuggling woman got a year in prison. It was considered quite the bust and even made the local news; we all listened to the radio describe a major drug operation intercepted. The public imagined Escobar, moving his narcotics through maximum-security state prisons. The reality would have been hundreds of pin-sized joints, furtively smoked by men set to die in prison who paid for the pleasure with stamps they had saved up. But the law's the law.

The FRP visits could be terminated for much less, however. Perhaps the most unfortunate episode I can recall involved a kid who hit his head in the first ten minutes of a trailer visit. When the convict's wife and child arrived, the inmate was so eager to bang his wife that he locked his ten-year-old outside to "play" on the icy paddock. The boy promptly gashed his forehead open. He tried to go back to his trailer but found the door was locked. He went to the other ones for help, and adults had to knock on his parents' door until the couple finally opened up. The cops had to be made aware. When the inmate suggested his son be taken to the prison infirmary for stitches, the cops decided to end the visit so the boy could be taken to the emergency room. It really wasn't much of a wound, but they wanted to teach the man a lesson.

One could pay ten dollars for a ten-pack of Polaroid film and the use of a beat-up camera. Until recently, when the fad returned, prison was one of the last sources for Polaroid pictures in the modern world. On trailers you could borrow these cameras, assuming you bought the film in advance. Whatever lurid ideas the conflation of caged heat and instant pictures may have inspired, the pictures were all scanned by the cops on the way out and anything with nudity confiscated. The legal logic is that such pictures have the possibility of being used for blackmail, while the moral outrage must be over the chance that immoral convicts share the photos as pornography. I could actually see the chances of both happening.

I truly valued the forty-hours hours Petra and I had together, and I'm glad I have photos that are a record of my prime physical condition as a memento. I came home with about a hundred of them.

2010

Music was also allowed to be brought to the trailers, to set the mood, I suppose. Prisoners were still using cassette tapes and Walkmans. This proved to be a thriving business opportunity; since cassettes were allowed to travel, there was a huge profit to be made in recording the audio from smuggled-in porn and selling "fuck tapes." Cassettes of recorded humans procreating were some of the rarest and most valuable contraband around. The image of men masturbating to these human rhythms coming from their Walkman headphones is a priceless one to me.

To answer the common question of how many times you could do it in forty-four hours, well, it's fourteen. I was only twenty-five, after all. Having sex in prison, with a woman, was the greatest of luxuries. Of course, some women get pregnant. I know men with three trailer babies, and I even met the final outcomes. There was one fellow in Green Haven who had been conceived there, thirty years earlier, when his father was a prisoner. He had the misfortune to say, "What do you want me to do, kill myself?" on the phone. It was during a fight with his girlfriend, but the cops on call-screening duty had to act anyway.

They raced to him and punched him in the face when they terminated the phone call, because although the cops knew the threat of suicide wasn't real, they still had to keep him in a paper smock for three days. He took it in stride, as he had always feared that it was his destiny to go to Green Haven anyway.

The trucks were also special because you could have real food. Planning the menus was an exquisite pleasure, not far from deciding on one's last meal before execution. I used Petra's visits to court death by overeating. Mostly we focused on red meat, fish, and seafood and vegetables. Petra used to pick up Chinese takeout on the way for lunch, but the rules changed and bringing in home cooking (a stretch, in this case) was banned. I only had borscht on my first trailer, but afterward we had the fun of cooking lamb chops together, boiling shrimp to eat with a movie (I subjected Petra to childhood landmarks like *The Goonies* and *The Warriors*; she made me watch *The Deer Hunter*), and drinking Russian mineral water compulsively. The only problem we ever had was the horror that two trout induced in a screener. It turned out that whole fish were not as familiar to the cops, who I had taken as all being outdoor types, as they were to me. The caviar was never even noticed, since it came in a can, but my skinny, fancy, big-city wife and her nasty sushi drew the usual class-conflict ire. They forgave me a little when they saw that I brought chewing tobacco with me.

Petra never ate too much on the visits but did show off her cooking prowess; chocolate coconut balls were a memorable accomplishment. We split the pictures we had taken between us, and planned the next trailer from the moment one ended. Everyone did; it really gave a lot of prisoners something to live for. I learned to stop planning a final breakfast, because we were too anxious at departing to eat it; buttermilk or kefir suited us fine.

Of course, this being prison, there was always something less pleasant behind the curtain. Trailer visits were the ultimate leash, ensuring participants in the program stayed on their best behavior. Any ticket (misbehavior report) resulting in more than fourteen days of keep-lock canceled your FRP visit. The punishments for even the lightest of tickets began at fifteen days of not going to the yard. I lost my first trailer with my first ticket, for getting a roll of tape out of an office. To be honest, it was a whole case of tape; each roll went for a pack each, because it was used to "laminate" porn into "bibles." Entire collections I've seen bound between the covers of a volume from *The Encyclopedia Britannica* were bound with tape and cost a lot. The bibles were thematic: butt shots, cum shots, interracial (big seller), belladonna, etc. Since the material was inevitably passed around, it was good advertisement for the binders. But I paid heavily for the theft. After the second infraction that led to losing the trailers for good when I got transferred to prisons without them a few years later, I was stuck only with "short eyes," or porn, for the entire latter half of my bid.

Not all prisons have trucks. For the most part none of the mediums do. Because I went to the box, I landed in joints that had so many disciplinary problems that there would have been little point in investing in the mobile homes. Sex offenders aren't allowed to go on trailers at all, so prisons with programs for them didn't bother funding what was essentially a disciplinary tool. And that describes the bittersweet sword trailers were, double-edged and Damoclean.

The truth is, there are many times in a prisoner's life that call for breaking the rules. The simple algebra of cost/benefit analysis demands that if someone degrades you, fight. The thirty days of keeplock, when you can't touch the yard or the mess hall, are ultimately worth it, because "holding down" an insult only invites another and another, escalating to losing your ass at its most extreme. If someone calls you a rat, you either draw blood or remain a rat, even though the possibility of a tough snitch is not unheard of. You don't have to win the fight or stab to kill, just show up. I speak from experience and I'll leave it at that.

AFTER LOSING THE TRAILERS more or less permanently, I missed my great wife greatly and physically. But the quality of my bid improved; that invisible policeman I'd carried around for years, running every situation by him, was now killed, dead, and by friendly fire at that. My conduct was no longer bound by the fear of losing trailer visits, and my life improved, except for the loss of future trailer visits.

The trucks are a rare feature of New York prisons; almost all state systems as well as the feds and counties did away with conjugal visits decades ago. I am grateful for the twelve times I managed to avail myself of it, and so was my Petra. While I always suspected it was her indecisiveness that preserved our marriage, the conjugal visits must have helped, as here we are here, together, now.

20.

LAZARUS

It all ended on a chilly February morning in 2014. The walls of Jeri-cho (Fishkill CF, in my case) did not come tumbling down. I was not freed by a mass amnesty, like half the Soviet Gulag upon Stalin's death in 1953. I did not escape, like the two men did from Clinton CF in 2015. The governor didn't sweep in with a clemency order, which so many of us dreamed about without ever once having witnessed it in the previous ten years. And it wasn't even a liberation of the soul, achieved through transcendence, that spiritually freed me. Ten years, three months, and six days had simply passed. The end of my exile, something I never dared imagined because it was easier to ac-cept my circumstances day by day, arrived very quietly. I was terrified.

There was a phone call, my name was called, I picked up my packed bags, and I walked away from the entire world I had known for a third of my life. Everyone acted as if I were being called down to the clinic or something. Some of the men in the dorm knew, and shook my hand or patted me on the back; I had done the serious hug-ging the night before. I didn't know anyone nasty enough to be jeal-ously angry at my departure, although stories of such reactions were well-known. Even though I was going home to my family, I felt as if I was leaving my actual kin behind. These men didn't judge me or doubt me at every meeting, like my parents had. They didn't fear me like I worried my wife now did. We ate together and shared our common lot as convicts with dirty jokes and tall tales. I loved these killers and thieves and even a molester with whom I had gotten close, against all odds because he told me the truth about his sin, unlike another. As much as I wanted to leave this horrible place that had done its best to destroy me as an individual, I dreaded leaving behind the people I knew here.

The internal hurricane that was to mark my return to the land of the living, Lazarus rising from the dead, began with such conflicted turmoil. I barely held the sobs in as I looked at my jailhouse friends, a pack of fat losers who had killed and stolen and more. I loved them. The last convict to whom I said goodbye was an old black porter mopping the floor of the room where you sign your release papers. We barely knew each other even by sight, but there was no one else. I didn't understand why but I suddenly loved him, too. He must have seen this sort of behavior before, because he kindly shook my hand.

The cops who had to do my paperwork and lead me out treated me differently than what I'd grown accustomed to. I knew how to have a friendly rapport with the COs, which depended on showing an awareness of our different places in life. But now the cops spoke to me as if I were just a regular guy. Had the ten years of aloofness and occasional derision been all an act? Were they taught to treat us the way they did? In any case, the final officer shook my hand, wished me good luck, and joked that he'd better not see me here ever again. I loved him, too.

My parents were waiting in the parking lot in a Mini Cooper. Now it was my turn to act. The odd eruptions of love I had been experiencing vanished. They did not emerge to hug me or welcome me or anything; it was cold, and I just got in the car. My mother let me sit in the front. I wished my wife were there, but an additional trip to pick her up in Brooklyn was deemed unnecessary. As we rolled away,

I saw the prison from the outside for the first time; I had arrived there at night the year before. I felt love again—for the stones that had held me captive! I feared madness but kept a calm face; that was one trick I learned early on.

We made small talk. The enormity of what was happening caused my psyche to split. I had long ago developed the ability to suppress my inner state from expressing itself on my face and could make whatever impression was necessary. My parents were acting reserved and clearly not looking to celebrate. I prayed that they were just acting and would suddenly explode in joy at my release, but instead we talked about what my father had seen in the newspaper that day. It was very hard to concentrate, but I did my best to mirror their affectation, manifesting good-humored optimism. One half of my divided self made jokes about not knowing how touchscreen phone gestures work as I called Petra to let her know they had really released me. The other half was silently screaming. When she squealed with delight my selves were momentarily united, but I was soon told I spoke too loudly inside the little car.

I bought coffee at a gas station and supplied the appropriate comment about my first purchase as a free man being overpriced. For one hundred miles I kept up this patter, a psyche in schism for my parents' sake. They had their reasons to worry. I might, after all, jump out and stick up the gas station where we stopped, or immediately go heroin shopping. For some reason, they insisted on behaving as if we had been reunited the morning after I was arrested. But a decade had passed, and the day that had made me tremble in anticipation had come.

Since they acted as if it were just another day, I did, too. I did not sing the way I wanted to, my sternum vibrating with the music of the spheres. I didn't kiss the free ground or shout at heaven. Having to dampen my heart poisoned my homecoming, but it was not for me to dictate how happy anyone should be to see me. And the relief at coming through the hellfire unscathed was just another emotion I painfully hid, while counting my change at the Amoco.

Silently, tearlessly, and while bantering, I wept. Great heaves roiled within me, an emotional storm composed of relief and disbelief; ecstasy and agony. Tears that don't flow down your face drip inside of you and feel like molten poison. And yet some of the storm was pride; even if it was being denied in totality by my parents, I knew that I had done something really hard: I had survived over a decade in hell, and I'd made it out. Not just alive, but unscathed, without a scar on my face or any great shame to bear. Of course I was ten years older, but I felt myself to be a better version of the person I had been before prison. I knew this was actually impossible, but what I really meant was that prison had not taken away from me what it tried to and had succeeded in doing to so many others. I was proud of never having lost my sense of humor. I had kept my sanity and been brave. I had fought my biggest enemy, my addiction. If anything, it was my parents who seemed more affected by my time in prison than I was. These two people whom I knew as progenitors, they had changed. Whereas once it had been the same things that made us rejoice, whether the Berlin Wall falling, Clinton's reelection, or lox on sale, I now didn't know or couldn't discern what made them happy.

Realistically my time in prison could have been so much worse. I read and wrote for ten years, keeping my head outside the walls as best as I could. I hadn't been stabbed or scarred. Most of the trouble I had, I had brought on myself. No one ever tried to rape me, and the very people I expected to hate me instead respected, liked, and sometimes loved me. God knows this wasn't how everyone's bid went, especially first timers, especially out-of-place educated Jews. I had been smart about it, made the right decisions, and done well.

But what had been the purpose of it all? Why did I have to go?

Surely making me exist in a twilight world segregated from the real one from the ages of twenty-five to thirty-five had some kind of point. Prison had definitely made a man out of the boy I had been when I had gone in, and I thought I had also become a better husband, son, and citizen than I'd ever been. It certainly wasn't thanks to the therapeutic programs prison offered. I spent a combined total of fourteen months in the six-month-long ASAT program, the adult substance and alcohol abuse therapy classes, and emerged with the same predilection to addiction that had brought me there in the first place.

Three years into my five years of parole, I had a relapse and got caught stealing coffee in a supermarket. It cost me a ninety-day parole violation, but I got sober again. The programs inside as well as the ones parole sent me to consisted of rote repetition of platitudes, which succeeded primarily in transferring federal funds to state coffers. I also completed the three-month Alternatives to Violence Project (AVP) session. AVP seemed remarkably unlikely to have any impact on anyone's capacity for violence. Everyone knew to take these programs at the end of one's bid, to avoid wasting time on them. After every fight, you'd have to take AVP again, the assumption being that you had missed something the first time around, and no one could do a bid without a scrap or two. My multiple times through the ASAT class were the result of similar logic, even though one of the times I had to take the half-year course again was because I couldn't pee on command for urinalysis.

If anyone really knew how to prevent addiction or stop violence, then addiction would stop being a problem and violence would disappear. For me, the primary thing that keeps me sober is the fear of consequence, and it's definitely day by day. I know it will remain so for the rest of my life.

Prison had tested me, but it had also furthered my education in the traditional sense. My incarceration gave me ten years to continue learning. This is a luxury that typically costs people a lifetime of student debt. I took advantage of the time by reading 1,046 books. While that was not the stated purpose of my incarceration, it was a personal decision that did, in fact, give me an answer to what the meaning of life was for me as a prisoner.

I pondered the enormous penal system, with its hundreds of facilities, thousands of trained staff, fifty-eight thousand wards, a fleet of buses and vans, packs of trained dogs, and millions spent on the economic black hole that is the Department of Corrections. Surely it had an official purpose, a *raison d'être* that informed its helmsmen? Someone was steering this leviathan somewhere, I hoped, because the lives wasted and misery it induced made it a costly ship to run, in human capital and every other kind, too.

The occasional peek behind the curtain into the administrative strategy—in other words, being in earshot of unguarded speech—gave me an impression of abject meanness. Much of the staff understood their mission simply to be punishment. It seemed as if "Corrections" was a euphemism for the goal of taking society's revenge on those who'd broken the social contract. So when my sneakers were rejected by the package room, or I couldn't have a hand uncuffed to wipe my ass after using the facilities on a transit bus, or I had to take ASAT a third time, it wasn't for any grander reason than simple punishment.

If the point of my ten-year incarceration was to impress on me that I had done wrong, it was a bleak deduction and monstrous waste of time. I knew I was wrong when robbing; I'd demonstrated contrition at the very scene of the crime, being the Apologetic Bandit and all. The rehabilitation I was put through had no effect on me (or anyone else, in my opinion), and the people most punished by my sentence were my innocent wife and family. Was the decade-long interruption in my life completely pointless?

Since prison is the rare milieu where the question of why one should read matters in a way that shapes lives, the possible answers are worth considering. Entertainment is the entry-level reason, followed by education. However, I am in the rare category of the genuinely overeducated. My ability to say something meaningful on most subjects and wing it with a high probability of success even if the topic is one I never bothered with only makes me a bore at parties. My dominance at *Jeopardy!* and Trivial Pursuit never got me a job or even earned me any love or admiration; irritation with a know-it-all was more common. After passing the halfway point of my bid and my thirtieth birthday, I ceased reading to learn more about things. I decided that a finer reason to read is to learn meanings. Of life, for example.

Douglas Adams said that that meaning is forty-two, which is as good an answer as any. I explored Nietzsche, Schopenhauer, and Heidegger, reading the latter on an exercise bike to double my pain. The philosophy of ethics particularly interested me, but the truth was that I was too dense to apply what I learned from these German philosophers to my own situation. Literature was easier for me to digest, so I found myself in *The Brothers Karamazov* and *Crime and Punishment* and Knut Hamsun's *Hunger*. It was in these great psychological novels of the nineteenth century that I discovered my flawed person. My narcissism and cowardice and compromises were all there, but the solutions—or at least a solution for me—were absent. The redemption I craved, the meaning of my ill-spent life, was not provided by Tolstoy or Dostoyevsky. I did not believe in god or destiny; only I was responsible for my actions, and it wasn't forgiveness I craved but meaning.

At one point I was almost converted to Stoicism, by Tom Wolfe of all people. As I mentioned earlier in this book, his novel *A Man in Full* captured the position of an incarcerated thinking man with incredible verisimilitude and suggested that the way to survive the experience intact was to become a Stoic, like Marcus Aurelius. Wolfe led me to reread Epictetus after my first exposure almost twenty years earlier. It helped, especially when I suffered from being treated unjustly. But I was no lifer, and as my remaining time dwindled, I realized I needed a better answer to the question of the meaning of my life. Stoicism understandably gives a man condemned to live out his life behind the wall a way to continue living in the face of hopelessness. But I was soon to be released to go live with my wife in Brooklyn. I needed more than the stiffest upper lip of them all.

In the end the answer I found applied to my life rather neatly. It would not do for most people. I never argue that Proust has the answer to the eternal question for everyone, but I will eagerly assert that it was Marcel who spent three thousand pages explaining the meaning of my life to *me*. I found redemption and sanity while I read the longest novel of them all in the box while Radar raged on the cot beneath me.

It was Orphu of Io who led me to Proust. My hyperliterate father had never read him and didn't recommend *Remembrance of Things Past* or *In Search of Lost Time* or *À la recherche du temps perdu*, by whatever title you know the book. My NYU education certainly didn't include such outmoded dinosaurs. Orphu of Io, the innermost of the Galilean moons of Jupiter, was a character in a science-fiction novel by Dan Simmons. He was a "moravec," an immortal living robot who looked like an SUV-sized scarab, sent to work in Jovian orbit. Like all of his kind, he was programmed to take an interest in an unfathomable area of human thought. Other moravecs studied Shakespeare and *Star Trek*, but Orphu of Io meditated on Proust. When another robot dismisses the writer as an aesthete, Orphu makes an impassioned defense of Proust's brilliance in finding ecstasy in existence, no matter how mundane it might seem. As the trajectory of my life had seemed a sad disappointment, I thought I should read this behemoth. Besides, when would I ever have the necessary time again?

I didn't know that *Remembrance of Things Past* would change my life. While the Simmons books *Ilium* and *Olympus* piqued my curiosity about Proust, I would ultimately have made it there on my own, given that I had devoted myself to a specialized project in my prison reading program. Proust was the culmination of a many-years-long effort to read the longest books of world literature. This meant spending months and three additional guidebooks to conquer James Joyce's *Ulysses*, though I pulled a Bartleby on *Finnegans Wake*, preferring not to. I read *Infinite Jest* with all of the footnotes; David Foster Wallace enabled me to laugh through one of the hardest times of my bid.

Dostoyevsky's *Brothers Karamazov* almost put me off from writing, since like an ur-novel, it contains all possible novels within it. Its brilliance made me despise my own prose. Not all the classics had as strong an effect on me. I read Boswell's cozy and meandering *Life of Johnson* because I figured it was too long for anyone else to have read, and doorstoppers like Murakami's *1Q84* were no threat to me, not after reading both volumes of Musil's *The Man Without Qualities*. Long books were a way of life, and moving from one to another felt like the alpinist's progression from peak to peak. They also managed to fill out parts of my life to which prison had introduced me and left for me to figure out. When I first had to deal with whether I was a Jew, Thomas Mann's four volumes of *Joseph and His Brothers* did more to enlarge my understanding of the question than the Torah. Of course, brilliance also came in sublime little packets. When I learned that the man I had become closest to over the years had neglected to tell me he was a pedophile Franciscan monk, it was *Lolita*'s Humbert Humbert who let me love a monster. This was a humbling and painful experience. How could I have misjudged a man so badly? And why did I still miss him? The man who had been the closest friend I had inside for the six months I knew him did not exist. He invented parts of himself for my benefit, like telling me he was in for vehicular homicide. And I went for it. The harshest lesson was that the heart can always disappoint you, especially when it's your own, but books are clear in their limitations. You find in them only what's there. In over a thousand that I read, sometimes I found great wisdom. This enormous catalog of books was *satori* in piecemeal portions. However, toward the end I found something a little more consequential. Proust gave meaning to my experience, to my time, my pain, to the whole lot.

Like many others drawn together so, we shared an enemy in Time. Proust describes it as the destroyer of joy in life and sapper of meaning. I simply had years of it to do, though in Proustian terms, we are all "doing" life sentences. The years are obviously the commodity taken away from a prisoner. They stand between him and happiness in the most concrete of ways, but Time is also the opponent of all life. Every passing second erodes whatever joy one has found and carries one closer to the grave. The fact that the passage of time inevitably leads to our deaths makes the conduct of our lives mean nothing. Belief in an afterlife is the tool with which religions enforce morals and submission, but it's hard for modern people to believe in that. Proust didn't, and became so depressed by the misery of mortal life that he retired to a cork-lined room, drank morphine cordials, and masturbated under a sheet when paid rent boys came to perform before him. And yet, in his work, this prisoner of time offers a solution.

The cruelty with which childhood and love can pass particularly concerned Proust. Not by coincidence, the happiness of childhood is the set of memories that torments prisoners as well. Every prisoner is a memory artist, a maestro at remembering. Much of Marcel's quest for happiness is as a memory master as well, even though the only cage in which he's locked is the present. *In Search of Lost Time* takes us through the red herring of defeating time with recollection. Ultimately Proust rejects memory, as must the prisoner. As did I.

Starting with the damned madeleines, Proust suggests perfectly summoning up happy memories as a way to be happy. Perfect recollection of the perfect moment seems to be a supernatural process available to those sensitive enough to do so. There are almost psychedelic episodes throughout the narrative that seem to show a flicker in space-time when an instance resonates in synchronicity with a prior one and an ecstatic unity across time and space is achieved. As prisoners are on the whole unable to attain such epiphanies, I read Proust with an eye toward practical use of his methods.

We are led through six volumes of the battle against Time by the memory artist. I was one, as we all were. I know what it means to compulsively recreate in the mind's eye, having had years of practice. I've had more sex in my head than in bed, and savored fine meals hundreds of times, clutching the memories even as time claws at them.

But in the seventh volume Proust takes a sudden turn. It is a subtle one, and yet no surprise to every memory artist with years of practice. No matter how good one is at remembrance, it is a barren occupation. It creates nothing, and mimics time in eating away one's allotment of years. After thousands of pages, Proust shows us that memory cannot defeat Time after all. The essence of life that even the best memory artist can squeeze out is vapid. The only power it has is to pervert and decay. Compulsively remembering revives joy into hysteria, wonder into obsession, and love into jealousy.

So, what then? Proust shows us that it is only art that can defeat Time. The grand novel concludes with Marcel going off to write the novel that the reader can begin reading anew. Even linearity is thus discarded. The novel ends with the author inviting the reader to return to the beginning. Many do, reading Proust continually throughout their lives. The message I received was different. To save myself, to make meaning of my life, I had to write.

I was thunderstruck by the implications of Proust. My bid was the perfect manifestation of the predations of Time, but there was an answer. Art would redeem the loss. Art alone could save my life.

The bid may have ended sadly for me, with my parents cold to the joy of my release, but I had a lovely wife who was waiting. And I didn't leave from within those walls empty-handed. Of course I had fifteen notebooks of journals, cases of correspondence, the manuscript of a novel, and half of a second one, but what I really had was within.

Omnia mea mecum porto, wrote Cicero; all that is mine I carry with me. And I had a book inside of me, one made of pain and fear and laughter and lots of other books. Memories, too, of course. I didn't lose my ability as a memory artist. So once my time inside ended on a February morning, I flirted with memory to rekindle the special moments and clever bits, edited out the cringe and complaining, and ultimately went home and wrote.

ACKNOWLEDGMENTS

To everyone who helped me bring this project into reality: my editor, Rick Kot, who culled so wisely; my parents, who bought me typewriter(s); my wife, Petra, who read everything first; my friends Jed Russel and Ryan Savoca, who kept me company and criticized intelligently; and to all the other people who I haven't named only because I forgot to . . . forgive me. Thank you all!

CHRONOLOGY

This work is not arranged chronologically, as a thematic structure seemed to have more promise of revealing the interesting and unexpected. These pages are a distillation of what I had to learn about prison, not an account of the travels of one D. Genis. Despite my unavoidable presence as narrator, whatever you glean about me is secondary to my intentions. Nevertheless, a brief road map can't hurt. Included is the following itinerary to give an account of my peregrinations:

I was arrested on November 13, 2003, and bounced between the Manhattan Robbery Squad headquarters on 11th Street—right next to where I misspent my youth learning to play eight ball at the long-shuttered pool hall Le Q—and Central Booking (the Tombs), where my bail was set at $150 grand, followed by my eventual conviction seven months later, compelled the movement described below:

- Rikers Island 11/03
- Downstate CF 5/04
- Green Haven CF 6/04
- Eastern CF 9/07
- Upstate SHU 10/09
- Coxsackie CF 3/10
- Greene SHU 7/10
- Five Points CF 10/10
- Cayuga CF 9/11
- Lakeview SHU 2/12
- Groveland CF 5/12
- Fishkill CF 8/13
- Home 2/20/2014